The High Middle Ages in England 1154–1377

CONFERENCE ON BRITISH STUDIES
BIBLIOGRAPHICAL HANDBOOKS

Editor: J. JEAN HECHT

Consultant Editor: G.R. ELTON

The High Middle Ages in England 1154-1377

BERTIE WILKINSON
Professor Emeritus, University of Toronto

CAMBRIDGE UNIVERSITY PRESS
CAMBRIDGE
LONDON · NEW YORK · MELBOURNE
for the Conference on British Studies

Published by the Syndics of the Cambridge University Press
The Pitt Building, Trumpington Street, Cambridge CB2 1 RP
Bentley House, 200 Euston Road, London NW1 2DB
32 East 57th Street, New York, NY 10022, USA
296 Beaconsfield Parade, Middle Park, Melbourne 3206, Australia

© Cambridge University Press 1978

First published 1978

Printed in Great Britain
at the University Press, Cambridge

Library of Congress Cataloguing in Publication Data
Wilkinson, Bertie, 1898–
The high Middle Ages in England, 1154–1377.
(Conference on British Studies. Bibliographical handbooks)
Bibliography: p.
Includes index.
1. Great Britain – History – Plantagenets, 1154–1377 –
Bibliography. I. Title. II. Series.
Z2017.W54 [DA205]   016.94203   77-8490
ISBN 0 521 21732 6

CONTENTS

PREFACE

The problem presented by a bibliography of the period 1154–1377 is not the lack of material but the abundance. The area to be included expands greatly: serious consideration has to be given to Scotland, Ireland, Wales and France, whilst the problem of foreign relations must include the papacy, the Netherlands, Germany and Spain. In view of this expansion of material, it is obvious that a great deal has to be omitted; but it still seems possible, by bearing in mind the purpose this series is intended to serve, to provide a guide that will be useful to both serious students and mature scholars. It is hard to omit a separate section on literature and forgo the companionship of writers like Chaucer and Langland, but some references to them have found a place in other sections below. On the other hand, I am delighted to have been able to offer a selection of sources and other writings on historiography, which is an important subject for any researcher in this period. It is hardly necessary to say that in this and other cases categorization must be decided on the simple basis of an assessment as to where the greatest importance of an item lies. The comments that have been made on some items are intended primarily as an aid to the serious student: the opinions of the experts in the field are easily accessible in learned periodicals. However, in making the comments I have tried, wherever it has been reasonably possible, to make a first-hand judgement of my own.

In preparing this volume, slim though it is, I have been indebted to many individuals and institutions. Professor Geoffrey R. Elton gave me wise advice at the outset, and Professor J. Jean Hecht not only advised me at that time but also went far beyond the call of duty in editorial assistance in the final stage. I was fortunate, also, in having Professor Bryce Lyon as the official reader of the MS., and no less fortunate in the friendship of Mrs Natalie Fryde, who put at my disposal not only her scholarly knowledge of Welsh history but also her command of the Welsh language. Among the institutions I thank for their assistance, financial and otherwise, are the Canada Council and the University of Toronto, who have continued for many years to give me generous support. Last, but not least, I wish to record the many contributions of my wife throughout the whole preparation of this volume. Her aid has extended to every aspect of our joint enterprise, and I particularly recall with pleasure the happy days we spent in the British Museum, using its unrivalled resources for the completion of this work.

Toronto   BERTIE WILKINSON

ABBREVIATIONS

AgHR	*Agricultural History Review*
AHR	*American Historical Review*
AngAntiq	*Anglesey Antiquarian Society Transactions*
ArchAel	*Archaeologia Aeliana*
ArchCamb	*Archaeologia Cambrensis*
ArchCant	*Archaeologia Cantiana*
BedsRec	*Bedfordshire Historical Record Society*
BBCS	*Bulletin of the Board of Celtic Studies*
BIHR	*Bulletin of the Institute of Historical Research*
BJRL	*Bulletin of the John Rylands Library*
CHJ	*Cambridge Historical Journal*
EcHR	*Economic History Review*
EGAW	*The English Government at Work, 1327–1336*, Medieval Academy of America Publications, 37, 48, 56, ed. William H. Dunham, William A. Morris, Joseph R. Strayer, and James F. Willard. Cambridge, Mass., 1940, 1947, 1950, 3 vols.
EHJT	*Historical Essays in Honour of James Tait*, ed. J. Goronwy Edwards, Vivian H. Galbraith, and Ernest F. Jacobs. Manchester, 1933.
EHR	*English Historical Review*
EPBW	*Essays in Medieval History Presented to Bertie Wilkinson*, ed. Thayron A. Sandquist and Michael R. Powicke. Toronto, 1969.
EPRP	*Essays in History Presented to Reginald Lane Poole*, ed. H.W. Charles Davis. Oxford, 1927.
EPTT	*Essays in Medieval History Presented to Thomas Frederick Tout*, ed. Andrew G. Little and Frederick M. Powicke. Manchester, 1925.
FS	*Franciscan Studies*
Hans.Gesch.	*Hansische Geschichtsblätter*
HMSO	Her Majesty's Stationery Office
JBAA	*Journal of the British Archaeological Association*
JBS	*Journal of British Studies*
JEH	*Journal of Ecclesiastical History*
Lancs.Antiq.	*Transactions of the Lancashire and Cheshire Antiquary Society*
Lancs.Historic.	*Transactions of the Lancashire and Cheshire Historic Society*
LQR	*Law Quarterly Review*
Med et Hum	*Medievalia et Humanistica*
MS	*Medieval Studies*
NLWJ	*Journal of the National Library of Wales*
PBA	*Proceedings of the British Academy*
PP	*Past and Present*
PRO	Public Record Office
Rev. Belge	*Revue Belge du philologie et d'histoire*
SHR	*Scottish Historical Review*
SPAG	*Medieval Studies Presented to Aubrey Gwynn, S.J.*, ed. John B. Morrall, Francis X. Martin, John A. Watt. Dublin, 1961.

S.P.C.K.	Society for the Promotion of Christian Knowledge
SPFP	*Studies in Medieval History Presented to Frederick Maurice Powicke,* ed. Richard W. Hunt, William A. Pantin, and Richard W. Southern. Oxford, 1948.
SPHJ	*Studies Presented to Sir Hilary Jenkinson,* ed. J. Conway Davies. 1957.
TRHS	*Transactions of the Royal Historical Society*
UBHJ	*University of Birmingham Historical Journal*
WHR	*Welsh Historical Review*
Yorks.Arch.J.	*Yorkshire Archaeological Journal*
Yorks.Arch.Rec.	*Yorkshire Archaeological Society Record Series*

EXPLANATORY NOTES

1. Abbreviations have been employed for the names of those serial publications and collections of essays, such as *Festschriften*, that are cited with particular frequency.
2. When no place of publication is cited, London is to be understood, except in the case of periodicals and other serials.

I. BIBLIOGRAPHIES

1   Anderson, Mary D. *et al. Writings on British history, 1901–1933*, Vol. 1, *Auxiliary sciences and general works* (including a select list of publications in these years since 1914); Vol. 2, *The Middle Ages 450–1485*. 1968. Royal Historical Society, 5 vols. H. Hale Bellot, A. Taylor Milne *et al. Writings on British history, 1934–1945*. 1937–60, 8 vols. The best modern guide.

2   Asplin, Peter W.A. *Medieval Ireland, c. 1170–1495: a bibliography of secondary works*. Dublin, 1971.

3   Bémont, Charles. 'Bulletin historique. Histoire de Grande-Bretagne. Moyen âge', *Revue historique*, 174 (1934), 41–77.

4   *Bibliotheca Celtica: a register of publications relating to Wales and the Celtic peoples and languages*. Aberystwyth, 1909–66. National Library of Wales, 28 vols.

5   Bland, Desmond S. *A bibliography of the inns of court and of chancery*. Selden Society, Supp. ser. 3 (1965).

6   Boehm, Eric H. *et al.* (eds.). *Historical periodicals an annotated world list of historical and related serial publications*. Santa Barbara, Cal., 1961.

7   Caenegem, Raoul C. van. *Introduction bibliographique à l'histoire du droit et à l'ethnologie juridique. Les îles britanniques*. Brussels, 1963.

8   Caron, Pierre and Jaryc Marc (eds.). *World list of historical periodicals and bibliographies*. Oxford, 1939.

9   Carty, James. *National Library of Ireland. Bibliography of Irish history, 1912–1921*. Dublin, 1936; James Carty *et al.* 'Writings on Irish history', *Irish historical studies* (1938–69), 1–16; Peter W.A. Asplin. *Medieval Ireland, c. 1170–1485: a bibliography of secondary works*. Dublin, 1971.

10 Chrimes, Stanley B. and Ivan A. Roots. *English constitutional history, a select bibliography*. Historical Association Helps for Students, no. 58 (1958). Still useful.

11 Courtauld Institute of Art. *Annual bibliography of the history of British art*. Cambridge, 1934–.

12 Cowley, John D. (ed.). *A bibliography of abridgements, digests, dictionaries and indexes of English law to the year 1800*. Selden Society. 1932.

13 Crompton, James. 'Chronique des travaux d'histoire du droit publiés en Angleterre du I-er Janvier 1939 à la fin de Juillet 1948', *Annales d'histoire du droit*, Pozan. 2 (1949), 514–39.

14 *Dictionary of Welsh biography down to 1940*. 1959. Contains valuable bibliographical notes.

15 Eager, Alan R. *A guide to Irish bibliographical material*. 1964.

16 Emmison, Frederick G. (ed.). *English local history handlist*. Historical Association Pamphlet, no. 69 (1965).

17 Ferriday, Peter *et al.* (eds.). *British humanities index*. 1963–.

18 Friend, William L. *Anglo-American legal bibliographies. An annotated guide*. Washington, D.C., 1944.

19 Graves, Edgar B. *A Bibliography of British History to 1485*. Oxford, 1975. A revision of Gross, 21.

20 Gross, Charles. *A bibliography of British municipal history*. Reprinted, with a Preface by Godfrey H. Martin. Leicester, 1966.

21 ——— *Sources and literature of English history from the earliest times to about 1485*. 1915. The standard work until the publication of Graves' revision.

22 Hancock, Philip D. *A bibliography of works relating to Scotland 1916–1950*. Edinburgh, 1959–60, 2 vols. Invaluable.

23 Hastings, Margaret. 'High history or hack history: England in the later Middle Ages', *Speculum*, 36 (1961), 225–53. Reprinted and enlarged in Elizabeth C. Furber (ed.). *Changing views on British history: essays on historical writing since 1939*. Cambridge, Mass., 1966, 58–100.

24 Historical Association. *Annual bulletin of historical literature*. Vol. 1 (1911–22)–Vol. 53 (1967). Quite invaluable for both European and British history.

25   Hodgson, Henry W. (ed.). *Bibliography of the history and topography of Cumberland and Westmorland.* Carlisle, 1969.
26   Holdsworth, William S. *Sources and literature of English law.* Oxford, 1925. General survey by a master.
27   Howe, George F. *et al.* (eds.). *The American Historical Association's guide to historical literature.* 1961. Has a useful section on the United Kingdom and the Republic of Ireland by Sidney A. Burrell.
28   Humphreys, Arthur L. *A handbook of county bibliography, being a biography of bibliographies relating to the counties and towns of Great Britain and Ireland.* 1917. Useful.
29   Jenkins, Rhys T. and William Rees (eds.). *Bibliography of the history of Wales...* 2nd ed., Cardiff, 1962, Supp. 3 (1969), ed. Emyr G. Jones, *BBCS*, 23 (1969), 263–83.
30   Jennings, W. Ivor. 'Legal history' in *Annual survey of English law.* 1929. (Continued by Theodore F.T. Plucknett. 1931 and 1932.)
31   Kimball, Elizabeth G. 'A bibliography of the printed records for the justices of the peace for counties', *University of Toronto Law Journal,* 6 (1946), 401–13.
32   Lyon, Bryce D. 'From Hengist and Horsa to Edward of Caernarvon: recent writings in English history' in Elizabeth C. Furber (ed.). *Changing views on British history: essays on historical writing since 1939.* Cambridge, Mass., 1966, 1–57. Covers the years 1939–62.
33   MacGregor, M. Blair. *The sources and literature of Scottish church history.* Glasgow, 1934. Comprehensive but uncritical.
34   Mainwaring, G. Ernest. *A bibliography of British naval history... a guide to printed and manuscript sources.* 1930.
35   Marwick, W. Hutton. 'A bibliography of Scottish economic history', *EcHR*, 3 (1931), 117–37. Comprehensive.
36   Milne, A. Taylor. *Index to periodicals* (Bibliographical Aids to Research 3), *BIHR*, 11 (1934), 165–80.
37   Otway–Ruthven, A. Jocelyn. 'Medieval Ireland (1169–1485)', *Irish Historical Studies*, 15 (1967), 359–65. A scholarly survey of thirty years work in medieval Irish history before 1967.
38   Plucknett, Theodore F.T. 'Bibliography and legal history', *Papers: bibliographical society of America*, 26 (1932), 128–42.
39   Potthast, August. *Bibliotheca historica medii aevi.* 2nd ed., Berlin, 1896. Invaluable: a new edition in progress, entitled *Repertorium fontium historiae medii aevi.* Two volumes have appeared (1962, 1967): to be used with some caution.
40   Rees, William. *A bibliography of published works on municipal history of Wales and the border... BBCS*, 2 (1925), 321–82; 3 (1927), 72.
41   Roth, Cecil. *Magna bibliotheca Anglo-Judica. A bibliographical guide to Anglo-Jewish history.* Jewish Historical Society. New ed. 1938. First compiled by Joseph Jacobs and Lucien Wolf in 1888.
42   Trautz, Fritz (ed.). 'Literaturbericht über die Geschichte Englands im Mittelalter: Veröffentlichungen 1945 bis 1962/63', *Historische Zeitschrift,* 2 (1965), 108–259.
43   U.S. Department of Health. *Bibliography of the history of medicine.* Washington, D.C., 1965–. Issued annually.
44   Willard, James F. and S. Harrison Thomson. *Progress of Medieval and Renaissance Studies in the United States and Canada.* Boulder, Colo., 1923–.
45   Williams, Eileen A. 'A bibliography of Giraldus Cambrensis *c.* 1147–*c.* 1223', *NLWJ*, 12 (1961), 97–141.

II. CATALOGUES, GUIDES, AND HANDBOOKS

46   Atkinson, Thomas D. *A glossary of terms used in English architecture.* 7th ed., 1948.

47 Bannister, Arthur T. *A descriptive catalogue of the manuscripts in the Here-ford cathedral library.* Hereford, 1927. Introduction by Montague R. James.

48 Barnes, Patricia M. *List of documents relating to the household and wardrobe: John—Edward I.* Public Record Office Handbooks, no. 7 (1964). HMSO.

49 Baudrillart, H.M. Alfred *et al.* (eds.). *Dictionnaire d'histoire et de géographie ecclésiastique.* Vol. 10. Paris, 1938. Includes articles on Thomas Brad-wardine (Irene Churchill); on Wulfstan Bransford, bishop of Worcester, 1339—49 (A. Hamilton Thompson); on Richard de Bury, bishop of Durham (Joseph de Ghellinck).

50 Baxter, James H. *et al. An index of British and Irish Latin writers, 400—1520.* Paris, 1932. From the *Bulletin du Cange*, 7 (1932), 110—210.

51 Bell, H. Idris. 'The Welsh manuscripts in the British museum collections', *Cymmrodorion Society Transactions for 1936*. 1937, 15—40.

52 ——— 'A list of original papal bulls and briefs in the department of manu-scripts, British museum', *EHR*, 36 (1921), 392—419.

53 Bickley, Francis (ed.). *Guide to reports of the royal commission on historical manuscripts 1870—1911.* Pt. 2. *Index of Persons*, 2nd section: Lever to Z. 1938. HMSO.

54 Bouwens, Bethell G. *Wills and their whereabouts.* Revised ed. by Anthony J. Camp. Canterbury, 1963.

55 Briggs, Helen M. and C. Hilary Jenkinson (eds.). *Surrey manorial accounts: a catalogue and index of the earliest surviving rolls down to the year 1300.* Surrey Record Society, 15 (1935).

56 *British Museum Catalogue of additions to the manuscripts, 1931—1935.* 1967.

57 Brooke, George C. *English coins.* 1932. Much of it lists and classified descriptions.

58 Burke, John B. and Ashworth P. Burke. *A genealogical and heraldic history of the peerage and baronage,* ed. E.M. Swinhoe. 94th ed., 1936.

59 Byrne, William J. *A dictionary of English law.* 1923.

60 Caenegem, Raoul C. van. *Quellenkunde des europäischen Mittelalters.* Göttingen, 1964. A valuable guide.

61 Cam, Helen M. 'On the material available in the eyre rolls', *BIHR*, 3 (1926), 152—60.

62 Cheney, Christopher R. *Handbook of dates for students of English history.* Royal Historical Society Handbook, no. 7, 2nd ed. 1961. An indispensable tool. Cf. 144.

63 Clay, Charles T. *A catalogue of the publications of the record series, 1885—1946. With an introductory chapter on its history compiled by Charles Travis Clay. Yorks.Arch.Rec.,* 113 (1948).

64 ——— and Edith M. Clay. *Consolidated index of persons and places to William Farrer (ed.). Early Yorkshire charters. Yorks.Arch.Rec.,* extra ser., 4 (1942).

65 Corder, Joan. *A dictionary of Suffolk arms.* Ipswich, 1965. An efficient list of heraldry.

66 Cowan, Ian B. *The parishes of medieval Scotland.* Scottish Record Society, 93 (1967). Contains list of all the parishes.

67 Cross, Frank L. (ed.). *The Oxford dictionary of the Christian church.* Oxford, 1957. A standard work.

68 Davis, Elwyn (ed.). *Celtic studies in Wales.* Cardiff, 1963. Includes studies in Welsh history and historians (Arthur H. Dodd); on Welsh laws (Hywel D. Emmanuel); and on literature (W.J. Gruffydd). A somewhat limited survey.

69 Davis, Godfrey R.C. *Medieval cartularies of Great Britain: a short catalogue.* 1958. A valuable help to research. Cartularies listed here are not given below.

70 Dawson, Warren R. *Manuscripta medica: a descriptive catalogue of the MSS. in the library of the Medical Society of London.* 1932.

71 Denholm-Young, Noël. 'Yorkshire monastic archives', *Bodleian Quarterly Record,* 87 (1935), 95—100.

72   Dew, Edward N. *Index to the registers of the diocese of Hereford, 1275–1535.* Hereford, 1925.
73   Easson, David E. *Medieval religious houses Scotland.* 1957. Mainly lists: learned and in many respects pioneer. Foreword by David Knowles.
74   Ekwall, B.O. Eilert. *The concise Oxford dictionary of English place-names.* 4th ed., Oxford, 1960.
75   Emden, Alfred B. *A biographical register of the university of Oxford to A.D. 1500.* Oxford, 1957–59, 3 vols. An invaluable work of reference. Additions and corrections in the *Bodleian Library Record,* 6 (1957–61), 668–88; 7 (1964), 149–64.
76   —— *A biographical register of the university of Cambridge to 1500.* 1963.
77   —— *A survey of Dominicans in England, based on the ordination lists and episcopal registers (1268 to 1538).* Rome, 1967.
78   Emmison, Frederick G. *Catalogue of Essex parish records, 1240–1894.* 2nd, revised ed., Chelmsford, 1966.
79   —— *Guide to the Essex record office.* 2nd, revised ed., Chelmsford, 1969.
80   Fisher, John L. *A medieval farming glossary of Latin and English words, taken mainly from Essex records.* 1968.
81   Floyer, John K. and Sidney G. Hamilton. *Catalogue of manuscripts preserved in the chapter library of Worcester cathedral.* Worcestershire Historical Society, 20 (1920).
82   Fox-Davies, Arthur C. *A complete guide to heraldry.* 1949. Fulfills its title.
83   Gardner, Samuel. *A guide to English Gothic architecture.* Cambridge, 1922. Numerous drawings and photographs.
84   —— *English Medieval sculpture.* Cambridge, 1951. The original handbook revised and enlarged.
85   Gibbs, Vicary *et al. The complete peerage of England, Scotland, and Ireland, Great Britain and the United Kingdom.* 1910–59, 13 vols. New ed. of Cokayne's *Complete Peerage,* revised and enlarged.
86   Grant, Francis J. *Manual of heraldry.* Revised ed. Edinburgh, 1924. Contains 350 illustrations.
87   Green, Francis (comp.). *National library of Wales. Calendar of deeds and documents.* 1921–31, 3 vols.
88   *Guide to seals in the Public Record Office.* 1968. HMSO. First published in 1954.
89   Hall, Hubert. *Repertory of British archives, Part I: England.* 1920.
90   Hampson, Ethel M. *Cambridge county records.* 1931.
91   Hand, Geoffrey J.P. 'Material used in "Calendar of documents relating to Ireland" ', *Irish Historical Studies,* 12 (1960), 94–104. A revision of the PRO *Calendar of documents relating to Ireland, 1171–1307.*
92   Harvey, John H. and Arthur Oswald (comps.). *English medieval architects. A biographical dictionary down to 1550.* 1954. A comprehensive and remarkable work.
93   Hearnshaw, Fossey J.C. *Municipal records.* Helps for Students of History, no. 2 (1918).
94   Hector, Leonard C. *et al. Guide to the contents of the Public Record Office.* 1963. HMSO, 2 vols.
95   HMSO. *British national archives: sectional list no. 24* (Record Publications). A revised list of governmental publications in the PRO, the RS, the Record Commission publications. Issued annually; *Reports of the deputy keeper of the public records, Ireland.* 1912–51; *Ancient monuments and public buildings* (Sectional list no. 27). Issued annually. *Guide to publications of the royal commission on ancient and historical monuments;* Royal Commission on Historical Monuments, *England. An inventory . . . in Oxford.* 1939. *Catalogue of works (other than parliamentary papers and acts of parliament) published by HMSO. Consolidated list, 1922–32.* 1922–33, 11 vols; *London Museum medieval catalogue.* Reprinted 1967; James H. Wylie and J. Wylie (eds.). *Report on the records of the city of Exeter.* 1916; *Eighteenth and twentieth reports.* 1917–18.
96   —— PRO lists and indexes. *Lists of diplomatic documents, Scottish documents and papal bulls.* Lists and Indexes, 49 (1923); *List Q revised. List*

of record publications. 1935; *Index of ancient petitions of the chancery and of the exchequer.* Revised eds., 1966 and 1969, 2 vols; *Index of ancient petitions.* Revised ed., 1969; *Supplementary list of accounts various of the exchequer.* 1969; *Supplementary list of rentals and surveys,* 14. In Supplementary series. 1969.

97   Irish Manuscripts Commission. *Catalogue of publications issued and in preparation, 1928–45.* Dublin, 1946.

98   Irwin, Raymond and Ronald Stavely (eds.). *The libraries of London.* 2nd ed., 1961. A good introduction to London's historical resources.

99   James, Montague R. *The wanderings and homes of manuscripts.* 1919.

100   —— *A descriptive catalogue of the Latin manuscripts in the John Rylands library at Manchester.* Manchester, 1921. Supplementary lists printed in *BJRL.*

101   —— 'Bury St Edmunds manuscripts', *EHR,* 41 (1926), 251–60. A complete list, as far as possible.

102   —— and Claude Jenkins. *A descriptive catalogue of the manuscripts in the library of Lambeth Palace.* 5 Pts. 1930–32.

103   Jeayes, Isaac H. *Descriptive catalogues of the charters and muniments belonging to the Marquis of Anglesey.* Collections for a history of Staffordshire ed. by the staff of the Staffordshire Record Society (1937). Kendal, 1937. A catalogue with abstracts. Preface on Burton Abbey to which charters, etc. refer, by Margaret Deansley.

104   Jenkins, Claude. *Ecclesiastical records . . . 1920.* Helps for Students of History, no. 18 (1920).

105   Jenkinson, C. Hilary. 'The records of the exchequer receipts from the English Jewry', *Jewish Historical Society,* 8 (1918), 19–62. Contains lists of special Jewish receipt rolls.

106   —— A manual of archive administration. 1922. Revised ed. 1937.

107   —— *Guide to the public records, Pt. 1, Introductory.* 1949. HMSO. Historical development and present functions.

108   —— *Guide to archives and other collections of documents relating to Surrey.* Surrey Record Society, 23.

109   Jones, Philip E. and Raymond Smith. *A guide to the records in the corporation of London records office and the guildhall library muniment room.* 1951. A systematic analysis.

110   Ker, Neil R. *Medieval libraries of Great Britain: a list of surviving books.* Royal Historical Society Guides and Handbooks, no. 3 (1941). 2nd ed., 1964.

111   —— 'Salisbury cathedral manuscripts and Patrick Young's catalogue', *Wiltshire Archaeological and Natural Magazine,* 53 (1949–50), 153–83.

112   —— '*Liber Custumarum* and other manuscripts formerly at the guildhall' (London). *Guildhall Miscellany,* 1 (1952–59), no. 3 (1954), 37–46. List of manuscripts.

113   —— *English manuscripts in the century after the Norman Conquest.* Oxford, 1960. Numerous plates excellent for paleography.

114   Kiralfy, Alfred K.R. and Gareth H. Jones. *General guide to the society's publications.* Selden Society, 1960. Covers vols. 1–79.

115   Kirby, John L. *A guide to historical periodicals in the English language.* Historical Association. 1970.

116   Kurath, Hans, Sherman M. Kuhn *et al.* (eds.). *Middle English dictionary.* Ann Arbor, Mich., 1952–. The best available.

117   Kuttner, Stephan G. *Reportorium der Kanonistik (1140–1234). Prodomus corporis glossarum.* Vol. 1. Vatican City, 1937. Includes a comprehensive survey of canonistic manuscripts in England. A very important book.

118   Latham, Ronald E. (ed.). *Revised medieval Latin word-list from British and Irish sources.* 1965. Basic.

119   Lawrence, Henry. *Yorkshire Archaeological Society.* Leeds, 1939. Analytical index of the first thirty volumes of the society.

120   Leach, Maria (ed.). *Standard dictionary of folklore, mythology, and legend.* New York, 1949–50, 2 vols.

121   Le Neve, John. *John Le Neve, fasti ecclesiae anglicanae, 1300–1541.* 1962–

69, 12 vols. Revised by Joyce M. Horn *et al.* Invaluable lists of ecclesiastical officials: a scholarly revision.

122   Little, Andrew G. *Franciscan papers, lists and documents.* Manchester, 1943.

123   London University, Institute of Historical Research. 'Historical manuscripts: accessions; migrations', *BIHR.* Published annually.

124   Major, Kathleen. *A handlist of the records of the bishop of Lincoln and of the archdeacons of Lincoln and Stow.* Lincoln, 1953.

125   Martin, Charles T. *List of ancient correspondence of the chancery and the exchequer.* Revised ed. 1970.

126   Masters, Betty R. 'The common sergeant', London city officers, I. *Guildhall Miscellany,* 2 (1967), 379–89. Lists 1319–1964.

127   —— 'The town clerk', London city officers. *Guildhall Miscellany,* 3 (1969), 55–74. From 1274–1954.

128   Matheson, Cyril. *Catalogue of the publications of Scottish historical clubs and societies, and of the papers relative to Scottish history issued by H.M. Stationery Office.* Aberdeen, 1928. From 1909–27.

129   Matthews, Leslie G. *The royal apothecaries.* 1967.

130   Milne, A. Taylor. *A centenary guide to the publications of the Royal Historical Society 1868–1968 and of the former Camden Society 1838–1897.* 1968.

131   Mullins, Edward L.C. *Texts and calendars: an analytical guide to serial publications.* Royal Historical Society Guides and Handbooks, no. 7 (1958). An annotated guide to governmental publications, such as Rolls Series and materials from PRO.

132   —— *Guide to the historical and archaeological publications of English and Welsh societies 1901–1933.* 1968. Supplements *BIHR,* 1–10.

133   Murray, Robert H. *The public record office, Dublin.* Helps for Students of History, 1918. A very small but useful pamphlet.

134   —— *A short guide to the principal classes of documents preserved in the public record office, Dublin.* Helps for Students of History, 7 (1919).

135   Mynors, Roger A.B. (ed.). *Durham cathedral manuscripts to the end of the twelfth century.* Oxford, 1939. Includes plates.

136   —— *Catalogue of the manuscripts of Balliol College.* Oxford, 1963.

137   Nas, Raoul *et al. Dictionnaire du droit canonique, contenant tous les termes du droit canonique, avec un sommaire de l'histoire et des institutions et de l'État actuel de la discipline.* Paris, 1935. Scholarly and invaluable.

138   O'Grady, Standish H., Robin Flower, and Mylos Dillon. *Catalogues of Irish manuscripts in the British museum.* 1926–53, 3 vols. Printed for the trustees. With valuable comments.

139   Ollard, Sidney L. *Fasti Wyndesorienses: the deans and the canons of Windsor.* Windsor, 1950.

140   —— *et al.* (eds.). *A dictionary of English church history.* 1912. 3rd ed. revised 1948. Valuable.

141   O'Rahilly, Thomas F. *et al. Catalogue of Irish manuscripts in the Royal Irish academy.* Vols. 1–27. Dublin, 1926–43. Index by Kathleen Mulchrone and Elizabeth Fitzpatrick. Dublin, 1948.

142   Owen, Edward. *A catalogue of the manuscripts relating to Wales in the British museum.* 1920–22, 4 vols.

143   Peek, Heather E. and Catherine P. Hall (eds.). *The archives of the university of Cambridge.* Cambridge, 1962.

144   Powicke, Frederick M. and Edmund B. Fryde. *Handbook of British Chronology.* Royal Historical Society Guides and Handbooks, no. 2. 2nd ed., 1961. An invaluable tool for research; includes lists of officers and ecclesiastics.

145   Reaney, Percy H. *A dictionary of British surnames.* 1958. An indispensable work of reference, the best of its kind. See also B.O. Eilert Ekwall. 'Variations in surnames in medieval London', *Bulletin de la société royale des lettres de Lund.* 1944–45, 307–62.

146   Ricci, Seymour de. *Census of medieval and Renaissance manuscripts in the United States and Canada.* New York, 1935–40, 3 vols.

147   Richardson, Henry G. and George O. Sayles. 'List of parliaments, 1258–

1832', *Interim report of the committee on House of Commons personnel and politics 1264–1832.* 1932. HMSO.

148 Russell, Josiah C. *Dictionary of writers of thirteenth century England.* Special Supp. no. 3, *BIHR.* 1936. Includes long series of biographies. By a remarkable scholar, but to be handled with some care.

149 ———— Supplements in *BIHR,* 16 (1938), 48–50; 18 (1940), 40–42; 20 (1942), 99–100; 22 (1944), 312–14.

150 Rye, Reginald A. *Catalogue of MSS. in the [London] university library . . . with a description of the . . . life of Ed. the Black Prince by Chandos the herald . . .* 1921.

151 ———— *The students' guide to the libraries of London . . .* 1908; 3rd ed., revised and enlarged 1927.

152 Saltmarsh, John. *The muniments of King's College* [Cambridge]. Cambridge, 1933.

153 Sayers, Jane E. *Estate documents at Lambeth palace library: a short catalogue.* Leicester, 1965.

154 ———— *Original papal documents in the Lambeth palace.* 1967. A catalogue.

155 Singer, Dorothea W. (ed.). 'Survey of medical manuscripts in the British Isles dating from before the sixteenth century'. *Proceedings of the Royal Society of Medicine,* 12 (1918). 96–107.

156 ———— and Annie Anderson. *Catalogue of Latin and vernacular alchemical manuscripts in Great Britain and Ireland dating from before the XVI century.* Brussels, 1928. 1931, 2 vols.

157 Somerville, Robert. *Handlist of Record Publications.* British Record Association Pamphlet, no. 3 (1951).

158 Stratton, Arthur. *Introductory handbook to the styles of English architecture.* 3rd ed., 1938, 2 vols.

159 Talbot, Charles H. and Eugene A. Hammond. *The medical practitioners in medieval London. A biographical register.* 1965.

160 Tanner, Lawrence E. *Westminster abbey. The library and muniments room.* 2nd ed., revised, Oxford, 1935.

161 Tavender, Augusta S. 'Medieval English alabasters in American Museums', *Speculum,* 30 (1955), 64–71. Lists the examples. Includes ten fine plates.

162 Taylor, Frank (ed.). 'Court rolls, rentals, surveys and analogous documents in the John Rylands Library', *BJRL,* 31 (1948), 345–78.

163 Thompson, A. Hamilton. *The Surtees Society 1834–1934 including a catalogue of its publications. Surtees Society, Publications for 1935,* 150 (1939).

164 Watt, Donald E.R. *Fasti ecclesiae Scoticanae Medii Aevi ad annum 1638.* (Second draft). Scottish Record Society, n.s. 1 (1969).

165 Wood, Herbert. *A guide to the records deposited in the public record office Ireland.* Dublin, 1919.

166 ———— 'Muniments of Edmund de Mortimer, third earl of March concerning his liberty of Trim', *Royal Irish Academy,* 40 (1931–32). Section 3, 312–55. Includes catalogue of deeds and transcripts of documents.

167 Wooley, R. Maxwell. *Catalogue of MSS. of Lincoln cathedral chapter library.* 1927.

168 Zupko, Ronald E. *A dictionary of English weights and measures from Anglo-Saxon times to the nineteenth century.* Madison, Wis., 1968.

III. GENERAL SURVEYS

169 Bloch, Marc. *La société féodale.* Paris, 1939–40, 2 vols. English trans. 1960. A landmark, written by a master. Trans. L.A. Manyon. *Feudal Society.* Chicago, 1961. Foreword by Michael M. Postan.

170 Boutruche, Robert. *Seigneurie et féodalité.* Vol. 1. Paris, 1959.

171 Bury, John B. *et al.* (eds.). *The Cambridge medieval history.* Vol. 6: *Victory of the papacy.* Cambridge, 1929. Vol. 7: *Decline of Empire and Papacy.* Cambridge, 1932. Weighty interpretation, now a little out of date.

172   Crump, Charles G. and Ernest F. Jacob. *The legacy of the middle ages.* Oxford, 1926. Some stimulating essays, including a contribution by Frederick M. Powicke on the Christian life.

173   Lagarde, Georges de. *La naissance de l'esprit laïque au décline du moyen âge.* New ed., Paris, 1956—63, 5 vols. A standard work. Vol. 5 on William Ockham in the ed. of 1963 is almost a new book.

174   McIlwain, Charles H. *The growth of political thought in the West.* 1932. Still a valuable survey.

175   Mitteis, Heinrich. *Lehnrecht und Staatsgewalt.* Weimar, 1933. Mainly European, but important for English historians.

176   Ullmann, Walter. *Medieval papalism; the political theories of the medieval canonists.* 1949. A valuable background, but sometimes out of touch with the realities of political life.

177   —— *Principles of government and politics in the Middle Ages.* New York, 1961. Ullmann's attempt to relate principles to politics has been strongly criticized.

178   *Victoria history of the counties of England*, ed. William Page *et al.* See Altschul 167—96, 199—200. Oxford, ed. Louis F. Salzmann, 1939; Dorset, ed. Ralph B. Pugh, 1968; Middlesex, ed. James S. Cockburn, 1969; Shropshire, ed. Alexander T. Gaydon, 1968; Southwark and the city, ed. David J. Johnson, 1969; Warwickshire, ed. William B. Stephens, 1969; General Introduction, Ralph B. Pugh, 1970.

IV. CONSTITUTIONAL AND ADMINISTRATIVE HISTORY

1 Printed Sources

179   Angus, William (ed.). 'Miscellaneous charters, 1315—1401, from transcripts in the collection of the late Sir William Fraser', *Publications of the Scottish Historical Society*, ser. 3, 21 (1933), 3—75.

180   Barnes, Patricia and Cecil F. Slade (eds.). *A medieval miscellany for Doris May Stenton.* Pipe Roll Society, 36 (1962). Contains charters from the period Henry I to Henry III.

181   Barrow, Geoffrey W.S. (ed.). *The acts of Malcolm IV, king of Scots, 1153—1165.* Edinburgh, 1960.

182   Bayley, Kennett E. (ed.). 'Two thirteenth century assize rolls for the county of Durham', *Surtees Society Miscellanea*, 2 (1916), 1—105.

183   Beardwood, Alice (ed.). *Records of the trial of Walter Langton bishop of Coventry and Lichfield 1307—1312.* Camden Society, ser. 4, 6 (1969). Throws much light on administrative practice under Edward I.

184   Bémont, Charles (ed.). *Un rôle Gascon de lettres closes expédiées par la chancellerie du prince Édouard (1254—5).* Paris, 1916. There is a valuable Introduction.

185   Bracton, Henry. *Bracton on the laws and customs of England* (Bracton de legibus et consuetudinibus Angliae), ed. and trans. Samuel E. Thorne. Cambridge, 1968, 2 vols. Revises and amends the ed. by George E. Woodbine, New Haven, Conn., 1915 and 1942, 4 vols., which it supersedes. A definitive ed.

186   Cam, Helen M. (ed.). *The eyre of London, 14 Edward II, A.D. 1321.* (Year Books of Edward II, Pts 1 and 2.) Selden Society, 26, 27 (1968—69), 2 vols.

187   Cantle, Albert (ed.). *The pleas of quo warranto for the county of Lancaster. Remains historical and literary connected with the palatine counties of Lancaster and Cheshire.* Chetham Society, n.s., 98 (1937).

188   Chaplais, Pierre (ed.). *English royal documents, 1199—1461.* Oxford, 1971. A beautiful ed.

189   Chew, Helena M. and Martin Weinbaum (eds.). *The London eyre of 1244.* London Record Society, 6 (1970).

190   Chrimes, Stanley B. and Alfred L. Brown (eds.). *Select documents of English constitutional history, 1307—1485.* 1961. A useful collection, with some careless headings.

191   Cooper [Lord] Thomas M. *Select Scottish cases of the thirteenth century.* Edinburgh, 1944. Condensed summary of cases with sixty-eight pages of Introduction.

192   ——— 'The register of brieves as contained in the Ayr MS., the Bute MS., and the Quoniam Attachiamenta', *Stair Society,* 10 (1946), 1—65.

193   Cuttino, George P. (ed.). *The Gascon calendar of 1322.* Camden Society, ser. 3, 70 (1949). From 1187 to 1331. Excellently edited; see also *English diplomatic administration, 1259—1330.* New York, 1971.

194   Dale, Marion R. (ed.). *Calendar of the cases from Derbyshire from eyre and assize rolls preserved in the public record office.* Heswall Hill, Cheshire, 1938. Compiled by Cecil E. Lugard.

195   Davies, J. Conway (ed.). *The Welsh assize roll (1277—84).* Board of Celtic Studies, History and Law Series, 7 (1940). An important source for the period.

196   ——— *The cartae antiquae rolls 11—20, printed from the original MSS. in the public record office.* Pipe Roll Society, 71 (for 1957), n.s. 33 (1960). These rolls are composed of medieval transcripts of charters, mainly royal grants of lands and liberties.

197   Davis, E. Jeffries and Martin Weinbaum (eds.). 'Sources for the London eyre of 1321', *BIHR,* 7 (1930), 35—38.

198   De Haas, Elsa and George D.G. Hall (eds.). *Early registers of writs.* Selden Society, 87 (1970). Contains the writs 'of course' current in England in the thirteenth century. Sent by Henry III to Ireland, so that justice could be done there more according to the custom of England.

199   Denholm-Young, Noël. *Magna carta and the other charters of English liberties in a revised text.* 1938; see also W. Ivor Jennings. *Magna carta and its influence on the world today.* 1965. HMSO. Arthur J. Collins. 'The documents of the great charter of 1215', *PBA,* 34 (1948), 233—79.

200   Deslisle, M. Léopold (ed.). *Recueil des actes de Henry II, roi d'Angleterre et duc de Normandie, concernant les provinces françaises et les affaires de France.* Revue et publiée par M. Élie Berger. Vol. 3 (tables). Paris, 1920.

201   Dunham, William H. (ed.). *Casus placitorum and reports of cases in the king's courts 1272—1278.* Selden Society, 69 (1952). A collection of cases made for men of the law, with an illuminating Introduction.

202   Edwards, J. Goronwy (ed.). *Calendar of ancient correspondence concerning Wales.* Cardiff, 1935.

203   ——— *Littere Wallie preserved in the Liber A in the public record office.* Cardiff, 1940. A book of records, ranging in date from 1241 to 1292, probably compiled for Edward I.

204   Emmanuel, Hywel D. (ed.). *The Latin Texts of the Welsh laws.* Cardiff, 1967. Of major importance for the study of medieval Welsh law; the text consists of five redactions dating from the twelfth to the fifteenth centuries, with Introduction and notes.

205   Fitz Nigel, Richard. *The course of the exchequer by Richard son of Nigel (text and translation of 'De necessariis observandis saccario qui vulgo dictatur Dialogus de Saccario'),* ed. Charles Johnson. 1950. A fine work of scholarship, with an excellent Introduction.

206   Flower, Cyril T. (ed.). *Public works in medieval law.* Vol. 2. Selden Society, 40 (1923). (Vol. 1 published in 1915.) A mine of information.

207   Fowler, G. Herbert. 'Roll of the justices in eyre at Bedford, 1227', *BedsRec,* 3 (1916), 1—206; also 'Calendar of the roll of the justices on eyre, 1247', *BedsRec,* 21 (1939).

208   Fowler, Robert C. *Calendar of chancery warrants preserved in the public record office, 1244—1326.* 1927. HMSO.

209   Furber, Elizabeth C. *Essex sessions of the peace, 1351, 1377—79.* Essex

Archaeological Society. Occasional Publications, no. 3 (1953). Illustrates lawlessness between 1349 and 1381.

210   Glanville, Ranulf de. *Tractatus de legibus et consuetudinibus regni Angliae qui Glanvilla vocatur (the treatise on the laws and customs of the realm of England commonly called Glanville),* ed. George D.G. Hall. 1965. An excellent ed., superseding earlier ones.

211   Gollancz, Marguerite (ed.). *Rolls of Northamptonshire sessions of the peace, 1320.* Northants Record Society Publications, 9 (1940).

212   Griffiths, John (ed.). 'Two early ministers' accounts for North Wales', *BBCS,* 9 (1937), 50–70. Chamberlain's accounts 1291–92; sheriff's accounts 1291–92.

213   Harvey, Charles and James MacLeod (eds.). *Calendar of writs preserved at Yester house 1166–1625.* Scottish Record Society, 42 (1930).

214   Hengham, Ralph de. *Radulphi de Hengham Summae,* ed. William H. Dunham. Cambridge, 1932. Definitive text. Indispensable.

215   HMSO. *Calendar, patent rolls, Edward III, 1374–7,* with appendixes for 1340 and 1345; *Calendar, charter rolls, 1341–1417; Close rolls of Henry III, 1242–72; Calendar, inquisitions misc. chancery.* 1–3. 1219–1377; Calendar, inquisitions post mortem. 9–14 (21–51 Edward III); *Curia regis rolls,* 1–15 Richard I–21 Henry III; *Calendar, chancery warrants, 1244–1445; Records of the Duchy of Lancaster,* 3 vols. The volumes were published between 1916 and 1969, with vol. 15 of the *Curia regis rolls* in the press.

216   Jenkins, Dafydd (ed.). *Llyfr Colan.* Cardiff, 1963. A fragment of the *Cyfraith Hywel* preserved in a thirteenth-century MS., including material from other sources.

217   Jenkins, J. Gilbert. *Calendar of the roll of justices on eyre, 1227, for Buckinghamshire.* Architectural and Archaeological Society for Buckinghamshire, Record Branch, 6 (1945).

218   Kaye, John M. *Placita corone, or la corone pledes devant justices.* Selden Society, Supp. ser. 4 (1966). The basic equipment of an ordinary thirteenth-century lawyer in an ordinary practice. The Introduction has novel views on the practice of criminal law.

219   Kimball, Elizabeth G. *Rolls of the Warwickshire and Coventry sessions of the peace, 1377–1397.* Dugdale Society, 6 (1939). Of great value for legal, social, and economic historians as well as for students of municipal institutions.

220   —— *Rolls of the Gloucestershire sessions of the peace, 1361–1398.* Bristol and Gloucestershire Archaeological Society, 62 (1942).

221   —— *Records of the sessions of the peace in Lincolnshire, 1381–96,* II: *the parts of Lindsey.* Lincoln Record Society, 56 (1962).

222   Landon, Lionel (ed.). *The cartae antiquae. Rolls 1–10.* Pipe Roll Society, n.s., 17 (1939). Mostly Angevin period, particularly John.

223   Leadam, Isaac and James F. Baldwin (eds.). *Select cases before the king's council, 1243–1482.* Cambridge, Mass., 1918. Valuable introduction.

224   Lugard, Cecil E. (ed.). *Trailbaston, Derbyshire.* Ashover, 1933–35, 3 vols. Concerned with 1297–1305.

225   —— *Calendar of cases for Derbyshire from eyre and assize rolls preserved in the P.R.O.* 1938. Introduction and transcript by Marion K. Dale.

226   Meekings, Cecil A.F. (ed.). *Crown pleas of the Wilshire eyre, 1249.* Archaeological Society, Record Branch, 16 (1961). Translated with an excellent Introduction.

227   Putnam, Bertha H. *Proceedings before the justices of the peace in the fourteenth and fifteenth centuries, Edward III to Richard III.* 1938. Breaks new ground and makes available valuable new material. Important commentary on the indictments by Theodore F.T. Plucknett, pp. cxxxiii to clxi; also *Yorkshire sessions of the peace 1361–1364. Yorks.Arch.Rec.,* 100 (1939). Expertly edited.

228   Richardson, Henry G. and George O. Sayles (eds.). *Rotuli parliamentorum hactenus inediti 1279–1373.* Camden Society, ser. 3, 51 (1935). Important new material.

229 ——— *Select cases of procedure without writ under Henry III*. Selden Society, 60 (1941). Valuable Introduction.
230 ——— *Parliaments and councils of medieval Ireland*. Vol. 1. Dublin, 1947. Stationery Office. Prints relevant documents with little comment. But a valuable selection.
231 ——— *Fleta*. Selden Society, 72 (1955). A definitive text with some flaws in translation.
232 ——— *The administration of Ireland, 1172–1377*. Dublin, 1963. Contains lists of officers of state, with illustrative documents.
233 Rogers, Ralph V. 'A source for Fitzherbert's "La Graunde abridgement" ', *EHR*, 56 (1941), 605–28. Prints three versions of a case in 1330–31.
234 Salter, Herbert E. *Facsimiles of early charters in Oxford muniments rooms*. Oxford, 1929. Dated up to 1251.
235 Sayles, George O. (ed.). 'The "Mad" parliament: parliamentary representation in 1294, 1295, and 1307', *BIHR*, 3 (1926), 110–15. Prints a facsimile.
236 ——— *Select cases in the court of king's bench under Edward I, II and III*. Selden Society, 55, 57, 58, 74, 76, 82 (1936–65), 6 vols. Valuable Introductions.
237 ——— *Analecta Hibernica*, 23 (1966). Contains documents illustrating legal proceedings against the first earl of Desmond, 1351.
238 Shanks, Elsie and Stroud F.C. Milsom (eds.). *Novae narrationes*. Selden Society, 80 (1963). Collections of formal statements with which plaintiffs opened their cases before the court, probably 1285–c. 1310. Includes a 'Commentary on the Actions'. A work of high scholarship.
239 Sillem, Rosamond (ed.). *Some sessions of the peace in Lincolnshire 1360–1375*. Lincoln Record Society, 30 (1936).
240 Sinclair, Walter (ed.). *A Lincolnshire assize roll for 1298*. Lincoln Record Society, 36 (1944).
241 Stenton, Doris M. (ed.). *The earliest Lincolnshire assize rolls, A.D. 1202–1209*. Lincoln Record Society, 22 (1926); *The earliest Northamptonshire assize rolls A.D. 1202 and 1203*. Northants Record Society, 5 (1930); *Rolls of the justices in eyre, Lincolnshire 1218–19 and Worcestershire 1221*. Selden Society, 53 (1934); *Rolls of the justices in eyre, being the rolls of pleas and assizes for Gloucestershire, Warwickshire and Shropshire, 1221, 1222*. Selden Society, 59 (1940). (Title corrected — for 'Staffordshire' read 'Shropshire'). Illuminating commentary on society; *Pleas before the king or his justices, 1198–1202 and 1198–1212*. Selden Society, 67–68, 83–84 (1953, 1967), 4 vols. Of outstanding importance.
242 Stenton, Frank M. (ed.). *Facsimiles of early charters from Northamptonshire collections*. Northants Record Society, 4, 5 (1930), 2 vols.
243 Stone, Edward (ed.). *Oxford hundred rolls of 1279*. Oxford Record Society, 46 (1968). *The hundred of Bampton*, ed. Edward Stone; the borough of Witney, ed. Patricia Hyde.
244 Thompson, A. Hamilton. *Northumbrian pleas from de banco rolls, 1 Edward I*. Durham, 1950.
245 Thomson, Walter S. (ed.). *A Lincolnshire assize roll for 1298 (P.R.O. assize roll no. 505)*. Lincoln Record Society, 36 (1944). Contains proceedings before a commission of oyer and terminer appointed April 4, 1298; deals with complaints against royal officials. A remarkable piece of work.
246 Thorne, Samuel E. *A discourse upon the exposition and understanding of statutes with Sir Thomas Egerton's additions*. San Marino, Cal. Thorne holds that English lawyers in the Middle Ages did not consider that parliament made new laws which the courts must enforce. His view is rejected by some English legal historians. See *EHR*, 58 (1943), 106–07. But Thorne's interpretation commands serious attention.
247 Turner, George J. (ed.). *Brevia placitata*. (Completed with additions by Theodore F.T. Plucknett.) Selden Society, 66 (1947). The *Brevia* was a legal treatise of the mid-thirteenth century. There is a valuable Introduction.
248 Willard, James F. 'Ordinance for the guidance of a deputy treasurer, 22

October 1305', *EHR*, 48 (1933), 84—89. The ordinances were made to operate during the absence of the treasurer.
249   *Year Books.* The year books of Edward II are published by the Selden Society, Vol. 9 (1926) to Vol. 81 (1964). The editors were George J. Turner, Theodore F.T. Plucknett, William C. Bolland, Paul Vinogradoff, Ludwig Ehrlich, M. Dominica Legge, William Holdsworth, John P. Collas. The series is magnificently edited and is invaluable.

2 General Surveys

250   Buckland, William W. and Arnold D. McNair. *Roman law and common law.* Cambridge, 1936.
251   Chrimes, Stanley B. *An introduction to the administrative history of medieval England.* Oxford, 1952. A useful synthesis.
252   Clanchy, Michael T. 'Law, government and society in medieval England', *History*, 59 (1974), 73—78.
253   Edwards, J. Goronwy. *The principality of Wales, 1267—1967: a study in constitutional history.* Caernavon, 1969. A reliable guide by a fine historian.
254   Fifoot, Cecil H.S. *History and sources of the common law: tort and contract.* 1949. From Glanvil to *c.* 1849.
255   Holdsworth, William S. *History of English law*, ed. Stanley B. Chrimes *et al.* 7th ed., 1956—66, 16 vols.
256   Jolliffe, John E.A. *The constitutional history of medieval England from the English settlements to 1485.* 1937, 4th ed., 1961. Scholarly and stimulating, but somewhat erratic.
257   Kantorowicz, Ernst H. *The king's two bodies: a study in medieval political theology.* Princeton, N.J., 1957. A long-awaited complement to Fritz Kern.
258   Kuttner, Stephan and John J. Ryan (eds.). *Proceedings of the second international congress of medieval canon law, Boston College 12—16 August, 1963.* Vatican City, 1965; especially Charles Duggan. 'The reception of canon law in England in the later twelfth century', pp. 391—97; Michael Sheehan. 'Canon law and English institutions: some notes on current research', pp. 391—97; Leonard Boyle. 'The "Summa summarum" and some other English works of canon law', pp. 415—56.
259   Lyon, Bryce D. *A constitutional and legal history of medieval England.* New York, 1960. A lucid textbook.
260   McIlwain, Charles H. *Constitutionalism: ancient and modern.* Ithaca, N.Y., 1947. By an eminent constitutionalist but containing some debatable views, especially about *gubernaculum* and *jurisdictio.*
261   Mackinnon, James and James A.R. Mackinnon. *The constitutional history of Scotland from the early times to the Reformation.* 1924.
262   Petit-Dutaillis, Charles *et al. Studies and notes supplementary to Stubbs' 'Constitutional History' down to the great charter.* Manchester, 1908—29, 3 vols. (Published in one vol. in 1930 and reprinted in 1968.) Some parts are now out of date.
263   Plucknett, Theodore F.T. *A concise history of the common law.* 5th ed., 1956. Still the best available.
264   Pollock, Frederick and Frederic W. Maitland. *The history of English law before the time of Edward I.* New ed., Cambridge, 1968, 2 vols., ed. Stroud F.C. Milsom. With a new Introduction and a select bibliography. A well-known masterpiece.
265   Post, Gaines. *Studies in medieval legal thought: public law and the state, 1100—1322.* Princeton, N.J., 1964. A scholarly discussion of the intellectual background to legal and political change.
266   Richardson, Henry G. and George O. Sayles. *The governance of medieval England from the conquest to magna carta.* Edinburgh, 1963. Learned and indispensable, but sometimes dogmatic and perverse.
267   Stenton, Doris M. *English justice between the Norman conquest and the great charter, 1066—1215.* Philadelphia, 1964. A judicious survey by a great expert, but saying little of *vis* and *voluntas, ira* and *malvolentia.*

268   Stubbs, William. *The constitutional history of England in its origin and developments.* Reprint of 6th ed., New York, 1967, 3 vols. A great classic, but Stubbs' method of approach has long been under attack (some of which is quite unwarranted), and much of the three vols. is out of date.

269   Taswell-Langemead, Thomas P. *English constitutional history.* 11th ed., 1960. Revised and enlarged by Theodore F.T. Plucknett. Compact and factual; a standard work.

270   Tout, Thomas F. *Chapters in the administrative history of medieval England.* Manchester, 1920—37, 7 vols. A great pioneer survey: influencing all future writing on the subject. It has been unduly criticized by some younger scholars.

271   Ullmann, Walter. *Principles of government and politics in the middle ages.* 2nd ed., 1966. A stimulating survey by an eminent scholar, but to be used with care.

272   ——— *The individual and society in the middle ages.* Baltimore, Md., 1966. Scholarly and thought-provoking, but overemphasizes the purely theoretical aspect of the problem.

3 Monographs

273   Ault, Warren O. *Private jurisdiction in England.* New Haven, Conn., 1923. Brings together much material in a difficult and important subject.

274   Barraclough, Geoffrey. *The earldom and county palatine of Chester.* Oxford, 1953. An expert study.

275   Bassett, Marjory. *Knights of the shire for Bedfordshire during the Middle Ages. BedsRec.*, 29 (1949).

276   Bellamy, John G. *The law of treason in England in the later Middle Ages.* Cambridge, 1970. A learned and important book; see also Ojars Kratins. 'Treason in middle English romances', *Philological Quarterly*, 35 (1966), 668—87; Samuel Rezneck. 'History of the parliamentary declaration of treason', *LQR*, 46 (1930), 81—102; Maurice H. Keen. 'Treason trials under the law of arms', *TRHS*, ser. 5, 12 (1962), 85—103. Important pioneer work.

277   Bisson, Thomas N. *Assemblies and representation in Languedoc in the thirteenth century.* Princeton, N.J., 1964. An important study; also 'The military origins of medieval representation', *AHR*, 71 (1966), 1199—1218; William N. Bryant. 'The financial dealings of Edward III with the county communities, 1330—1360', *EHR*, 83 (1968), 760—71; Helen M. Cam. 'The evolution of the medieval English franchise', *Speculum*, 32 (1957), 427—42; also 'Representation in the city of London in the Middle Ages', *Album E. Lousse*, in *Studies presented to the international commission for representative and parliamentary institutions.* Louvain, 1963, 109—23; Ludwig Riess. *The history of English electoral law in the Middle Ages*, trans. and enlarged Kathleen Wood-Legh. Cambridge, 1940. First published in German in 1885. The work has been partly superseded by more recent research; Edward E. Miller. *The origins of parliament.* 1960. Historical Association Leaflet, 44; George P. Cuttino. 'Medieval parliament reinterpreted', *Speculum*, 41 (1966), 681—87; also 'A reconsideration of the *modus tenendi parliamentum*', in Francis L. Utley (ed.). *The forward movement of the century.* Columbus, Ohio, 1961, 31—60; William A. Morris. 'The date of the "modus tenendi parliamentum" ', *EHR*, 49 (1934), 407—22; William A. Morris. 'Magnates and community of the realm in parliament, 1264—1327', *Med et Hum*, 1 (1943), 58—94; Henry G. Richardson and George O. Sayles. *The early statutes.* 1934; Henry G. Richardson and George O. Sayles. *Parliaments and great councils in medieval England.* 1961. (Parliament is regarded as essentially an afforced meeting of the council); J. Goronwy Edwards. ' "Re-election" and the medieval parliament?', *History*, 11 (1926), 204—10; also *The commons in medieval parliaments.* 1958 (Emphasises the importance of "intercommuning"); also *Historians and the medieval parliament.* Glasgow, 1960; Robert S. Rait. *The parliaments of Scotland.* Glasgow, 1924; Maude V.

Clarke. *Medieval representation and consent, a study of early parliaments in England with special reference to the "modus tenendi parliamentum".* 1936; also 'Irish parliaments in the reign of Edward II', *TRHS*, ser 4, 9 (1926), 29–62; J. Enoch Powell and Keith Wallis. *The house of lords in the Middle Ages.* 1968; Edmund B. Fryde. 'Parliament and the French war, 1336–40', *EPBW*, 250–81; Josiah C. Russell. 'Early parliamentary organization', *AHR*, 43 (1937), 1–21; George L. Haskins. 'The petition of representatives in the parliaments of Edward I', *EHR*, 53 (1938), 1–20; Theodore F.T. Plucknett. 'Parliament', *EGAW*, 1, 82–128; Albert F. Pollard. 'The medieval under-clerks of parliament', *BIHR*, 16 (1938), 65–87; also 'The clerical organization of parliament', *EHR*, 57 (1942), 31–58; 'Receivers of petitions and clerks of parliament', *EHR*, 57 (1942), 202–26; 'The clerk of the crown', *EHR*, 57 (1942), 312–33; Thor Thorgrimsson. 'Plenum parliamentum', *BIHR*, 32 (1959), 69–82; John Taylor. 'The manuscripts of the *modus tenendi parliamentum*', *EHR*, 83 (1968), 673–88; Henry G. Richardson. 'John of Gaunt and the parliamentary representation of Lancashire', *BJRL*, 22 (1938), 175–222; 'The Irish parliaments of Edward I', *Proceedings of the Royal Irish Academy*, 38 (1928–29), 128–47; Henry G. Richardson and George O. Sayles. 'Problems presented by the early statutes', *LQR*, 50 (1934), 201–23, 540–71 (Discuss MSS.); Henry G. Richardson and George O. Sayles. 'Parliamentary documents from formularies', *BIHR*, 11 (1933–34), 147–62. (Print extract from 1338); Henry G. Richardson and George O. Sayles. 'The parliament of Carlisle, 1307 – some new documents', *EHR*, 53 (1938), 425–37; and 'The earliest known official use of the term "parliament" ', *EHR*, 82 (1967), 747–50; John S. Roskell. 'The problem of the attendance of the lords in medieval parliaments', *BIHR*, 29 (1956), 153–204. (Shows the lack of attendance by peers.); John S. Roskell. 'Sir Peter de la Mare, speaker for the commons in parliament in 1376 and 1377', *Nottingham Medieval Studies*, 2 (1958), 24–37; and 'Perspectives in English parliamentary history', *BJRL*, 46 (1963–64), 448–75; and 'A consideration of certain aspects and problems of the English modus tenendum parliamentum', *BJRL*, 50 (1967–68), 411–42; also George O. Sayles. 'Representation of cities and boroughs in 1268', *EHR*, 40 (1925), 580–85 (Contains some important facts); 'Parliamentary representation in 1294, 1295, and 1307', *BIHR*, 3 (1925–26), 110–15. (With facsimiles); Reginald F. Treharne. 'The nature of parliament in the reign of Henry III', *EHR*, 74 (1959), 590–610; Kathleen Wood-Legh. 'Sheriffs, lawyers, and belted knights in the parliaments of Edward III', *EHR*, 46 (1931), 372–88; Kathleen Wood-Legh. 'The knights' attendance in the parliaments of Edward III', *EHR*, 47 (1932), 398–413; Bertie Wilkinson, *The creation of medieval parliaments.* New York, 1972; George O. Sayles. *The king's parliament of England.* New York, 1974.

278   Bolland, William C. *The year books.* Cambridge, 1921. A general introduction by an authority on the subject; also *A manual of year book studies.* Cambridge, 1925.

279   —— *The general eyre.* Cambridge, 1922.

280   Boussard, Jacques. *Le gouvernement d'Henri II Plantagenêt.* Paris, 1956. trans. Jean Penfold 1959. Ambitious, but not very reliable.

281   Brown, Ronald S. *The serjeants of the peace in medieval England and Wales.* Manchester, 1936. A careful study, breaking new ground.

282   Caenegem, Raoul C. van. *Royal writs in England from the conquest to Glanvill: studies in the early history of the common law.* Selden Society, 77 (1959). An exhaustive survey of Roman and Canon law influences on the early common law.

283   Cam, Helen M. *Studies in the hundred rolls.* Oxford, 1921. An important addition to knowledge of local government.

284   —— *Law-finders and law-makers in medieval England: collected studies in legal and constitutional history.* New York, 1963. Twelve articles and papers published or read between 1943 and 1961.

285   Clarke, Maude V. *Medieval representation and consent: a study of early parliaments in England.* 1936. Important in its time, but now somewhat dated.

286   —— *Fourteenth century studies*, ed. Ione S. Sutherland and May McKisack. Oxford, 1968. First published 1937. Includes 'The impeachment of Latimer'.

287   Cohen, Hermann J. *A history of the English bar and attornatus to 1450.* 1929. An indispensable work of reference for legal history.

288   Davies, J. Conway (ed.). *Studies presented to Sir Hilary Jenkinson.* Oxford, 1957. Some important essays on justice, finance, and administration.

289   Dawson, John P. *A history of lay judges.* Cambridge, Mass., 1960. A comprehensive survey, with stress laid on the English courts, especially manorial.

290   De Haas, Elsa. *Antiquities of bail. Origins and historical development in criminal cases to the year 1275.* New York, 1940; and George D.G. Hall. *Early registers of writs.* Selden Society, 87 (1970).

291   Denholm-Young, Noël. *Collected papers on medieval subjects.* Oxford, 1946. Includes articles on Richard de Bury; the *Cursus*; two papers on *Fleta*; the Barons' wars; the honour of Walbrook; the Bermondsey library.

292   Ehrlich, Ludwig. *Proceedings against the crown (1216—1377).* Oxford, 1921. A scholarly essay.

293   Ellis, Geoffrey. *Earldoms in fee, a study in peerage law and history.* 1963.

294   Ellis, Thomas P. *Welsh tribal law and custom in the Middle Ages.* Oxford, 1926, 2 vols.

295   Flower, Cyril T. *Introduction to the Curia Regis rolls, 1199—1230 A.D.* Selden Society, 62 (1944). Expert discussion.

296   Fox, Levi. *The administration of the honour of Leicester in the fourteenth century.* Leicester, 1940. A scholarly work.

297   Galbraith, Vivian H. *Studies in the public records.* 1948. Reprinted 1949. A small book by a great expert, discussing the medieval system of keeping government records.

298   Gooder, Arthur. *The parliamentary representation of the county of York, 1258—1832.* Vol. 1. *Yorks.Arch.Rec.*, 91 (1935).

299   Gray, Howard L. *The influence of the commons on early legislation: a study of the fourteenth and fifteenth centuries.* Cambridge, Mass., 1932. Pioneer work that contains much valuable material.

300   Hand, Geoffrey J. *English law in Ireland.* Cambridge, 1967. An authoritative history of the medieval Irish legal system at its peak.

301   Harding, Alan. *Social history of English law.* Harmondsworth, 1966. Has some good comments and is easy to read; *The law courts of medieval England.* New York, 1973.

302   Hewitt, Herbert J. *Cheshire under the three Edwards.* Cheshire Community Council. 1969.

303   Hill, Mary C. *The king's messengers 1199—1377. A contribution to the history of the royal household.* 1961. Scholarly and breaks new ground.

304   Holdsworth, William S. *The influence of the legal profession on the growth of the English constitution.* Oxford, 1924; also *Sources and literature of English law.* Oxford, 1925. A good introduction by a great authority; see also his *Some makers of English law.* Cambridge, 1938, including Glanvil, Bracton, and Edward I.

305   Holt, James C. *Magna carta.* Cambridge, 1965. By the leading authority; also *Magna carta and the idea of liberty.* New York, 1972; for the charter MSS, see Noël Denholm-Young above no. 199 and John C. Fox. 'The originals of the great charter of 1215', *EHR*, 39 (1924), 321—36; C.R. Cheney. 'The twenty-five barons of magna carta', *BJRL*, 50 (1967—68), 280—307. Argues that the safeguard clause led the pope to condemn the charter; Michael T. Clanchy. 'Magna carta, clause thirty-four', *EHR*, 79 (1964), 532—47; Vivian H. Galbraith. 'A draft of Magna carta (1215)', *PBA*, 53 (1967), 344—60; James C. Holt. 'The making of Magna carta', *EHR*, 72 (1957), 401—22; also Holt. 'Rights and liberties in Magna carta', in *Album Helen M. Cam*, Vol. 1, *Studies presented to the international commission for representative and parliamentary institutions*, 23. Louvain, 1960, 57—

15

69; Faith Thompson. *The first century of magna carta.* Minneapolis, Minn., 1925; Samuel E. Thorne. 'What magna carta was', in Samuel E. Thorne *et al. The great charter.* New York, 1965, 3—20; Léon Leclère. 'La grande charte de 1215 est-elle un "illusion"?' *Mélanges d'histoire offerts à Henri Pirenne.* Brussels, 1926; Sidney Painter. 'Magna carta', *AHR*, 53 (1947), 42—49; Frederick M. Powicke. 'Per iudicium parium vel per legem terrae', in Henry E. Malden (ed.). *Magna carta commemoration essays.* 1917, 96—121; Paul Vinogradoff. 'Magna carta, c. 39. *nullus liber homo*, etc.?' in Henry E. Malden (ed.). *Magna carta commemoration essays.* 1917, 78—95; Henry G. Richardson. 'The morrow of the great charter', *BJRL*, 28 (1944), 422—43; Christopher R. Cheney. 'The eve of magna carta', *BJRL*, 38 (1955—56), 311—41; Naomi D. Hurnard. 'Magna carta, clause 34', *SPFP*, 157—79; Bryce D. Lyon. 'The lawyer and magna carta', *Rocky Mountain Law Review*, 23 (1951), 416—33; Charles H. McIlwain. 'Magna carta and common law', in Henry E. Malden (ed.). *Magna carta commemoration essays.* 1917, 122—79. Law of the realm bulked larger than the law of the Crown in the 'fundamental law', and included magna carta; Edward Miller. 'The background of magna carta', *PP*, 23 (1962), 72—83, a review article.

306 Hornyold-Strickland, Henry. *Biographical sketches of the members of parliament of Lancashire (1290—1550).* Chetham Society, 5 (1935).

307 Hoyt, Robert S. *The royal demesne in English constitutional history, 1066—1272.* Ithaca, N.Y., 1951. Valuable pioneer work.

308 Hughes, Dorothy. *A study of social and constitutional tendencies in the early years of Edward III.* 1915. An unduly neglected volume, still valuable.

309 Hunnisett, Roy F. *The medieval coroner.* Cambridge, 1961. A much needed monograph.

310 Hurnard, Naomi D. *The king's pardon for homicide before A.D. 1307.* Oxford, 1969. An important and interesting pioneer study.

311 Jolliffe, John E.A. *Angevin kingship.* 1955, 2nd ed., 1963. Original suggestive, and erratic, but still important.

312 Kantorowicz, Ernst H. *Selected studies.* New York, 1965. Contains '*Pro patria mori* in medieval political thought', pp. 138—50; 'The prologue to *Fleta* and the school of Petrus de Vinea', pp. 308—24.

313 Keeney, Barnaby C. *Judgment by peers.* 1949. The only modern survey of the topic. It has minor defects but it provides a new start in the study.

314 Kern, Fritz. *Kingship and law in the Middle Ages*, trans. Stanley B. Chrimes. Oxford, 1949. Second impression. A standard work, though modified by more recent work; also Barnaby C. Keeney. 'The medieval idea of the state: the great cause 1291—92', *University of Toronto Law Journal*, 8 (1949), 48—71; see also J.T. Durkin. 'Kingship in the vision of Piers Plowman', *Thought*, 14 (1939), 413—21; Ernst H. Kantorowicz, above no. 257; Ewart Lewis. 'King above the law? "Quod principi placuit in Bracton" ', *Speculum*, 39 (1964), 240—69; Bryce D. Lyon. 'What made a medieval king constitutional?', *EPBW*, 157—75; Samuel J.T. Miller. 'The position of the king in Bracton and Beaumanoir', *Speculum*, 31 (1956), 263—96; Gaines Post. 'Bracton on kingship', *Tulane Law Review*, 42 (1968), 519—54; John E.A. Jolliffe, above no. 311; John C. Dickinson. 'The medieval conception of kingship and some of its limitations, as developed in the *Policraticus of John of Salisbury*', *Speculum*, 1 (1926), 308—37; Beryl Smalley. 'The king's two bodies', *PP*, 20 (1961), 30—35.

315 Kimball, Elizabeth G. *Serjeanty tenure in medieval England.* New Haven, Conn., 1936. The best analysis up to date.

316 Maitland, Frederic W. *Selected historical essays*, ed. Helen M. Cam. Cambridge, 1957. Includes 'The history of a Cambridgeshire manor'; 'Leet and tourn'; 'Introduction to memoranda de parliamento, 1305'; 'English law 1307—1600'; 'Round's *Commune of London*'; 'William Stubbs, bishop of Oxford'; and 'Mary Bateson'.

317 Maxwell-Lyte, Henry C. *Historical notes on the use of the great seal of England.* 1926. HMSO. A great pioneer work, badly organized. See also Hedwig Ohnesorge. *Die Siegel als Mittel der Königlichen Prärogative in*

England im 13 u. 13 Jahrhundert. Berlin, 1928; also C. Hilary Jenkinson. 'A seal of Edward II for Scottish affairs', *Antiquaries Journal*, 11 (1931), 229—39. Includes text of charters and letters patent with plates of seals; see also C. Hilary Jenkinson. 'The great seal of England: some notes and suggestions', *Antiquaries Journal*, 16 (1936), 8—28; Bertie Wilkinson. 'A letter of Edward III', *EHJT*, 305—13.

318 Morris, William A. *The early English county court.* Berkeley, Cal., 1925. Still valuable; also *The medieval English sheriff to 1300.* Manchester, 1927. Reprinted 1968. A standard work, but somewhat uneven and lacking in interpretation. See also 'The sheriff', *EGAW*, 2, 41—108.

319 Patourel, John H. le. *The medieval administration of the Channel Islands, 1199—1399.* Oxford, 1937. Scholarly and suggestive.

320 Petit-Dutaillis, Charles. *La monarchie féodale en France et en Angleterre X^e— XIIe siècle.* Paris, 1933. Stimulating but now considerably out of date, trans. E.D. Hunt. New York, 1964.

321 Plucknett, Theodore F.T. *The medieval bailiff.* 1954. The best account.

322 ——— *Early English legal literature.* Cambridge, 1958. Plucknett's views on Bracton have been criticised.

323 Pugh, Ralph B. *Itinerant justices in English history.* Exeter, 1967. Slight but expert. See also Ralph B. Pugh. *Imprisonment in medieval England.* Cambridge, 1968. An authoritative survey. Now the standard work.

324 Putnam, Bertha H. *Early treatises on the justices of the peace.* Oxford, 1924; *Kent keepers of the peace 1316—17.* Kent Archaeological Society Records, 13 (1933). Describes a step in the gradual transition from Keepers towards Justices of the Peace; 'The transformation of the keepers of the peace into the justices of the peace, 1327—1380', *TRHS*, ser. 4, 12 (1929), 19—48. An important article; also 'Records of the keepers of the peace and their supervisors, 1307—27', *EHR*, 45 (1930), 435—44; 'Chief justice Shareshull and the economic and legal codes of 1351—1342', *University of Toronto Law Journal*, 5 (1944), 251—81. Treats Shareshull the innovator; 'Shire officials: keepers of the peace and justices of the peace', *EGAW*, 3, 185—217; also Alan Harding. 'The origins and early history of the keeper of the peace', *TRHS*, ser. 5, 10 (1960), 85—109; Leo F. Page. *Justice of the Peace.* 1936.

325 Sanford, Frederic R. *Origins of the early English maritime and commercial law.* New York, 1930.

326 Sayles, George O. *The medieval foundations of England.* 1948.

327 Somerville, Robert. *History of the duchy of Lancaster.* Vol. 1, *(1265—1603).* 1953. The standard work.

328 Squibb, George D. *The high court of chivalry, a study of civic law in England.* Oxford, 1959. The court was established shortly after Crecy. The volume corrects many older views.

329 Stenton, Doris M. *King John and the courts of justice.* Oxford, 1958. Offprint, *PBA*, 44 (1959); also Ralph V. Turner. *The king and his courts: the role of John and Henry III in the administration of justice, 1199—1240.* Ithaca, N.Y., 1968. Emphasises personal authority of the king; Francis J. West. *The justiciarship in England, 1066—1232.* Cambridge, 1966; and Francis J. West. 'The *curia regis* in the late twelfth and early thirteenth centuries', *Historical Studies, Australia and New Zealand,* 6 (1954), 173—85.

330 Stewart-Brown, Ronald. *The serjeants of the peace in medieval England and Wales.* Manchester, 1936. Explores a neglected subject, with sound scholarship.

331 Sutherland, Donald W. *Quo warranto proceedings in the reign of Edward I (1278—1294).* Oxford, 1963. Throws much light on Edwardian government and the Edwardian Crown.

332 Tout, Thomas F. *Collected papers,* ed. James Tait *et al.* Manchester, 1932—34, 3 vols. Include 'The Welsh shires: a study in constitutional history'; 'Flintshire, its history and records'; 'Wales and the March during the barons' wars'; 'John Halton bishop of Carlisle'; 'The household of chancery and its disintegration'; 'The fair of Lincoln and the "Histoire de

Guillaume le Maréchal" '; 'The tactics of the battles of Boroughbridge and Marlaix'; 'Some neglected fights between Crecy and Poitiers'; 'Firearms in England in the fourteenth century'; 'The communitas bacheleriae angliae'; 'A thirteenth century phase'; 'The Westminster chronicle attributed to Robert of Reading'; 'The study of medieval chronicles'; 'The place of St Thomas of Canterbury in history. A centenary study'; 'Medieval town-planning'; 'A medieval burglary'; 'Medieval forgers and forgeries'; 'The captivity and death of Edward of Carnarvon'; 'The English civil service in the fourteenth century'; 'Some conflicting tendencies in English administrative history during the fourteenth century'; 'The beginnings of a modern Capital: London and Westminster in the fourteenth century'.

333 Trabut-Cussac, Jean-Paul. *L'administration anglaise en Gascogne sous Henry III et Édouard I de 1254 à 1307.* Geneva 1792.

334 Vinogradoff, Paul. *Collected papers.* 1928, 2 vols. Include 'The Roman element in Bracton's treatise', I, 237—44; 'Magna carta, clause 39', II, 207—21; 'Les maximes dans l'ancien droit commun anglais', II, 239—47; bibliography, II, 479—500.

335 Waters, William H. *The Edwardian settlement of North Wales in its administrative and legal aspects, 1284—1343.* Cardiff, 1935. An important book based on much research in unpublished records.

336 Wedgwood, Josiah C. *Staffordshire parliamentary history from the earliest times to the present day.* Vol. 1, *1213—1603.* 1917. William Salt Archaeological Society Collections for 1917—20, 3 vols.

337 White, Albert B. *Self-government at the king's command.* Minneapolis, Minn., 1933. Useful; now partly superseded.

338 Wilkinson, Bertie. *Constitutional history of medieval England.* 1948—50, 3 vols. Has been described as 'well-balanced, imaginative work of primary importance'. George F. Howe *et al.* (eds.). *American Historical Association's guide to historical literature.* New York, 1961, 185. At the beginning of each chapter of the *Constitutional history,* there is a list of recent publications concerned: Vol. 1. Ending of the minority of Henry III, 68—69; the crisis of 1223—334, 99; the paper constitution of 1244, 117; the provisions of Oxford, 131—32; the crisis of 1297, 187. Vol. 2: the coronation of Edward II, 85; the ordinances of 1311, 112; the statute of York, 134; the deposition of Edward II and the accession of Edward III, 157; the crisis of 1341, 176; the Good parliament, 204; the crisis of 1386—87, 227; the parliament of 1388, 252; the deposition of Richard II, 284. Vol. 3: kingship, 72—73; the king's administration, 112; the king's justice, 151; king and community, 186—87; representation and consent and the beginning of parliament, 233—34; parliament to the death of Edward I, 264—65; parliament in the fourteenth century, 322—23; church and state, 376—67. (These items are not listed elsewhere in this handbook.)

339 Willcock, I.D. *The origins and development of the jury in Scotland.* Edinburgh, 1966.

340 Williamson, John B. *The history of the temple, London, from the institution of the knights of the temple to the close of the Stuart period.* 1924. A scholarly book.

341 Wolffe, Bertram P. *The royal demesne in English history: the crown estate from the conquest to 1509.* Athens, Ohio, 1971.

342 Young, Charles R. *The English borough and royal administration.* Durham, N.C., 1961. A careful study, but adds little new to the subject.

4 Biographies

343 Bolland, William C. *Chief justice Sir William Bereford.* Cambridge, 1924. Printed lecture, lively and learned.

344 Boussard, Jacques. 'Ralph Neville, évêque de Chichester et chancelier d'Angleterre (1244) d'après sa correspondence', *Revue historique,* 176 (1935), 217—33.

345 Keally, Edward J. *Roger of Salisbury, viceroy of England.* Berkeley, Cal., 1972.

346   Magrath, John R. 'Sir Robert Parving, knight of the shire for Cumberland and chancellor of England', *Transactions of the Cumberland and Westmorland Antiquarian and Archaeological Society*, n.s., 19 (1919), 30—91. Reprinted in book form, Kendal, 1919.

347   Putnam, Bertha H. *The place in legal history of Sir William Shareshull, chief justice of the king's bench, 1350—61*. Cambridge, 1950. A learned appreciation of one of the most influential justices of Edward III's reign.

348   Stones, Edward L.G. 'Sir Geoffrey le Scrope (*c.* 1280 to 1340), chief justice of the king's bench', *EHR*, 69 (1954), 1—17. Valuable preliminary study.

5 Articles

349   Adler, Michael. 'The testimony of the London Jewry against the ministers of Henry III', *Jewish Historical Society*, 14 (1941), 141—85. Quotes extracts.

350   Baldwin, James F. 'The king's council', *EGAW*, 1, 129—61.

351   Balfour-Melville, Evan W.M. 'Burgh representation in early Scottish parliaments', *EHR*, 59 (1944), 79—87. Significant formulae.

352   Bannister, Arthur T. *et al. Camden Miscellany*, 15 (1929). A group of significant essays, including a survey of the estates of the bishopric of Hereford, second half of the thirteenth century, and a case in July 1361 which refers to equity and the law of the sea.

353   Barrow, Geoffrey W.S. 'The Scottish judex in the twelfth and thirteenth centuries', *SHR*, 45 (1966), 16—35.

354   Beardwood, Alice. 'Royal mints and exchanges', *EGAW*, 3, 35—66.

355   ——— 'Trial of Walter Langton, bishop of Lichfield, 1307—12', *Transactions of the American Philosophical Society*, ser. 2, 54, Pt. 3 (1964), 3—45. An important examination of royal administration and justice.

356   Bellamy, John G. 'Appeal and impeachment in the good parliament', *BIHR*, 39 (1966), 35—46; see Gabrielle Lambrick. 'The impeachment of the abbot of Abingdon in 1368', *EHR*, 82 (1967), 250—76. Throws light on the origins and nature of impeachment.

357   Blair, Claude H.H. 'Wardens and deputy wardens of the Marches of England towards Scotland in Northumberland and the English wardens of Berwick upon Tweed', *ArchAel*, 28 (1950), 18—95.

358   Bolland, William C. 'The training of a medieval justice', in Percy H. Winfield *et al.* (eds.). *Cambridge legal essays presented to Doctor Bond*. Cambridge, Mass., 1926, 57—70. Mainly thirteenth century.

359   ——— 'Some notes on the year books and plea rolls', *LQR*, 43 (1927), 60—73.

360   Brown, R. Allen. 'The "treasury" of the later twelfth century', *SPHJ*, 35—49.

361   Caenegem, Raoul C.J. van. 'La paix publique dans les iles britanniques du XIe au XVIIIe siècle', *Recueils de la société Jean Bodin*, 15 (1961), 5—26. By a distinguished scholar.

362   Cam, Helen M. 'Shire officials: coroners, constables and bailiffs', *EGAW*, 3, 143—83.

363   Chaplais, Pierre. 'The chancery of Guyenne 1289—1453', *SPHJ*, 61—96. An expert analysis.

364   ——— 'Privy seal drafts, rolls and registers (Edward I—Edward III)', *EHR*, 73 (1958), 270—73. Establishes the keeping of files of drafts for writs of privy seal in these reigns.

365   ——— 'Master John de Branketre and the office of notary in chancery, 1355—1375', *Journal of the Society of Archivists*, 4 (1971), 169—99; see also Christopher R. Cheney. *Notaries public in England in the thirteenth and fourteenth centuries*. New York, 1972.

366   Cheney, Christopher R. 'The "paper constitution" preserved by Matthew Paris', *EHR*, 65 (1950), 213—21.

367   Chew, Helena M. 'The ecclesiastical tenants-in-chief and writs of military summons', *EHR*, 41 (1926), 161—69. Either tenure was not the basis of parliamentary summons; or, if it was, tenure 'per baroniam' was not tenure by knight service.

368   Cheyette, Frederic. 'King, courts, cures, and sinecures: the statute of provisors

and the common law', *Traditio*, 19 (1963), 295—49. Compares the
growth of 'Gallicanism' in France with that of 'Anglicanism' in England.

369 —— 'Custom, case law, and medieval constitutionalism: a re-examination',
Political Science Quarterly, 78 (1963), 362—90.

370 Churchill, E.F. 'The dispensing power and the defence of the realm', *LQR*,
37 (1921), 412—41.

371 Clanchy, Michael T. 'The franchise of return of writs', *TRHS*, ser. 5, 17
(1967), 59—79.

372 Clementi, Dione. 'That the statute of York of 1322 is no longer ambiguous',
Album Helen M. Cam. Vol. 2: *Studies presented to the international
commission for representative and parliamentary institutions*, 25. Louvain,
1961. See also John H. Trueman. 'The statute of York and the ordinances
of 1311', *Med et Hum*, 10 (1956), 64—81; Gaines Post. 'The two laws and
the statute of York', *Speculum*, 29 (1954), 417—32; also 'Status id est
magistratus; l'état, c'est moi; and status regis; the "Estate Royal", (1100—
1322)', *Studies in Medieval and Renaissance History*, 1 (1964), 3—103.
Deals especially with the Statute of York and the question of alienability;
also Joseph R. Strayer. 'The statute of York and the community of the
realm', *AHR*, 47 (1941), 1—22. Part of a lively and important debate.

373 Crump, Charles G. 'What became of Robert Rag, or some chancery blunders',
EPTT, 335—45. Ingenious and scholarly analysis of a law suit involving
forgery in the fourteenth century, with extract from the *Coram rege* roll.

374 Cuttino, George P. 'King's clerks and the community of the realm', *Speculum*,
29 (1954), 395—416. Throws light on the background and the recruitment of the king's clerks in the thirteenth century.

375 Davies, J. Conway. 'Felony in Edwardian Wales', *Cymmrodorion Society
Transactions*. 1916—17, 145—96.

376 —— 'The statute of Lincoln, 1316, and the appointment of sheriffs', *LQR*,
33 (1917), 78—86.

377 —— 'Common law writs and returns: Richard I to Richard II', *BIHR*, 26
(1953), 125—56; 27 (1954), 1—34.

378 Davies, Robert R. 'The twilight of Welsh law, 1284—1536', *History*, 51
(1966), 143—64.

379 —— 'The law of the March', *WHR*, 5 (1970—01), 1—31. Discusses the
relationship with English common law.

380 Denholm-Young, Noël. 'The cursus in England', in Frederick M. Powicke
(ed.). *Oxford essays in medieval history presented to Herbert Edward
Salter*. Oxford, 1934, 68—103. Throws light on a little-known subject.

381 —— 'Who wrote Fleta?', *EHR*, 58 (1943), 1—12, 252—57. Possibly
Matthew de Scaccario. See also Boris M. Komar. 'Two claims to Fleta's
honors', *West Virginia Law Quarterly*, 30 (1924), 167—85. (Text 1525)

382 —— 'A letter from the council to Pope Honorious III, 1220—21', *EHR*,
60 (1945), 88—96.

383 Ditmas, Edith M.R. 'The curtana or sword of mercy', *JBAA*, ser. 3, 29
(1966), 122—33.

384 Dix, Elizabeth J. 'The origins of the action of trespass on the case', *Yale Law
Review*, 46 (1937), 1142—76. Argues against emphasis on Westminster
II.

385 Dowdall, Harold C. 'The word "state" ', *LQR*, 39 (1923), 98—125.

386 Duggan, Charles. 'Richard of Ilchester, royal servant and bishop', *TRHS*, ser.
5, 16 (1966), 1—21. Richard played an important part in the Henry II—
Becket dispute.

387 Dunham, William H. 'The chronology of Hengham's dismissal', *EHR*, 47
(1932), 88—93.

388 Eastman, Albert E.W. 'The history of trial by jury', *National Bar Journal*, 3
(1945), 87—113.

389 Edwards, J. Goronwy. 'The royal household and the Welsh lawbooks', *TRHS*,
ser. 5, 13 (1963), 163—76. Includes information about the thirteenth
century.

390 —— 'The historical study of the Welsh lawbooks', *TRHS*, ser. 5, 12 (1962),
141—55.

391 ———— 'Studies in the Welsh laws since 1928', *WHR*, Special no. (1963), 1–19.

392 Edwards, R. Dudley. 'Magna carta hiberniae', in John Ryan (ed.). *Essays and studies presented to Prof. Eoin MacNeill.* Dublin, 1948, 307–18.

393 Ehrlich, Ludwig. 'Petitions of right', *LQR*, 45 (1929), 60–85. In the period 1276 to 1349, there were all kinds of petitions in parliaments. From 1349 to the latter fifteenth century, only in parliament if the matter could not be settled elsewhere.

394 Evans, David L. 'Some notes on the history of the principality in the time of the Black Prince, 1343–76', *Cymmrodorion Society Transactions*, 1925–26, 25–110. One of the best surveys of the administration of Wales in the fourteenth century.

395 Fox, Levi. 'Administration of the Leicester honour of the fourteenth century', *TLAS*, 20 (1940), 289–374.

396 Fraser, Constance M. 'Edward I of England and the regalian franchise of Durham', *Speculum*, 31 (1956), 329–42. Edward had no objection in principle to the franchise; also 'Prerogative and the bishops of Durham', *EHR*, 74 (1959), 467–76.

397 Galbraith, Vivian H. 'The death of a champion', *SPFP*, 283–95. Illustrates the last days of the civil duel; prints original sources.

398 ———— 'Osbert, dean of Lewes', *EHR*, 69 (1954), 289–302. Disproves the existence of an inquest in 1161 anticipating that of 1170.

399 ———— 'Statutes of Edward I: Huntington library MS. N. M. 25782', *EPBW*, 176–91. Discusses papal contribution to constitutional advance in thirteenth century. Appendix (pp. 187–91) by George D.G. Hall.

400 Gardiner, Dorothy A. 'The history of belligerent rights on the high seas in the fourteenth century', *LQR*, 48 (1932), 521–46.

401 Gibson, S.T. 'The escheatries, 1327–41', *EHR*, 36 (1921), 218–25.

402 Grassi, J.L. 'Royal clerks from the archdiocese of York in the fourteenth century', *Northern History*, 5 (1970), 12–33.

403 Graves, Edgar B. 'The legal significance of the statute of *praemunire*, 1353', in Charles H. Taylor (ed.). *Haskins anniversary essays.* Boston, 1929, 57–80.

404 Gutteridge, Harold C. 'The origin and historical development of the profession of notaries public in England', in Percy H. Winfield *et al.* (eds.). *Cambridge legal essays presented to Doctor Bond.* Cambridge, Mass., 1926, 123–37.

405 Gwynn, Aubrey O. 'Edward I and the proposed purchase of English law for the Irish, *c.* 1276–80', *TRHS*, ser. 5, 10 (1960), 111–27. The proposal was bound to fail.

406 Hamil, Frederick C. 'The king's approvers: a chapter in the history of English criminal law', *Speculum*, 7 (1936), 238–58. Interesting details regarding a little-known medieval practice.

407 Hand, Geoffrey J.P. 'Procedure without writ in the court of the justiciar of Ireland', *Proceedings of Royal Irish Academy*, 62 (1961–62), 9–20. Prints criticisms temp. Edward I.

408 ———— 'The status of the native Irish in the lordship of Ireland, 1272–1331', *Irish Jurist*, n.s. (1966), 93–115. Discusses their position relative to English law.

409 ———— 'Common law in Ireland in the 13th and 14th centuries', *Journal of the Royal Society of Antiquaries, Ireland*, 97 (1969), 97–111.

410 Harriss, Gerald L. 'The commons' petition of 1340', *EHR*, 78 (1963), 625–54.

411 Haskins, George L. 'Three early petitions of the commonalty', *Speculum*, 12 (1937), 314–18. Shows that petitions which can be glossed as from the *communitas Angliae* under Edward I may not have been from the representatives or even a majority of them.

412 ———— 'Three English documents relating to Francis Accursius', *LQR*, 54 (1938), 87–94.

413 Hill, Mary C. 'Jack Faukes, king's messenger, and his journey to Avignon in 1343', *EHR*, 57 (1942), 19–30.

414 —— 'King's messengers and administrative developments in the thirteenth and fourteenth centuries', *EHR*, 61 (1946), 315—28.

415 Holdsworth, William S. 'The history of remedies against the crown', Pt. 1, *LQR*, 38 (1922), 141—64.

416 Holt, James C. 'The carta of Richard de la Haye, 1166: a note on "continuity" in Anglo-Norman feudalism', *EHR*, 84 (1969), 289—97.

417 Hoyt, Robert S. 'The nature and origins of the ancient demesne', *EHR*, 65 (1950), 145—74. Argues that it was a creation of the Angevin monarchy.

418 Hunnisett, Roy F. 'The origins of the office of coroner', *TRHS*, ser. 5, 8 (1958). Argues for the importance of changes in 1194; also 'Pleas of the crown and the coroner', *BIHR*, 32 (1959), 117—37; and 'The medieval coroners' rolls', *American Journal of Legal History*, 3 (1959), 95—124, 205—21. Gives list of extant rolls before 1422.

419 Hurnard, Naomi D. 'The jury of presentment and the assize of Clarendon', *EHR*, 56 (1941), 374—410. A valuable contribution.

420 —— 'The Anglo-Norman franchises', *EHR*, 64 (1949), 289—323; 433—60. Questions the theory of Henry II's attack on the franchises. Important.

421 —— 'Did Edward I reverse Henry II's policy on seisin?', *EHR*, 69 (1954), 529—53. Argues against the view that he did.

422 Isaacs, Nathan. 'The statutes of Edward I — their relation to finance and administration', *Michigan Law Review*, 19 (1921), 804—18.

423 Jenkins, Dafydd. 'Legal and comparative aspects of the Welsh laws', *WHR*, special supp. (1963), 51—61.

424 —— 'Law and government in Wales before the act of union', *Welsh Studies in Public Law* (1970), 7—29. A most useful recent synthesis.

425 Jenkinson, C. Hilary and Mabel H. Mills. 'Rolls from a sheriff's office of the fourteenth century', *EHR*, 43 (1928), 21—32.

426 Johnson, Charles. 'The collectors of lay taxes', *EGAW*, 2, 201—26.

427 —— 'Notes on thirteenth century judicial procedure', *EHR*, 62 (1947), 508—21. Very helpful notes.

428 Johnson, John H. 'The system of account in the wardrobe of Edward II', *TRHS*, ser. 4, 12 (1929), 75—104. Analysis by an expert.

429 —— 'The king's wardrobe and household', *EGAW*, 1, 206—49.

430 Johnston, William J. 'The parliament of the pale', *LQR*, 34 (1918), 291—303.

431 Johnstone, Hilda. 'The parliament of Lincoln of 1316', *EHR*, 36 (1921), 53—57; 480. Straightens out chronology; see also Henry G. Richardson and George O. Sayles. 'The parliament of Lincoln, 1316', *BIHR*, 12 (1934—35), 105—07.

432 —— 'The wardrobe and household of Henry, son of Edward I', *BJRL*, 7 (1922—23), 354—420. Prints record.

433 —— 'The queen's exchequer under three Edwards', *EHJT*, 143—55.

434 —— 'The queen's household', *EGAW*, 1, 250—99.

435 —— 'The chamber and the castle treasures under King John', *SPFP*, 117—42. New evidence of John's administrative innovations.

436 —— 'The *camera regis* under Henry II', *EHR*, 68 (1953), 1—21; 337—62. Henry's *camera* anticipated that of John.

437 Jones-Pierce, Thomas. 'The laws of Wales, the kindred and the blood feud', *UBHJ*, 3 (1952), 119—37.

438 —— 'Social and historical aspects of the Welsh laws', *WHR*, 1 (1960—63), special no. (1963), 33—49.

439 —— 'The law of Wales — the last phase', *Transactions of the Cymmrodorion Society*, (1963), 7—26.

440 Jones, William R. 'Bishops, politics, and the two laws: the *Gravamina* of the English clergy, 1237—1399', *Speculum*, 41 (1966), 209—45. Shows how the advantage in a long conflict over jurisdiction always lay with the secular power.

441 Kaye, John M. 'The early history of murder and manslaughter', *LQR*, 83 (1967), 365—95; 565—601. Pt. 1 to 1380. Important.

442 Keeney, Barnaby C. 'Petitions in the parliament held at Westminster, Epiphany—Candlemas, 1327', *Huntington Library Quarterly*, 5 (1942), 338—48. Note and documents.

443 Keigwin, Charles A. 'The origin of equity', *Georgetown Law Library*, 28 (1930), 15—35, 92—119, 215—40; 29 (1931), 48—65, 165—84.

444 Kerr, Charles. 'The origin and development of the law merchant', *Virginia Law Review*, 15 (1929), 350—67.

445 Langbein, Irwin L. 'The jury of presentment and the coroner', *Columbia Law Review*, 32 (1935), 1329—65.

446 Lapsley, Gaillard. 'John de Warenne and the quo warranto proceedings in 1279', *CHJ*, 2 (1926—28), 110—32. Convincingly argues against Round's reasons for rejecting the story of the rusty sword. (*Peerage and Pedigree*, 1, 321—22.)

447 ———— 'Buzones', *EHR*, 47 (1932), 177—93; 545—67.

448 Latham, Lucy C. 'Collections of wages of the knights of the shire in the 14th and 15th centuries', *EHR*, 48 (1933), 455—64.

449 Levett, Ada E. 'The summons to a great council, 1213', *EHR*, 31 (1916), 85—90. Shows that the king summoned knights to the council; also 'Clerical proctors in parliament and knights of the shire, 1280—1374', *EHR*, 48 (1933), 443—55.

450 Lewis, Norman B. 'Simon Burley and Baldwin of Raddington', *EHR* 52 (1937), 662—69. Prints an indenture. Baldwin was a civil servant in the late fourteenth century.

451 Lloyd, John E. 'Edward I's commission of enquiry, 1280—81. An examination of its origin and purpose', *I Cymmrodorion*, 25 (1915), 1—20; 26 (1916), 252. The results of this enquiry provide one of our major sources of information about Welsh government and law.

452 Loomis, Roger S. 'Chivalric and dramatic imitations of Arthurian romance', in Wilhelm R.W. Koehler (ed.). *Medieval studies in memory of A. Kingsley Porter*. Cambridge, Mass., 1939. Vol. 1, 79—97. Throws light on the round tables of Edward I.

453 Lowry, Edith C. 'Clerical protectors in parliament and knights of the shire, 1280—1374', *EHR*, 48 (1933), 443—55. An additional note by Ada E. Levett. *EHR*, 48 (1933), 455.

454 Lucas, Henry S. 'The machinery of diplomatic intercourse', *EGAW*, 1, 300—31.

455 Lunt, William E. 'The consent of the English lower clergy to taxation during the reign of Henry III', in *Persecution and liberty: essays in honor of George Lincoln Burr*. New York, 1931, 117—69; 'The consent of the English lower clergy to taxation, 1166—1216', in Edwin F. Gay (ed.). *Facts and factors in economic history*, Cambridge, Mass., 1932, 62—89; 'The collectors of clerical subsidies', *EGAW*, 2, 227—80.

456 Lydon, James F. 'William of Windsor and the Irish parliament', *EHR*, 80 (1965), 252—67. Important comments on the powers of representatives.

457 Lyon, Bryce D. 'Fact and fiction in English and Belgian constitutional law', *Med et Hum*, 10 (1956), 82—101.

458 ———— 'Medieval constitutionalism: a balance of power', *Album Helen M. Cam*. Vol. 2. *Studies presented to the international commission for representative and parliamentary institutions*, 25. Louvain, 1961, 157—83. A well-made and important point.

459 Marshall, D.W. Hunter. 'Two early English occupations in Scotland — their administrative organization', *SHR*, 25 (1927), 20—40. In 1174—89.

460 Mate, Mavis. 'A mint of trouble, 1279—1307', *Speculum*, 44 (1969), 201—12. Interesting illustration of some of the difficulties of medieval administration.

461 Meekings, Cecil A.F. 'Martin Pateshull and William Raleigh', *BIHR*, 26 (1953), 157—80. Richardson's criticism of Maitland not sustained.

462 Meyer, Erwin T. 'Boroughs', *EGAW*, 3, 105—141.

463 Mills, Mabel H. 'The medieval shire house (*domus vicecomitis*)', *SPHJ*, 254—71.

464 Milsom, Stroud F.C. 'Trespass from Henry III to Edward III', *LQR*, 74 (1958), 194—224, 407—36, 561—90.

465 Morris, William A. '*Plenus comitatus*', *EHR*, 39 (1924), 401—03. Brief but important, though questionable.

466   Myers, Alec R. 'The English parliament and the French estates general in the Middle Ages', *Album Helen M. Cam.* Vol. 2. *Studies presented to the international commission for representative and parliamentary institutions,* 25. Louvain, 1961. 139–53. Some helpful generalizations.

467   Neilson, G. Nellie. 'Brus *versus* Balliol, 1291–1292: the model for Edward's tribunal', *SHR,* 16 (1918), 1–14.

468   —— 'The forests', *EGAW,* 1, 394–467.

469   —— 'The court of common pleas', *EGAW,* 3, 259–85.

470   —— 'The early pattern of the common law', *AHR,* 49 (1944), 199–212.

471   Otway-Ruthven, A. Jocelyn. 'The request of the Irish for English law, 1277–80', *Irish Historical Studies,* 6 (1949), 261–70. Prints two documents with translations.

472   —— 'The native Irish and English law in medieval Ireland', *Irish Historical Studies,* 7 (1950), 1–16. A scholarly survey.

473   —— 'The constitutional position of the great lordships of South Wales', *TRHS,* ser. 5, 8 (1958), 1–20. Stresses their independence: a valuable contribution.

474   —— 'The medieval county of Kildare', *Irish Historical Studies,* 16 (1959), 181–99.

475   —— 'The medieval Irish chancery', *Album Helen M. Cam.* Vol. 2. *Studies presented to the international commission for representative and parliamentary institutions,* 24. Louvain, 1961, 117–38.

476   —— 'The chief governors of medieval Ireland', *Journal of the Royal Society of Antiquaries, Ireland,* 95 (1965), 227–36.

477   Patourel, John H. le. 'The medieval administration of Sark', *Société guernesaise, Reports and Transactions,* 12 (1936), 310–36.

478   Pegues, Frank. 'The *clericus* in the legal administration of thirteenth-century England', *EHR,* 71 (1956), 529–59. The keeper of the rolls and writs of the Bench played a part in the formation of legal literature.

479   Picciotto, Cyril M. 'The legal position of the Jews in pre-expulsion England as shown by the plea rolls of the exchequer', *Jewish Historical Society* 9 (1922), 67–84.

480   Plucknett, Theodore F.T. 'Case and the statute of Westminster II', *Columbia Law Review,* 31 (1931), 780–995; also 'Case and Westminster II', *LQR,* 52 (1936), 220–24; see also, for a slightly less convincing interpretation. P.A. Landon. 'The action on the case and the statute of Westminster II', *LQR,* 50 (1936), 68–78.

481   —— 'New light on the old county court', *Harvard Law Review,* 42 (1929), 639–75.

482   —— 'Place of the legal profession in the history of English law', *LQR,* 48 (1932), 328–40. Does not contain much that is new.

483   —— 'Relations between Roman law and English common law down to the sixteenth century', *University of Toronto Law Journal,* 3 (1939), 24–51.

484   Pollock, Frederick. 'The origins of the inns of court', *LQR,* 48 (1932), 163–70.

485   Poole, Reginald L. 'The early lives of Robert Pullen and Nicholas Breakspear, with notes on other Englishmen at the papal court about the middle of the twelfth century', *EPTT,* 61–70.

486   Powell, W. Raymond. 'The administration of the navy and the stannaries, 1189–1216', *EHR,* 71 (1956), 177–88. A scheme evolved under John whereby stannaries and navy were placed under a single official and revenue from the former went directly to support the latter.

487   Powicke, Frederick M. 'Master Simon the Norman', *EHR,* 58 (1943), 330–43. Important for politics and administration about 1240.

488   —— 'Writ for enforcing watch and ward, 1242', *EHR,* 57 (1952), 469–73 and *EHR,* 58 (1943), 128. Corrects Stubbs' *Select charters.*

489   Prentout, Henri. 'De l'origine de la formule *dei gratia* dans les chartes d'Henri II', *Académie mediévale de Caen.* (1918–20), 341–93.

490   Prestwich, Michael C. 'Exchequer and wardrobe in the later years of Edward I', *BIHR,* 46 (1973), 1–10.

491   Pugh, Ralph B. 'The king's prisons before 1250', *TRHS*, ser. 5, 5 (1955), 1–22. Important discussion.

492   Raban, Sandra. 'Mortmain in medieval England', *PP*, 62 (1974), 3–26.

493   Radding, Charles M. 'Glanvill on the common law: *lax terrae* and *jus regni*'. *University of Pennsylvania Law Review*, 82 (1933), 26–36.

494   ——— 'The origins of Bracton's *Addicio de cartis*', *Speculum*, 44 (1969), 239–46.

495   Reinhardt, John F. 'The status of the crown in the time of Bracton', *Temple University Law Quarterly*, 17 (1943), 242–70.

496   Reuschlein, Harold G. 'Who wrote *The Mirror of Justices*? A note upon the suggestions of Maitland, Pollock and Leadham', *LQR*, 58 (1941), 265–79. Questions Maitland's view and suggests a professional pleader.

497   Richardson, Henry G. 'Early coronation records', *BIHR*, 13 (1935–6), 129–45 and *BIHR*, 14 (1936–37), 1–9, 145–48; also 'The coronation in medieval England', *Traditio*, 16 (1960), 111–202; 'The coronation of Edward I', *BIHR*, 15 (1937–38), 94–99; 'Early coronation records, the coronation of Edward II', *BIHR*, 16 (1938–39), 1–11. Contributions to a lively debate; Robert S. Hoyt. 'The coronation oath of 1308', *Traditio*, 11 (1955), 235–57; Robert S. Hoyt. 'The coronation oath of 1308', *EHR*, 71 (1956), 352–83; Bertie Wilkinson. 'Notes on the coronation records of the fourteenth century', *EHR*, 70 (1955), 582–600; John Brückmann. 'The ordines of the third recension of the medieval English coronation order', *EPBW*, 99–115. Argues convincingly, as against Henry G. Richardson, that a third recension was used in the coronations of the twelfth and thirteenth centuries.

498   ——— *Bracton and the problem of his text*. Selden Society, supp. ser. 12 (1964). A contribution to a wide-ranging debate. See also Wiebke Fesefeldt. *Englische Staatstheorie des 13 Jahrhunderts: Henry Bracton und seine Werke*. Göttingen, 1962; Ernst H. Kantorwicz. *Bractonian problems*. Glasgow, 1941; Henry G. Richardson. 'Studies in Bracton', *Traditio*, 6 (1948), 61–104; and *Traditio*, 14 (1958), 399–400; and Henry G. Richardson. 'Azo, Drogheda and Bracton', *EHR*, 59 (1944), 22–47; Gaillard Lapsley. 'Bracton and the authorship of the *Addicio de Cartis*', *EHR*, 62 (1947), 1–20. Fritz Schultz. 'Critical studies on Bracton's treatise', *LQR*, 59 (1943), 172–80; and 'A new approach to Bracton', *Seminar*, 2–3 (1944–45), 41–50; and 'Bracton as a computist', *Traditio*, 3 (1945), 265–306; Brian Tierney. 'Bracton on government', *Speculum*, 38 (1963), 295–317; Gaines Post. 'A Romano-canonical maxim, *quod omnes tangit* in Bracton', *Traditio*, 4 (1946), 197–251.

499   ——— 'The letters and charters of Eleanor of Aquitaine', *EHR*, 74 (1959), 193–213. Some information about the clerks who served her, with an Appendix on the queen's gold.

500   ——— 'The chamber under Henry II', *EHR*, 69 (1954), 596–611. Argues strongly, and on the whole convincingly, but with undue acerbity.

501   Riddell, William R. 'Wager of battle in A.D. 1200', *Illinois Law Review*, 20 (1926), 31–42.

502   ——— 'Erring judges of the fourteenth century', *Illinois Law Review*, 21 (1927), 543–58.

503   Roderick, Arthur J. 'The four cantreds: a study in administration', *BBCS*, 10 (1940), 246–56. A useful article about the much disputed 'frontier' area in north-east Wales.

504   ——— 'The feudal relationship between the English crown and the Welsh princes', *History*, 37 (1952), 201–12.

505   Rogers, Ralph V. 'Law reporting and the multiplication of law reports in the fourteenth century', *EHR*, 66 (1951), 481–506. Discusses the origin of the year book MSS. centered on reports of cases in 1330.

506   Round, J. Horace. ' "Barons" and "knights" in the great charter', in Henry E. Malden (ed.). *Magna carta commemoration essays*. For the Royal Historical Society, 1917, 46–77. A clearing up of confusion by a master hand.

507 ——— ' "Barons" and "peers" ', *EHR*, 33 (1918), 453—71. The barons
regarded (with earls and prelates) as 'peers', receiving special summons to
the upper house, in the first half of the fourteenth century.

508 Russell, Josiah C. 'The canonization of opposition to the king in Angevin
England', in Charles H. Taylor (ed.). *Haskins anniversary essays*, Boston,
1929, 279—90.

509 ——— 'Ranulf de Glanville', *Speculum*, 45 (1970), 69—79.

510 ——— 'The significance of charter witness lists in thirteenth-century
England', *New Mexico Normal University Bulletin*, supp. to no. 99
(1930); *Speculum*, 14 (1939), 108—09; 'Attestation of charters in the
reign of John', *Speculum*, 15 (1940), 480—98. Argues convincingly that
witnesses to charters normally saw them and heard them read; also 'Social
status at the court of king John', *Speculum*, 12 (1937), 319—29. A preliminary study. See also George L. Haskins. 'Charter witness lists in the
reign of king John', *Speculum*, 13 (1938), 319—25.

511 Salzmann, Louis F. 'Mines and stanneries', *EGAW*, 3 67—104.

512 Sandys, Agnes. 'The financial and administrative importance of the London
temple in the thirteenth century', *EPTT*, 147—62.

513 Sayles, George O. 'The court of king's bench in law and history', Selden
Society Lecture, 1959 (1962). By a great expert; see also Brian Kemp.
'Exchequer and bench in the later twelfth century — separate or identical
tribunals?', *EHR*, 88 (1973), 559—73.

514 ——— 'The legal proceedings against the first earl of Desmond', *Analecta
Hibernica*, 23 (1966), 3—47 [1329—1356].

515 Scammell, Jean V. 'The origin and limitations of the liberty of Durham',
EHR, 81 (1966), 449—73. Important comments on this and other palatin-
ates.

516 Schlaugh, Margaret. 'Chaucer's doctrine of kings and tyrants', *Speculum*, 20
(1945), 133—57.

517 Sharp, Margaret. 'The administrative chancery of the Black Prince before
1362', *EPTT*, 321—33.

518 Sheehan, Michael. 'English law in medieval Ireland', *Archivum Hibernicum,
Irish Historical Records*, 23 (1960), 167—75. Prints two illustrative documents.

519 Simmons, Thomas W. 'Chancery and exchequer clerks serving as attorneys
1327—1336', *University of Colorado Studies*, 22 (1935), 381—96.

520 Southern, Richard W. 'A note on the text of "Glanville", *De legibus et consuetudinibus regni Angliae*', *EHR*, 65 (1950), 81—89.

521 Steel, Anthony. 'The practice of assignment in the later fourteenth century',
EHR, 43 (1928), 172—80. A contribution to the understanding of the
complicated procedures of the exchequer; and 'Distribution of assignment
in the treasurer's receipt roll, Michaelmas, 1364—5', *CHJ*, 2 (1928), 178—
85. A helpful discussion.

522 Stevenson, Edward R. 'The escheator', *EGAW*, 2, 109—67.

523 Stones, Edward L.G. 'Two records of the "great cause" of 1291—92', *SHR*,
35 (1956), 89—109. Prints an important document.

524 ——— 'The text of the writ *"Quod omnes tangit"* in Stubbs's Select charters', *EHR*, 83 (1968), 759—76. Makes a small but important correction
of Stubbs' version.

525 ——— and George Rudisill. 'Taxation and community in Wales and Ireland,
1272—1327', *Speculum*, 29 (1954), 410—16. Observations on the meaning of *communitas* in Ireland, Wales and England, particularly under
Edward I.

526 Taylor, Mary M. 'Justices of assize', *EGAW*, 3, 219—57.

527 Teresa, May. 'The Cobham family in the administration of England, 1200—
1400', *ArchCant*, 82 (1969), 1—31.

528 Treharne, Reginald F. 'An unauthorized use of the great seal under the pro-
visional government in 1259', *EHR*, 40 (1925), 403—11.

529 ——— 'The constitutional problem in thirteenth century England', *EPBW*,
46—78. Expresses the final judgment of a distinguished scholar.

530 Trueman, John H. 'The privy seal and the English ordinances of 1311', *Speculum*, 31 (1956), 611—25.
531 Updegraff, Clarence M. 'The interpretation of "issue" in the statute *De donis*', *Harvard Law Review*, 39 (1926), 200—20.
532 Vinogradoff, Paul. 'Ralph de Hengham as chief justice of the common pleas', *EPTT*, 189—96.
533 Watt, John A. 'English law and the Irish church: the reign of Edward I', *SPAG*, 133—67.
534 Weinbaum, Martin. 'Die Anfänge der englischen Zentralverwaltung', *Schmollers Jahrbuch*, 56 (1932), 601—18.
535 White, Albert B. 'Was there a "common council" before parliament?', *AHR*, 25 (1919), 1—17. This important article is now dated, but it has been unduly ignored.
536 Wilkinson, Bertie. 'The seals of the two benches under Edward III', *EHR*, 42 (1927), 347—401.
537 ———— 'The chancery', *EGAW*, 1, 162—205.
538 ———— 'The government of England during the absence of Richard I on the third crusade', *BJRL*, 28 (1944), 485—509.
539 Willard, F. 'Taxation boroughs and parliamentary boroughs, 1294—1336', *EHJT*, 417—35. Discusses the method of classification.
540 Winfield, Percy H. 'The history of maintenance and champerty', *LQR*, 35 (1919), 50—72.
541 Wright, Elizabeth C. 'Common law in the thirteenth-century English royal forest', *Speculum*, 3 (1928), 166—91. In the ordinary course, forest pleas were heard in the forest courts, criminal or civil pleas in common law courts.
542 Zane, John M. 'The attaint', *Michigan Law Review*, 15 (1917), 127—48; 16 (1918), 1—20.

V. POLITICAL HISTORY

1 Printed Sources

543 Anstruther, Robert (ed.). *Radulfi Nigri chronica. The chronicles of Ralph Niger*. Caxton Society, 13 (1851). Reprinted New York, 1967. Ralph was critical of Henry II.
544 Appleby, John T. (ed.). *Cronicon Richardi divisensis de tempore regis Richardi primi*. 1963.
545 Aspin, Isabel S.T. (ed.). *Anglo-Norman political songs*, Anglo-Norman texts, 11. Oxford, 1953. Supersedes all previous editions.
546 Bagley, John. *Historical interpretation: sources of English medieval history, 1066—1540*. Penguin ed., Baltimore, Md., 1965. An extended bibliographical essay providing an introduction to the sources, with selections.
547 Balfour-Melville, Evan W.M. (ed.). 'Papers relating to the captivity and release of David II [1355 to 1357] ', *Publications of the Scottish Historical Society*, ser. 3, 50 (1958), 3—56.
548 Barrow, Geoffrey W.S. (ed.). *Regesta regum Scottorum: Vol. 1, the acts of Malcolm IV, 1153—1165*. Edinburgh, 1960. The first volume of an important new series; and Geoffrey W.S. Barrow and W.W. Scott (eds.). *The acts of William I, king of Scots, 1165—1214*. Edinburgh, 1971.
549 Bock, Friedrich. 'An unknown register of the reign of Edward III', *EHR*, 45 (1930), 353—72. Of considerable significance.
550 ———— 'Some new documents illustrating the early years of the Hundred Years War', *BJRL*, 15 (1931), 60—99. Prints treaty of alliance between Edward III and Charles de Blois, 1 March, 1353, and an unratified treaty between Edward and John of France, 6 April, 1354.
551 Briggs, Helen M. (ed.). *Here may a young man see how he should speak subtly in court. Translated from a thirteenth or fourteenth century manuscript*. 1936. Foreword by C. Hilary Jenkinson. A very brief tract.

552   Brooks, Eric St John (ed.). *Unpublished charters relating to Ireland, 1177–82 from the archives of the city of Exeter. Proceedings of the Royal Irish Academy*, 43 (1936), 313–66.

553   Carr, Antony D. *Some Edeyrnion and Dinmael documents. BBCS*, 21 (1965), 242–50. Sheds some light on the handful of Welsh lords who survived the Edwardian conquest.

554   Chaplais, Pierre (ed.). *The war of Saint-Sardos (1323–1325); Gascon correspondence and diplomatic documents.* Camden Society, ser. 3, 87 (1954). Important documents well edited.

555   —— *Treaty rolls preserved in the public record office.* Vol. 1, *1234–1325.* 1955. HMSO. A valuable collection of documents. *Foedera* is expertly calendared, and other documents given in full.

556   —— *Diplomatic documents preserved in the public record office.* Vol. 1, *1101–1272.* 1964. HMSO. Brilliantly assembled documents of great historical importance.

557   *Chronicle of Melrose* [731–1275]. Facsimile in collotype. Introduction by Alan O. and Marjorie O. Anderson. 1936. After the middle of the twelfth century, it is an original authority. Provides material for a new ed. An index of more than a hundred pp. Specially important for Scotland and Northern England.

558   Craster, Herbert H.E. and Mary E. Thornton (eds.). *The chronicle of St. Mary's abbey, York. From Bodley MS. 39.* Surtees Society, 148 (1934). Covers the thirteenth and fourteenth centuries.

559   Cuttino, George P. 'An unidentified Gascon register', *EHR*, 54 (1939), 293–99. Transcripts and summary.

560   —— 'A memorandum book of Elias Joneston', *Speculum*, 17 (1942), 74–85. Memorandum of documents regarding Gascony delivered to the Treasurer and Chamberlains of the exchequer on 10 June, 1317.

561   —— 'Another memorandum book of Elias Joneston', *EHR*, 63 (1948), 90–103. The record relates to the duchy of Aquitaine in 1303–1336.

562   —— *The Gascon calendar of 1332.* Camden Society, ser. 3, 70 (1949). Contains important extracts from miscellaneous books in the PRO: exchequer treasury of receipt.

563   Denholm-Young, Noël. 'Documents of the barons' wars', *EHR*, 48 (1933), 558–75. Throws important light on events.

564   —— (ed. and trans.). *The life of Edward II by the so-called monk of Malmesbury.* Oxford. 1957. One of the most important sources for the reign of Edward II; attributed by Denholm-Young to Master John Walwayn, D.C.L.

565   Dickinson, William C. *et al.* (eds.). *A source book of Scottish history.* Vol. 1, *From the earliest times to 1424.* 2nd ed., Edinburgh, 1958. A valuable collection.

566   Edwards, J. Goronwy (ed.). *Calendar of ancient correspondence concerning Wales.* Board of Celtic Studies, History and Law ser., no. 2. Cardiff, 1935. Excerpts from a volume temp. Edward I. One of the most important single collections for the history of Wales in the thirteenth century.

567   Freeman, Alexander M. (ed.). *Annála Connacht: the annals of Connacht* (A.D. 1224–1544). Dublin, 1944.

568   Galbraith, Vivian H. (ed.). *The anonimalle chronicle, 1333–1381.* Manchester University Historical ser., no. 175. Manchester, 1927. Probably completed by 1399. A rare modern discovery, brilliantly edited. Of special value for the Good Parliament and the Peasants' Revolt.

569   —— 'Extracts from the *Historia Aurea* and a French "Brut" ', [1317–47], *EHR*, 43 (1928), 203–17.

570   —— 'The St Edmundsbury chronicle, 1296–1301', *EHR*, 58 (1943), 51–78. Printed for the first time: contains interesting material.

571   Griffiths, John (ed.). 'Documents relating to the Rebellion of Madoc, 1294–5', *BBCS*, 8 (1936), 147–60. These are exchequer accounts and include a list of Welsh prisoners.

572   Guisborough, Walter of. *The chronicle of Walter of Guisborough, previously edited as the chronicle of Walter of Hemingford or Hemingburgh*, ed.

Harry Rothwell. Camden Society, ser. 3, 89 (1957). Expert editorial work. The chronicle is important after 1272.

573 Haskins, George L. 'A chronicle of the civil wars of Edward II', *Speculum*, 14 (1939), 73—81. Text, with no comment on the interesting wording of the scribe on the condemnations of Gaveston and Despensers.

574 Hinnse, S.O. (ed.). *Miscellaneous Irish annals (A.D. 1114—1437).* Dublin, 1947.

575 Hubert, Merton J. (trans.). *The crusade of Richard the Lion-Heart by Ambroise.* Notes and documentation by John L. La Monte. New York, 1941.

576 Jones, Thomas (ed.). 'Cronica de Wallia and other documents from Exeter Cathedral library MS. 3514', *BBCS*, 12 Pt. 1 (1946), 27—44. The *Cronica de Wallia* is one version of the chief surviving native chronicle which in other versions is known as 'Brut y Tywysogion'. The major text is attributed to a Cistercian monk of Whitland in Carmarthenshire, writing in 1277; also *Brut y Tywysogion (Peniarth MS. 20 version).* Board of Celtic Studies, History and Law ser., no. 11 (1952). The Bruts (two versions: Peniarth's and Red Book of Hergest) are the (sole) basic native chronicle. 'Annales Cambriae' and 'Cronica de Wallia' are further versions. They are Welsh texts of the lost Latin chronicle. See also Thomas Jones (ed.). *Brut y Tywysogion or the chronicle of the princes: Red Book of Hergest version.* Cardiff, 1955. Down to 1197 (one version) and 1282 (two versions). A basic narrative source of Welsh history.

577 Mellows, William T. (ed.). *The Peterborough chronicle of Hugh Candidus.* Oxford, 1949. Written in the twelfth century. Additions and changes by Robert of Swaffham in the thirteenth, and in the register of Walter of Whittlesey in the fourteenth century.

578 Myers, Alec R. (ed.). *English historical documents.* Vol. 4, *1327—1485.* General ed. David C. Douglas, 1969. A comprehensive and scholarly selection, superseding all predecessors.

579 Ockham, William of. *Guillelmi de Ockham opera politica,* ed. Jeffrey O. Sikes *et al.* Manchester, 1940—63, 3 vols. A great work, illuminating the development of medieval thought.

580 ——— *Wilhelm von Ockham als politischer Denker und sein 'Breviloquium de principatu tyrannico',* ed. Richard Scholz. Leipzig, 1944. Prints text of *Breviloquium.*

581 O'Grady, Standish H. and Robin Flower (eds.). *Gaithréim Toirdealbhaigh.* Irish Texts Society, 26—27 (1929). Dates from about the year 1360. Tells of local war from 1276—1318. A rare Gaelic genre.

582 Perroy, Édouard (ed.). *The diplomatic correspondence of Richard II.* Camden Society, ser. 3, 48 (1933). Some new material: a very fine ed.

583 Renouard, Yves (ed.). *Gascon rolls preserved in the public record office, 1307—1317.* 1962. HMSO. Includes itineraries for the two journeys of Edward II to France, 1308 and 1313.

584 Roberts, Richard A. (ed.). *Edward II, the lords ordainers, and Piers Gaveston's jewels and horses.* Camden Miscellany, 15. Camden Society, ser. 3, 41 (1929). More general and important than the title would suggest.

585 Ross, Thomas W. (ed.). *A satire of Edward III's England.* Colorado Springs, Colo., 1966. A critical ed.

586 Russell, Josiah C. and John P. Heironimus (ed.). *The shorter Latin poems of Master Henry Avranches relating to England.* Medieval Academy of America. Cambridge, Mass., 1935.

587 Salisbury, Edward. 'A political agreement of June, 1318', *EHR*, 33 (1918), 78—83. Prints the agreement between the Middle party and the court, of vital importance in relation to the treaty of Leak; also J. Goronwy Edwards. 'The negotiating of the treaty of Leak, 1318', *EPRP*, 360—78.

588 Salisbury, John of. *The statesman's book of John of Salisbury,* ed. John C. Dickinson. New York, 1927. Edits the fourth, fifth and sixth bks., together with selections from the seventh and eighth. There is a translation and a good Introduction.

589 Smith, J. Beverley. 'Offra principis Wallie domino regni', *BBCS*, 21 (1966),

362—67. A new document illuminating the struggle between Llywelyn ap Gruffyd and Edward I.

590   Stones, Edward L.G. (ed. and trans.). *Anglo-Scottish relations, 1174—1328: some selected documents.* 1965. Presents some documents which are not well-known.

591   Taylor, John (ed.). *The Kirkstall abbey chronicle.* Thoresby Society, 42 (1952). The two fourteenth-century chronicles contain material for Edward III's wars in France and the policies of Richard II.

592   Wallingford, John of. 'The chronicle of John of Wallingford', ed. Richard Vaughan, *EHR*, 73 (1958), 66—77. With variations from Matthew Paris. Of limited interest, except *sub anno* 1258, where there is a reference to the French *parlementum.*

593   Webster, Bruce (ed.). *Handlist of the acts of David II. Regesta regum Scottorum, 1329—1371.* Edinburgh, 1958—.

2 Surveys

594   Barlow, Frank. *The feudal kingdom of England, 1042—1216.* 2nd ed. 1962. Best modern survey.

595   Barrow, Geoffrey W.S. *Feudal Britain. The completion of the medieval kingdoms, 1066—1314.* 1957. An excellent survey.

596   Bateson, Edward *et al. A history of Northumberland.* Newcastle-upon-Tyne. 1893—1940, 15 vols. Continues history by J. Hodgson.

597   Bryant, Arthur. *The age of chivalry.* 1963. Written by a brilliant writer, but one who has specialized in modern history. Covers the period from Edward I to Henry IV.

598   *County Histories of Scotland.* Edinburgh and London, 1896—.

599   Courteault, Paul. *Histoire de Gascoigne et de Béarn.* Paris, 1938. Includes 'La Gascoigne de 1137 à 1447'; also *Pour l'histoire de Bordeaux et du sudouest.* Bordeaux, 1934.

600   Darby, H. Clifford (ed.). *An historical geography of England before A.D. 1800.* Cambridge, 1936. By the greatest experts in the field. Contents include 'The economic geography of England, A.D. 1000—1250'; 'Fourteenth-century England'; 'Medieval foreign trade: western ports'; 'Medieval foreign trade: eastern ports'.

601   Davis, H.W. Charles. *England under the Normans and Angevins, 1066—1272.* 13th ed., 1949. Still offers insights, but largely superseded.

602   Edwards, J. Goronwy. *The principality of Wales 1267—1967.* Caernarvon, 1969. A valuable survey by a leading expert of Welsh history.

603   Keen, Maurice H. *England in the later Middle Ages: a political history.* 1973; also John J. Palmer. *England, France and Christendom.* 1972.

604   Lloyd, John E. *A history of Wales from the earliest times to the Edwardian conquest.* 3rd ed., 1939; reprinted 1968, 2 vols. Monumental tomes by a most important Welsh historian. Others have tried to whittle it away; but it has, in general, been added to rather than replaced.

605   —— *et al. Histories of Carmarthenshire, of Merioneth, of Caernarvonshire, of Glamorgan.* 1935—71.

606   McKisack, May. *The fourteenth century. Oxford History of England.* Vol. 5. Oxford, 1959. The standard survey, based on sound scholarship.

607   Otway-Ruthven, A. Jocelyn. *A history of medieval Ireland.* 1968. The standard work. Supersedes all earlier vols.

608   Poole, Austin L. *From Domesday book to magna carta, 1087—1216.* Oxford, 1951; 2nd ed., Oxford, 1955. An authoritative survey.

609   Powicke, Frederick M. *The thirteenth century, 1216—1307.* Oxford, 1951. An outstanding survey and a masterpiece of interpretation; and Powicke's *King Henry III and the lord Edward: the community of the realm in the thirteenth century.* Oxford, 1947, 2 vols.

610   Schuyler, Robert L. *et al.* (eds.). *The making of English history.* New York, 1952. Prints significant articles by writers like McIlwain, Neilson, Templeman, Tout, and Thorndike.

611   Tout, Thomas F. *The history of England from the accession of Henry III to*

the death of Edward III (1216—1377). 2nd ed., 1920. Still has value; written by an outstanding expert.
612 Wilkinson, Bertie. *The later Middle Ages in England, 1216—1485.* 1969. A broad survey of politics and other main aspects of life.
613 Williams, H. *An introduction to the history of Wales.* Vol. 2, *The Middle Ages, Part 1, 1066—1284.* Cardiff, 1948.

3 Monographs

614 Appleby, John T. *England without Richard, 1189—1199.* Ithaca, N.Y., 1965. A very readable study.
615 Armstrong, Olive. *Bruce's invasion of Ireland,* 1924. Sharply criticized in Geoffrey W.S. Barrow. *Robert Bruce and the community of the realm of Scotland.* 1965. The best up to date.
616 Beckett, James C. (ed.). *Historical Studies,* 7 (1969). Includes Geoffrey Barrow on the reign of William the Lion, King of Scotland; and Wilfred L. Warren on the interpretation of twelfth-century Irish history.
617 Bloch, Marc. *Les rois thaumaturges; étude sur le caractère surnatural attribué à la puissance royale particulièrement en France et en Angleterre.* Strasbourg, 1924. An influential survey.
618 Boussard, Jacques. *La comté d'Anjou sous Henri Plantagenêt et ses fils, 1151—1204.* Paris, 1938.
619 Buchan, James W. *et al.* (eds.). *A history of Peeblesshire.* Glasgow, 1925—27.
620 Davies, J. Conway. *The baronial opposition to Edward II, its character and policy.* Cambridge, 1918; New impression, Cambridge, 1967.
621 Davis, H.W. Charles (ed.). *Essays in history presented to Reginald Lane Poole.* Oxford, 1927. Reprinted Oxford, 1967.
622 Dept, Gaston. *Les influences anglaise et française dans le comté de Flandre au début au XIIIe siècle.* Paris, 1928.
623 Fowler, Kenneth. *The age of Plantagenet and Valois: the struggle for supremacy 1328—1498.* New York, 1967. A survey of diplomacy, politics and war. Popular but scholarly.
624 Francesco, Ugo Aldo de. *Enrico III d'Inghilterra, Bonifacio di Savoia e la loro politico verso Frederico II de Suevia . . .* Naples, 1939.
625 Harvey, John H. *The Plantagenets.* 2nd ed., New York, 1959.
626 Holt, James C. *The northerners: a study in the reign of king John.* Oxford, 1961. Solid information and penetrating judgments.
627 Jacob, Ernest F. *Studies in the period of baronial reform and rebellion, 1258—1267.* Oxford, 1925. An important study, but now partly superseded.
628 Jones, William H. *History of Swansea and of the lordship of Gower from the earliest times to the XIVth century.* Carmarthen, 1920.
629 Landon, Lionel. *The itinerary of Richard I, with studies of certain matters of interest connected with his reign.* Pipe Roll Society, n.s., 13 (1935). Invaluable for all students of the reign.
630 Lloyd, John E. (ed.). *A history of Carmarthenshire, from prehistoric times to the act of union (1536).* Cardiff, 1935—39, 2 vols. A standard work.
631 Maddicott, John R. *Thomas of Lancaster 1307—1322. A study of the reign of Edward II.* Oxford, 1970.
632 Nicholson, Ranald. *Edward III and the Scots: the formative years of a military career, 1327—1335.* Oxford, 1965. A sound pioneer investigation, but with not much on the formation of Edward's military career.
633 Painter, Sidney. *The reign of king John.* 1950. A survey of lasting value.
634 Perroy, Édouard. *The Hundred Years' War,* trans. Warre B. Wells. Oxford, 1951. (Original French ed., Paris, 1945). Introduction by David C. Douglas. Still the best general account. See also George P. Cuttino. 'Historical revision: the causes of the Hundred Years' war', *Speculum,* 31 (1956), 463—77. The cosmopolitanism and suzerainty of 1259 became the nationalism and sovereignty of 1339; also Kenneth Fowler (ed.). *The Hundred Years' War.* 1971. Contains excellent articles by Kenneth Fowler (1—28, 184—209); John le Patourel (28—50); John Palmer (51—75);

Herbert J. Hewitt (75—96); Colin F. Richmond (96—122); Michael Powicke (122—35); Philippe Contamine (135—63); Christopher T. Allmand (163—84).

635 Petit-Dutaillis, Charles. *Le déshéritement de Jean sans terre et le meutre d'Arthur de Bretagne.* Paris, 1925. Exhaustive analysis; John R.S. Phillips. *Aymer de Valence, earl of Pembroke, 1307—1324: baronial politics in the reign of Edward II.* New York, 1972; also 'The "middle party" and the negotiating of the treaty of Leake, August, 1318: a reinterpretation', *BIHR*, 46 (1973), 1—27.

636 Powicke, Frederick M. *The loss of Normandy, 1189—1204: studies in the Angevin empire.* 2nd ed., Manchester, 1913; reprinted New York, 1961. Wide-ranging and scholarly. A fine pioneer work which has never been superseded.

637 —— and Reginald F. Treharne and Charles H. Lemmon. *The battle of Lewes 1264: its place in English history.* Lewes, 1964. Three separate contributions, the longest by Reginald F. Treharne, on why the battle matters in English history.

638 Pugh, Thomas B. (ed.). *Glamorgan county history.* Vol. 3, *The Middle Ages.* Cardiff, 1971. An authoritative and invaluable survey, some minor defects.

639 Rait, Robert S. and George S. Pryde. *Scotland.* 1934. Foreword by Herbert A.L. Fisher.

640 Rees, William. *Historical map of south Wales and the border in the fourteenth century.* Southampton, 1933. Ordnance Survey Office. Much more important than the title suggests, containing valuable information useful to students of social and political history.

641 Renouard, Yves (ed.). *Bordeaux sous les rois d'Angleterre.* Bordeaux, 1965. An important study; also *Études d'histoire médiévale II: septième partie: sud-ouest et relations Franco—Anglaises.* Paris, 1968.

642 Russell, Peter E. *The English intervention in Spain and Portugal in the time of Edward III and Richard II.* Oxford, 1955. An important book, filling a large gap in the history of English foreign policy and war; also Instituto de Coimbra. 'Comemoração das seculares relações entre a Inglaterra e Portugal', *Instituto*, ser. 4, 1937, 111—96. Historical review and bibliography of English works on Portugal; Edgar Prestage. 'The Anglo-Portuguese alliance', *TRHS*, ser. 4, 17 (1934), 69—100. Relations since the twelfth century discussed by an expert; and 'L'alliance Anglo-Portugaise', *Revue d'histoire diplomatique*, 50 (1936), 27—53.

643 Snellgrove, Harold S. *The Lusignans in England, 1247—1258.* Albuquerque, N.M., 1950. Useful survey. According to Frederick Powicke, it clinches Henry Richardson's arguments for marriage of Isabella to the son of her former fiancé; also Henry G. Richardson. 'The marriage and coronation of Isabelle of Angoulême', *EHR*, 61 (1946), 289—314 and *EHR*, 65 (1950), 360—71; Fred A. Cazel and Sidney Painter. 'The marriage of Isabella of Angoulême', *EHR*, 63 (1948), 83—89; *EHR*, 67 (1952), 233—35.

644 Stones, Edward L.G. *Anglo-Scottish relations, 1174—1328.* 1965. A most important survey. Reprinted with corrections, Oxford, 1971.

645 Sturler, Jean V. de. *Les relations politiques et les échanges commerciaux entre le Duché de Brabant et l'Angleterre au moyen âge.* Paris, 1936.

646 Tourneur-Aumont, Jean M. *La bataille de Poitiers (1356), et la construction de la France.* Paris, 1940.

647 Tout, Thomas F. *The place of Edward II in English history.* 1913; 2nd ed., Manchester, 1914; 3rd ed., Manchester, 1936. Revised by Hilda Johnstone. Still invaluable, though much of the interpretation has been questioned. However, the most recent reactions have gone too far. The work still represents an outstanding pioneer work.

648 Trautz, Fritz. *Die Könige von England und das Reich, 1272—1377, mit einem Rückblick auf ihr Verhältnis zu den Staufern.* Heidelberg, 1961. A lengthy work of exact scholarship.

649 Treharne, Reginald F. *The baronial plan of reform, 1258—1263.* Including the Raleigh lecture on history delivered to the British academy, 1954.

Publications of the University of Manchester, Historical ser. 62. First ed., Manchester, 1932; reprinted New York, 1971. A fine detailed study, somewhat idealistic.

650   Tuck, Anthony. *Richard II and the English nobility*. New York, 1974. Valuable.

651   Tucoo-Chala, Pierre. *Gaston Febus et la vicomté de Béarn, 1343–1391*. Bordeaux, 1961. Important for English as well as French history; also *La vicomté de Béarn et la problème de sa souveraineté*. Bordeaux, 1961. In the form of a collection of the more important documents, with a long Introduction.

652   Wolf, Ilse. *Heinrich II von England als Vasall Ludwigs VII von Frankreich*. Würzburg, 1936.

4 Biographies

653   Appleby, John T. *John king of England*. 1960. A scholarly popularization. See also James C. Holt in an authoritative pamphlet, *King John*. Historical Association General ser., 53 (1963); also Wilfred L. Warren. *King John*. New York, 1960. A book for the general reader; well balanced and readable.

654   Cartellieri, Alexander. 'Richard Löwenhertz', in *Probleme der Englischen Sprache und Kultur; Festschrift für Johannes Hoops zum 60 Geburtstag*. Heidelberg, 1925. An authoritative little study.

655   Denholm-Young, Noël. *Richard of Cornwall*. New York, 1947. A good biography.

656   Ellis, Clarence. *Hubert de Burgh: a study in constancy*. 1952.

657   Fergusson, James. *Alexander the third, king of Scotland*. 1937.

658   —— *William Wallace, guardian of Scotland*. 1938; New ed., Stirling, 1948.

659   Fowler, Kenneth. *The king's lieutenant Henry of Gosmont first duke of Lancaster, 1310–1361*. New York, 1969. A scholarly biography.

660   Henderson, Philip. *Richard coeur de lion*. 1958.

661   Johnstone, Hilda. *Edward of Carnarvon 1284–1307*. Manchester, 1946. A careful study, yielding little of significance.

662   —— 'Isabella, the she-wolf of France', *History*, 21 (1936), 208–18.

663   Kay, Frederick G. *Lady of the sun: the life and times of Alice Perrers*. New York, 1966. A good popular account.

664   Keally, Edward J. *Roger of Salisbury viceroy of England*. Berkeley, Cal., 1972.

665   Kelly, Amy. *Eleanor of Aquitaine and the four kings*. New York, 1957. First published, Cambridge, Mass., 1950. A sound literary work, showing much historical research; see also Régine Pernoud. *Aliénor d'Aquitaine*. Paris, 1965. Scholarly and important.

666   Labarge, Margaret W. *Simon de Monfort*. 1962. A good study.

667   Lewis, Frank R. 'William de Valence (*c*. 1230–1296)', *Aberystwyth Studies*, 13 (1934), 11–35; 14 (1936), 69–92. William was a royalist in the barons' wars.

668   McNulty, Joseph. 'Henry de Lacy, earl of Lincoln, 1251–1311', *LancsAntiq*, 51 (1937), 19–43.

669   Middleton, Arthur. *Sir Gilbert de Middleton and the part he took in the rebellion in the north of England in 1317*. Newcastle-upon-Tyne, 1918. A thorough investigation.

670   Norgate, Kate. *Richard the lion heart*. 1924. A scholarly work. Still useful.

671   Painter, Sidney. *William Marshal, knight errant, baron and regent of England*. [Reprint] Baltimore, Md., 1968. First published Baltimore, 1933. The standard biography.

672   Smith, Armitage S. *John of Gaunt, king of Castile and duke of Lancaster, earl of Derby, Lincoln and Leicester, seneschal of England*. New York, 1964. First published 1904. Now much out of date, but not quite superseded.

673   Stones, Edward L.G. *Edward I*. Oxford, 1968. A good short biography.

674   White, Geoffrey H. 'The career of Waleran count of Meulan and earl of Worcester (1104–1166)', *TRHS*, ser. 4, 17 (1934), 19–48.

POLITICAL HISTORY

675   Young, Charles R. *Hubert Walter, lord of Canterbury and lord of England.*
         Durham, N.C. 1968. Sound.

5 Articles

676   Barraclough, Geoffrey. 'Edward I and Adolf Nassau. A chapter of medieval
         diplomatic history', *CHJ*, 6 (1940), 225–62.
677   —— 'The earldom and county palatine of Chester', *LancsHistoric*, 103
         (1951–52), 23–57. Reprinted Oxford, 1953.
678   Barrow, Geoffrey W.S. 'The Scottish clergy in the war of independence', *SHR*,
         41 (1962), 1–22. Important article: the clergy played a significant role.
679   —— 'The Anglo-Scottish border', *Northern History*, 1 (1966), 21–42.
         Breaks new ground.
680   Baylen, Joseph O. 'John Maunsell and the Castillian treaty of 1254: a study
         of a clerical diplomatic', *Traditio*, 17 (1961), 482–91. John helped Henry
         to commit the kingdom to an ambitious foreign policy without the con-
         sent of the 'community of the realm'.
681   Bayley, Charles C. 'The campaign of 1375 and the good parliament', *EHR*,
         55 (1940), 370–83.
682   Bean, John M.W. 'The Percies and their estates in Scotland', *ArchAel*, ser. 4,
         35 (1957), 48–99.
683   Blackley, F. Donald. 'Isabella and the bishop of Exeter', *EPBW*, 220–235.
         An important revision of Isabella's actions in the last months of her hus-
         band's reign.
684   Born, Lester K. 'The perfect prince: a study in thirteenth- and fourteenth-
         century ideals', *Speculum*, 3 (1928), 470–504. Includes John of
         Salisbury and Gerald of Wales.
685   Broome, Dorothy M. 'The ransom of John II, king of France, 1360–70',
         Camden Miscellany, 13. Camden Society, ser. 3, 37 (1926), i–xxvi, 1–
         44. Prints lengthy documents relative to the payment of the ransom.
686   Carr, Antony D. 'Wales and the Hundred Years' War', *WHR*, 4 (1964), 21–
         46.
687   Cate, James L. 'The English mission of Eustace of Flay (1200–1202)',
         Mélanges d'histoire offerts à Henri Pirenne. Brussels, 1937, 67–89.
688   Chaplais, Pierre. 'English arguments concerning the feudal status of Aquitaine
         in the fourteenth century', *BIHR*, 21 (1946–48), 203–213. Prints a rel-
         evant document; 'Réglement des conflits internationaux franco-anglais au
         XIVe siècle (1293–1377)', *Le moyen âge*, 57 (1951), 269–302. Includes
         documents; 'The making of the treaty of Paris (1259) and the royal style',
         EHR, 67 (1952), 235–53. Clarifies procedure.
689   —— 'Le duché-pairie de Guienne', *Annales du Midi*, 69 (1957), 5–38.
690   —— 'Some private letters of Edward I', *EHR*, 77 (1962), 79–86. Prints
         drafts of seven letters which throw light on Edward's personality.
691   Cheney, Christopher R. 'The alleged deposition of king John', *SPFP*. An
         important correction of the view that John was deposed by Innocent III.
692   Clanchy, Michael T. 'Did Henry III have a policy?', *History*, 53 (1968), 203–
         16. Argues in favour.
693   Clarke, Maude V. 'William of Windsor in Ireland, 1369–76', *Proceedings of
         the Royal Irish Academy*, 41 (1932–4), 55–130. Includes a transcription
         of parliament and council proceedings – chancery.
694   Coulton, George G. 'Nationalism in the Middle Ages', *CHJ*, 5 (1935–37),
         15–40.
695   Cuttino, George P. 'Bishop Langton's mission for Edward I 1296–7', *Univer-
         sity of Iowa Studies in the Social Sciences*, 11 (1941), 147–83.
696   —— 'The process of Agen', *Speculum*, 19 (1944), 161–78. Discusses the
         important conference of 1332 which revealed the conflicting French and
         English concepts of sovereignty and suzerainty helping to produce the
         Hundred Years' War. Prints texts.
697   Denholm-Young, Noël. 'Edward I and the sale of the Isle of Wight', *EHR*, 44
         (1929), 433–38.

698 ———— 'Robert Carpenter and the provisions of Westminster', *EHR*, 50 (1935), 22—35.

699 ———— 'A letter from the council to Pope Honorius III, 1220—21', *EHR*, 60 (1945), 88—96.

700 ———— 'The song of Carlaverock and the parliamentary roll of arms as found in Cott. MS. Calig. A XVIII, in the British museum', *PBA*, 47 (1962), 251—62. Suggested date for roll, 1307—1308.

701 Déprez, Eugene. 'La conférence d'Avignon (1344)', *SPFP*, 301—20. Suggests reasons for failure of Pope Clement VI to obtain peace.

702 Dickinson, Joycelyne G. ' "Blanks" and "blank charters" in the fourteenth and fifteenth centuries', *EHR*, 66 (1951), 375—87; also Donald E. Queller. 'Diplomatic *"blancs"* in the thirteenth century', *EHR*, 80 (1965), 476—91. Offers conclusive proof of their use, with particular reference to England.

703 Doudelez, G. 'Les résultats de la bataille de Bouvines et l'exécution du traité de Melun par la Flandre', *Revue des questions historiques*, 128 (1937), 7—27, 22—62. Some significant conclusions.

704 Dunlop, Robert. 'Some notes on Barbour's *Bruce*', *EPTT*, 277—90. Sharply criticises Olive Armstrong.

705 Dunning, Patrick J. 'Innocent III and the Irish kings', *JEH*, 10 (1957), 17—32.

706 Edwards, J. Goronwy. 'Sir Gruffydd Llwyd', *EHR*, 30 (1915), 589—601. Includes an account of the defeat of the enemies of Edward II in 1321—22 by the rising of his Welsh supporters.

707 ———— '*The itinerarium regis Ricardi* and the *Estoire de la guerre sainte*', *EHJT*, 59—79. Argues convincingly for the idea of an independent derivation from a common original.

708 ———— 'The treason of Thomas Turberville, 1295', *SPFP*, 296—309. Probably the earliest notable instance of treason by spying.

709 Galbraith, Vivian H. 'Good kings and bad kings in English medieval history', *History*, 30 (1945), 119—32.

710 Gibb, Hamilton A.R. 'English crusaders in Portugal', in Edgar Prestage (ed.). *Chapters in Anglo-Portuguese relations*. Watford, 1935, 1—23.

711 Goodman, Anthony. 'Sir Thomas Hoo and the parliament of 1376', *BIHR*, 41 (1968), 139—49. Stresses the importance of Sir Thomas' contribution to the movement against Latimer.

712 Grassi, J.L. 'William Airmyn and the bishopric of Norwich', *EHR*, 70 (1955), 550—61.

713 Griffiths, John. 'The revolt of Madog ap Llywelyn 1294—5', *Transactions of the Caernarvonshire Historical Society*, 16 (1935), 12—25.

714 Griffiths, Ralph A. 'Gentlemen and rebels in late medieval Cardiganshire', *Ceredigion*, 5 (1964—67), 142—68.

715 ———— 'The revolt of Rhys ap Maredudd, 1287—88', *WHR*, 3 (1946—47), 121—43.

716 Guillemain, Bernard. 'Les tentatives pontificales de médiation dans le litige franco-anglais de Guyenne du XVe siècle', *Bulletin philosophique et historique du comité des travaux historiques et scientifiques*. Paris, 1957, 423—32.

717 Haskins, George L. 'The Doncaster petitions, 1321', *EHR*, 53 (1938), 478—85. Prints important documents.

718 Hérubel, Marcel A. 'Bordeaux et les ports de la Gironde an moyen âge', *Revue maratime*, n.s., 176 (1934), 461—83; 177 (1934), 347—63.

719 Hollister, C. Warren. 'King John and the historians', *JBS*, 1 (1961), 1—19; and Thomas K. Keefe. 'The making of the Angevin empire', *JBS*, 12 (1973), 1—25.

720 Holmes, George A. 'A protest against the Despensers, 1326', *Speculum*, 30 (1955), 207—12. Illustrates the cruelty and injustice of the government.

721 ———— 'The rebellion of the earl of Lancaster, 1328—9', *BIHR*, 28 (1955), 84—89. Clarifies chronology and prints a royal manifesto.

722 Holt, James C. 'King John's disaster in the Wash', *Nottingham Medieval Studies*, 5 (1961), 75—86.

723   Hubert, Merton J. 'Le miracle de Déols et la trêve conclude en 1187 entre les rois de France et d'Angleterre', *Bibliothèque de l'école des chartes*, 96 (1935), 285—300. Prints interesting document.

724   Jacob, Ernest F. 'The complaints of Henry III against the baronial council in 1261', *EHR*, 41 (1926), 559—71. Prints text.

725   Jamison, Evelyn M. 'Alliance of England and Sicily in the second half of the XIIth century', *Journal of the Warburg and Courtauld Institute*, 6 (1943), 20—32.

726   Jeulin, Paul. 'Un grand "honneur" anglais. Aperçus sur le "comté" de Richmond en Angleterre, possession des ducs de Bretagne 1069/71—1398', *Annales de Bretagne*, 42 (1935), 265—302.

727   Johnston, Samuel H.F. 'The lands of Hubert de Burgh', *EHR*, 50 (1935), 418—32.

728   Johnstone, Hilda. 'Poor relief in the royal households of thirteenth-century England', *Speculum*, 4 (1929), 149—66. The contributions of the royal family were very substantial.

729   Kingsford, Charles L. 'John de Benstede and his mission for Edward I', *EPRP*, 332—59.

730   Leicht, Pietro S. 'The principo politico medievale', *Rendiconti dell' Academia de Lincei*, ser. 5, 29 (1920), 232—45. Refers to *quod omnes tangit*.

731   Lewis, Alun. 'Roger Leyburn and the pacification of England, 1265—7', *EHR*, 54 (1939), 193—214. Prints Leyburn's household accounts.

732   Lewis, Ceri W. 'The treaty of Woodstock, 1247: its background and significance', *WHR*, 2 (1964—65), 37—65. Reveals a keen and perceptive intelligence on the part of the royal councillors.

733   Lewis, Frank R. 'History of Llanbadarn Fawr Cardiganshire in the later Middle Ages', *Cardiganshire Antiquarian Society*, 13 (1938), 16—41.

734   ——— 'A history of the lordship of Gower from the missing cartulary of Neath abbey', *BBCS*, 9 (1938), 149—64. He uses a seventeenth-century transcript of the cartulary from the Bodleian library.

735   Lewis, Norman B. 'Article VII of the impeachment of Michael de la Pole in 1386', *EHR*, 42 (1927), 402—07.

736   Lloyd, John E. 'Edward I and the county of Flint', *Journal of the Flintshire Historical Society*, 6 (1916—17), 15—25.

737   ——— 'The mother of Gruddydd ap Llywelyn', *BBCS*, 1 (1923), 335—38.

738   ——— 'The death of Llywelyn ap Gruffydd', *BBCS*, 5 (1931), 249—53.

739   Lodge, Eleanor C. 'Edward I and his tenants-in-chief', *TRHS*, ser. 4, 7 (1924), 1—26. Discusses the royal inquest of 1273.

740   Lucas, Henry S. 'Diplomatic relations of Edward I and Albert of Austria', *Speculum*, 9 (1934), 124—34. Prints a document from the PRO exchequer accounts.

741   ——— 'Diplomatic relations between England and Flanders from 1329 to 1336', *Speculum*, 11 (1936), 59—87. Important study. Prints a notorial act of 1334.

742   ——— 'John of Avesnes and Richard of Cornwall', *Speculum*, 23 (1948), 81—101. Concerning Richard's attempt to gain the German crown.

743   Lyon, Bryce D. 'Un compte de l'exchequier relatif aux relations d'Édouard Ier d'Angleterre avec le duc Jean II de Brabant', *Bulletin de la commission royale d'histoire de Belgique*, 120 (1955), 1—27.

744   McFarlane, Kenneth B. 'Had Edward a policy towards the earls?', *History*, 50 (1935), 145—59. Denigrates Edward.

745   ——— 'An indenture of agreement between two English knights for mutual aid and counsel in peace and war, 5 December, 1298', *BIHR*, 38 (1965), 200—10. An important early example helping to remove the identification of such agreements with the troubles of Edward II's reign. See also Norman B. Lewis. 'An early indenture of military service, 27 July, 1287', *BIHR*, 13 (1935—36), 85—89; and also 'An early fourteenth-century contract for military service', *BIHR*, 20 (1944), 110—18. William la Zouche undertook to serve the king for a year with thirty men-at-arms; 'Indentures of retinue with John of Gaunt . . . enrolled in chancery, 1367—1399', *Camden Miscellany*, 22. Camden Society, ser. 4, 1 (1964), 1—77.

746 Mackenzie, Hugh C. 'Anti-foreign movement in England in 1231–2', in Charles H. Taylor (ed.). *Haskins anniversary essays*. Boston, 1929, 183–203.
747 McKisack, May. 'London and the succession to the crown during the Middle Ages', *SPFP*, 76–89.
748 ——— 'Edward III and the historians', *History*, 45 (1960), 1–15. Makes some reassessment of Edward.
749 Marc-Bonnet, Henri. 'Richard de Cornouailles et la couronne de Sicile', in *Mélanges d'histoire du moyen âge ... à ... Louis Halphen*. Paris, 1951, 483–89. Important consequences of Richard's claim.
750 Maude, Ralph. 'David, the last prince of Wales: the ten "lost" months of Welsh history', *Transactions of the Cymmrodorian Society*, (1968) Pt. 1, 43–62.
751 Nicholson, Ranald. 'An Irish expedition to Scotland in 1335', *Irish Historical Studies*, 13 (1963), 197–211. Strongly criticises the policy of Edward III in organising the expedition.
752 Nitze, William A. 'The exhumation of king Arthur at Glastonbury', [in 1191], *Speculum*, 9 (1934), 355–61. Monastic propaganda by the Angevin rulers.
753 Offler, Hilary S. 'England and Germany at the beginning of the Hundred Years' War', *EHR*, 54 (1939), 608–31. Discusses the failure of the vicarate, and the changed situation from 1337–40 to 1348.
754 Otway-Ruthven, A. Jocelyn. 'The character of the Norman settlement in Ireland', *Irish Historical Studies*, 5 (1965), 75–84.
755 Palmer, John J.N. 'Articles for a final peace between England and France, 16 June, 1393', *BIHR*, 39 (1966), 180–85.
756 ——— 'Anglo-French peace negotiations, 1390–1393', *TRHS*, ser. 5, 16 (1966), 81–94.
757 Patourel, John le. 'Edward III and the kingdom of France', *History*, 43 (1958), 173–89. Convincing analysis of the reality of Edward's claim to the French throne.
758 ——— 'The treaty of Brétigny, 1360', *TRHS*, ser. 5, 10 (1960), 19–39. The articles of Brétigny were, for the first time, a matter of give and take, in which both sides made important concessions. A convincing argument.
759 ——— 'The Plantagenet dominions', *History*, 50 (1965), 289–308.
760 Perroy, Édouard. 'Charles V et la traité de Brétigny', *Le moyen âge*, ser. 2, 29 (1928–29), 255–81. Prints eighteen original documents.
761 ——— 'France, England and Navarre from 1359 to 1364', *BIHR*, 13 (1935–36), 151–54. Prints two interesting documents.
762 Poole, Austin L. 'Richard I's alliance with the German princes in 1194', *SPFP*, 90–99. Relieves Richard of the charge of bad faith.
763 Powicke, Frederick M. 'Some observations on the baronial council (1258–1260) and the provisions of Westminster', *EPTT*, 119–34. Important analysis of events.
764 ——— 'Guy de Montfort (1265–1271)', *TRHS*, ser. 4, 18 (1935), 1–23.
765 ——— 'The archbishop of Rouen, John de Harcourt, and Simon de Montdort in 1260', *EHR*, 51 (1936), 108–113.
766 ——— 'The murder of Henry Clement and the pirates of Lundy Island', *History*, 25 (1941), 285–310.
767 Queller, Donald F. 'Thirteenth-century diplomatic envoys: *nuncii* and *procuratores*', *Speculum*, 35 (1960), 196–213. Clears up confusion regarding types of diplomatic envoys.
768 Reid, W. Stanford. 'Trade, traders and Scottish independence', *Speculum*, 29 (1954), 210–22.
769 ——— 'English stimulus to Scottish nationalism, 1286–1370', *Dalhousie Review*, 38 (1958), 189–203. Considers Bannockburn decisive.
770 Renouard, Yves. 'Les papes et le conflit franco-anglais en Aquitaine de 1259 à 1327', *École de Rome Mélanges*, 51 (1934), 258–92.
771 Rothwell, Harry. 'Edward I's case against Philip the Fair over Gascony in 1292', *EHR*, 42 (1927), 572–82. Prints an important document.
772 ——— 'Edward I and the struggle for the charters 1297–1305', *SPFP*, 319–

32. The struggle is presented as the end of a chapter dominated by the Great Charter.

773 Russell, Josiah C. 'London and thirteenth century anti-royal methods', *Southwestern Social Science Quarterly*, 12 (1931), 156—68.

774 Sanders, Ivor J. 'The texts of the treaty of Paris, 1259', *EHR*, 66 (1951), 81—97. Indictment of Simon de Montfort's policy. Prints text of treaty. A definitive study.

775 Sayles, George O. 'The formal judgment on the traitors of 1322', *Speculum*, 16 (1941), 57—63. Interesting details of unrest in 1324—5.

776 —— 'The seizure of wool at Easter 1297', *EHR*, 67 (1952), 543—47. Prints a writ to the chancellor.

777 Scammell, Jean V. 'Robert I and the north of England', *EHR*, 73 (1958), 385—403. A good analysis of conditions in the north from 1311—1328.

778 Schnith, Karl. 'Staatsordnung und Politik in England zum Anfang des 14 Jahrhunderts', *Historisches Jahrbuch*, 88 (1968), 36—53. Argues that under Edward II it was not the relations between king and parliament that mattered, but new perspectives of *lex, ratio, natura*, and *necessitas*. A doubtful thesis.

779 Smith, J. Beverley. 'The lordship of Glamorgan', *Morgannwg*, 2 (1958), 9—38. Establishes the partial nature of Fitzhamon's conquest. Final phase only by the Clares, between 1245 and 1289.

780 —— 'The origins of the revolt of Rhys ap Maredudd', [1287], *BBCS*, 21 (1965), 151—63. Some new evidence on an attempt by Edward I to stop this revolt.

781 —— 'The Welsh Dominicans and the crisis of 1277', *BBCS*, 22 (1968), 353—57.

782 Smith, William J. 'The "revolt" of William de Somertone', *EHR*, 69 (1954), 76—83. Throws light on local organization and method in opposition to Edward II.

783 Southern, Richard W. 'England and the continent in the twelfth century: II, popular and unpopular kings', *Listener*, 77 (1967), 494—95.

784 Stephens, George R. 'A note on William Cassingham', *Speculum*, 16 (1941), 216—23. A valuable footnote on an obscure hero of the civil war after magna carta.

785 Stones, Edward L.G. 'The English mission to Edinburgh in 1328', *SHR*, 28 (1929), 121—32.

786 —— 'The treaty of Northampton 1328', *History*, 38 (1953), 54—61.

787 Sturler, Jean V. de. 'Les relations politiques de l'Angleterre et du Brabant sous Édouard I et Édouard II', *Revue Belge*, 11 (1932), 626—50.

788 —— 'Une démarche politique inconnue de Jean III duc de Brabant (1337—1338)', *Revue Belge*, 14 (1935), 1319—27. John did homage to Edward in 1337.

789 Tanquerey, Frédéric J. 'The conspiracy of Thomas Dunheved, 1327', *EHR*, 31 (1916), 119—24. Prints a letter showing the temporary escape of Edward II from Berkeley castle.

790 Templeman, Geoffrey. 'Edward I and the historians', *CHJ*, 10 (1950), 16—35. An excellent survey of modern writings on Edward; 'Edward III and the beginnings of the Hundred Years' War', *TRHS*, ser. 5, 2 (1952), 69—88; also Philippe Wolff. 'Un problème d'origins: la Guerre de Cent ans', *Hommage à Lucien Febvre. Éventail de l'histoire*. Vol. 2, 141—48. Paris, 1953.

791 Tomkinson, A. 'Retinues at the tournament of Dunstable, 1309', *EHR*, 74 (1959), 70—89. Suggests that grouping of magnates at Dunstable may have reflected the grouping in contemporary politics.

792 Trabut-Cussac, Jean-Paul. 'Les cartulaires gascons d'Édouard II, d'Édouard III et de Charles VII', *Bibliothèque de l'École des Chartes*, 111 (1954), 5—106.

793 —— 'Bordeaux dans les rôles gascons d'Édouard II (1307—1317)', *Annales du Midi*, 77 (1966), 83—98.

794 Treharne, Reginald F. 'The significance of the baronial reform movement 1258—67', *TRHS*, ser. 4, 25 (1943), 35—72. Reiterates his somewhat

idealistic interpretation of the movement. Failure came from internal
division and betrayal.

795 —— 'The mise of Amiens, 23 January 1264', *SPFP*, 223—239. Justifies
Simon de Montfort's rejection of the mise. See also Peter Walne, 'The
barons' argument at Amiens, January, 1264', *EHR*, 69 (1954), 418—25;
EHR, 73 (1958), 453—59.

796 —— 'The Franco-Welsh treaty of alliance in 1212', *BBCS*, 18 (1958), 60—
75. Can be described as the oldest surviving witness to an independent
foreign policy pursued by a medieval Welsh ruler (Llywelyn ap Iorwerth,
writing to Philip Augustus). Prints and discusses the letter.

797 Trueman, John H. 'The personnel of medieval reform: the English Lords
Ordainers of 1310', *MS*, 21 (1959), 247—71. Tends to paint a somewhat
bright picture of the Ordainers.

798 Walker, R.F. 'Hubert de Burgh and Wales, 1218—1232', *EHR*, 87 (1972),
465—94.

799 Watt, Donald E.R. 'Sources for Scottish history of the fourteenth century in
the archives of the Vatican', *SHR*, 32 (1953), 101—22.

800 Watt, John. 'Negotiations between Edward II and John XXII concerning
Ireland', *Irish Historical Studies*, 10 (1956), 1—15. An appeal by Edward
for support, which paints a black picture of the Irish.

801 Webster, Bruce. 'David II and the government of fourteenth-century Scotland', *TRHS*, ser. 5, 16 (1966), 115—130.

802 Williams, Gwyn A. 'The succession to Gwynedd; 1238—47', *BBCS*, 20
(1964), 393—413.

VI. SOCIAL HISTORY

1 Printed Sources

803 Adler, Michael (ed.). 'Inventory of the property of the condemned Jews
(1285). Part of a pipe roll in the P.R.O.', *Jewish Historical Society
Miscellany*. Pt 2 (1935), 56—71. Notes and text.

804 Ballard, Adolphus and James Tait. *British borough charters*. Cambridge, 1913,
1923, 2 vols. From 1042—1307. Indispensable for the subject. Continued
in Martin Weinbaum. *British borough charters, 1307—1660*. Cambridge,
1943.

805 Barraclough, Geoffrey. *Early Cheshire charters*. Lancashire and Cheshire
Record Society. Oxford, 1957. Twenty-one plates, thirty charters, mostly
of the twelfth century.

806 Blagg, Thomas M. (ed.). *Abstracts of the inquisitiones post mortem and other
inquisitions relating to Nottingham*. Vol. 3. Thoroton Society, Record
ser. 6 (1939). [1321—1350].

807 Boulton, Helen E. (ed.). *The Sherwood forest book*, Thoroton Society, 23
(1964). Originally designed as a work of reference in the administration
of the forest. Contains material from Edward I and Edward III.

808 Brown, William N. and Charles T. Clay *et al.* (eds.). *Early Yorkshire deeds*.
Yorks.Arch. Rec., 39 (1909—).

809 Chew, Helena M. (ed.). *London possessory assizes, a calendar*. Vol. 1. London
Record Society, 1 (1965). Covers second half of fourteenth and first half
of fifteenth centuries. Useful introduction; and William Kellaway (ed.).
London assize of nuisance, 1301—1431. London Record Society, 10
(1973).

810 Dilks, Thomas B. (ed.). *Bridgwater borough archives, 1200—1377*. Somerset
Record Society, 48 (1934).

811 Douglas, David C. (ed.). *Feudal documents from the abbey of Bury St
Edmunds*. First published 1958 in British Academy Records of the Social
and Economic History of England and Wales, no. 8 (1932). From the
conquest to 1180. Invaluable for social and economic history.

812   Du Boulay, Francis R.H. (ed.). *Kent records. Documents illustrative of medieval Kentish society.* Kent Archaeological Society Records, 18 (1964). Contains list of archbishop of Canterbury's tenants by knight service in the reign of Henry II; the pipe roll account of the see of Canterbury after the death of archbishop Pecham, 1292—95; the Kent lay subsidy roll of 1334—35; the earliest Canterbury freemen's rolls, 1298—1363.

813   Edwards, J. Goronwy (ed.). *Flint pleas, 1283—5.* Flintshire Historical Society, Record Series, 8 (1924).

814   —— *Calendar of the Coleman deeds relating to Flintshire.* Flintshire Historical Society, Record Series, 1 (1924).

815   Evans, David L. (ed.). *Flint ministers' accounts 1328—53.* Flintshire Historical Society, Record Series, 2 (1929).

816   Farr, Brenda (ed.). *The rolls of Highworth hundred, 1275—1287.* Wiltshire Archaeological and Natural History Society, 21, 22 (1966—68), 2 vols. 1275—87. Introduction and text.

817   Farrer, William (ed.). *Feudal Cambridgeshire.* Cambridge, 1920. Calendar of records, mainly twelfth and thirteenth centuries, intended as a source of reference for baronial, honorial and manorial history.

818   —— and Charles T. Clay (eds.). *Early Yorkshire charters. Yorks.Arch.Rec.,* extra ser. (1914—65), 12 vols.

819   Fowler, G. Herbert (ed.). *Rolls from the office of the sheriff of Beds. and Bucks., 1332—4.* Bedfordshire Historical Society, Quarto Memoirs, 3 (1929).

820   —— '*Tractatus de Dunstaple et de Hocton*'. *BedsRec*, 19 (1937), 1—99. A treatise of *c.* 1290 concerning the priority of Dunstable and its lands in Houghton Regis (Hocton).

821   Fraser, Constance M. (ed.). *Ancient petitions relating to Northumberland, 13th to 15th centuries.* Surtees Society, 176 (1966). A scholarly collection.

822   Furley, John S. (ed.). *The ancient usages of the city of Winchester from the Anglo-French version preserved in Winchester college.* Oxford, 1927. The customs of the city probably set down about 1275. Text and translation.

823   Gidden, Harry W. (ed.). *The book of remembrance of Southampton.* Southampton, 1927—28, 2 vols. Important but badly edited. Earliest document 1310.

824   Harding, Norah D. (ed.). *Bristol Charters 1155—1373.* Bristol Record Society, 1 (1930).

825   Hervey, Francis (ed.). *The Pinchbeck register, relating to the abbey of Bury St. Edmunds, etc.* 1925, 2 vols. An important source of information: begun in 1334.

826   HMSO. *Calendar of inquisitions for the reign of Edward III.* 1916. Includes inquisitions post mortem; *Inquisitions and assessments relating to feudal aids, 1284—1431.* 1920; *The register of Edward the Black Prince.* Pts 1—4. 1930—65.

827   Hopkins, Albert W. (ed.). *Selected rolls of the Chester city courts of the late XIII and early XIV centuries.* Chetham Society, Ser. 3, 2 (1950).

828   Ingleby, Holcombe (ed.). *The red register of King's Lynn.* King's Lynn, 1922, 2 vols. Transcribed by Robert F. Isaacson. Mainly deeds and wills, 1307—72. Provides the anatomy of an important town, especially in the fourteenth century.

829   Jack, R. Ian.'Records of Denbighshire lordships. II. The lordship of Dyffryn Clwyd in 1324', *Transactions of the Denbighshire Historical Society,* 17 (1968), 7—54.

830   Johnstone, Hilda (ed.). *Letters of Edward prince of Wales 1304—1305.* Roxburghe Club. Cambridge, 1931. Brief but expert Introduction.

831   Kingsford, Charles L. (ed.). *The Stonor letters and papers 1290—1483.* Vol. 1. Camden Society, ser. 3, 29 (1919).

832   Lloyd, Lewis C. and Doris M. Stenton (eds.). *Sir Christopher Hatton's book of seals.* Oxford, 1950. Transcriptions and plates of charters, twelfth to seventeenth centuries.

833   McNeill, Charles and A. Jocelyn Otway-Ruthven (eds.). *Dowdall deeds.* Dublin, 1960. Of value to Irish social historians. Seven hundred documents, half before 1400.

834   MacNiocaill, Gearóid (ed.). *The red book of earls of Kildare.* Dublin, 1964. Stationery Office. Compiled early sixteenth century, but the earliest document was *c.* 1189.

835   Martin, Geoffrey H. *The early rolls of the borough of Ipswich.* University of Leicester, Department of English, Local History Occasional Papers, 5 (1954).

836   Mellows, William T. (ed.). *Henry of Pytchley's book of fees.* Northants Record Society, 2 (1927). Probably from documents collected 1346—48, mainly regarding lands held of Peterborough abbey by knight service.

837   Murray, Katherine M.E. (ed.). *Register of Daniel Rough common clerk of Romney, 1353—80.* Kent Archaeological Society, Records Branch, 16 (1945). Translation and Introduction.

838   Owen, Henry. *A Calendar of the public records relating to Pembrokeshire.* 1914—18, 3 vols.

839   Palmer, William M. (ed.). *Cambridge borough documents.* Cambridge, 1931.

840   Patourel, John le. *Documents relating to the manor and borough of Leeds, 1066—1400.* Thoresby Society, 45 (1957). A good pioneer work; Angelo Raine. *York Civic Records.* Vols. 1—4. *York.Arch. Rec.*, 98, 103, 106, 108 (1939—43), 4 vols.

841   Patterson, Robert B. (ed.). *Earldom of Gloucester charters . . . of the earls and countesses . . . to A.D. 1217.* New York, 1973.

842   Salter, Herbert E. *et al.* (eds.). *Formularies which bear on the history of Oxford c 1204—1420.* Oxford Historical Society, n.s., 4 and 5 (1942), 2 vols.

843   Sausmarez, Havilland de (ed.). *The extentes of Guernsey, 1248 and 1331, and other documents relating to ancient usages and customs of that island.* Guernsey, 1934.

844   Schopp, Jacob W. (ed.). *The Anglo-Norman custumal of Exeter.* Milford, 1925. Introduction by Jacob W. Schopp and Ruth C. Easterling. Important source: written between 1230 and 1257.

845   Shickle, Charles W. (ed. and trans.). *Ancient deeds belonging to the corporation of Bath, 13—16 centuries.* Bath Record Society, 1 (1921).

846   Smith, J. Beverley (ed.). 'The Arundel charters to the lordship of Chirk in the fourteenth century', *BBCS*, 23, Pt. 2 (1969), 153—66.

847   Stenton, Frank M. (ed.). *Facsimiles of early charters from Northamptonshire.* Northants Record Society, 4—5 (1930). Lay and ecclesiastical charters eleventh to thirteenth centuries.

848   Stewart-Brown, Ronald. (ed.). *Calendar of county court, city court, and eyre rolls of Chester, 1259—97, with an inquest of military service, 1288.* Manchester, 1925. A valuable source with an illuminating introduction. The earliest surviving roll is for 1259—60.

849   Thomas, Arthur H. (ed.). *Calendar of early mayor's court rolls preserved among the archives of the corporation of the City of London at the Guildhall, A.D. 1298—1307.* Cambridge, 1924. A most valuable collection of material.

850   ——— *Calendar of the pleas and memoranda rolls . . . of the city of London.* Cambridge, 1926—29, 2 vols. 1323—81.

851   Tupling, George H. (ed.). *South Lancashire in the reign of Edward II as illustrated by the pleas at Wigan recorded in Coram rege roll no. 254.* Chetham Society, ser. 3, 1 (1949). Transcripts, translations and calendar. Well edited, and amply fulfilling its purpose.

852   Turner, George J. and Herbert E. Salter (eds.). *The register of St. Augustine's abbey, Canterbury, commonly called the black book.* 1924. British Academy records of the social and economic history of England and Wales. Vol. 3. Illustrates Kentish customs.

853   Veale, Edward W.W. (ed.). *The great red book of Bristol.* Bristol Record Society, 2, 4, 8, 16, 18 (1931—53), 5 vols. (Pt. 1 Introduction: burgage tenure in medieval Bristol.) Pt. 3 contains the second part of the Introduction.

854   Walker, David (ed.). 'Charters of the earldom of Hereford. 1095–1205', *Camden Miscellany*, 22 (1964).
855   White, Newport B. (ed.). *The red book of Ormond.* Dublin, 1932. From Kilkenny castle. A 14th century cartulary.
856   White, Terence H. (ed. and trans.). *The book of beasts.* New York, 1954. Dated at the end of the twelfth century. (The MS. was reproduced in facsimile by Montague R. James for the Roxburghe Club in 1928.) Some lack of expertness, but opens a door to medieval lore.
857   Wilson, James M. (ed.). *The Worcester liber albus.* 1920. S.P.C.K. Selected entries 1331–38. Translations to be handled with care.
858   Wood, Herbert *et al.* (eds.). *Calendar of justiciary rolls, or proceedings of the justiciar of Ireland, I–VII years of Edward II.* Dublin, 1956. Stationery Office. Throws much light on Irish society in the part where English authority prevailed.

2 Surveys

859   Adler, Michael. *Jews of medieval England.* Jewish Historical Society, 1939.
860   Bean, John M.W. *The decline of English feudalism, 1215–1540.* Manchester, 1968. A somewhat misleading title: deals with the development of the feudal lord's fiscal rights over the tenants.
861   Beresford, Maurice W. *New towns of the Middle Ages: town plantation in England, Wales and Gascony.* 1967. From conquest to mid-fourteenth century. Highly illuminating.
862   Coulton, George G. *Medieval panorama; the English scene from conquest to reformation.* Cambridge, 1938. Still of value: written in Coulton manner; also *Social life in Britain from the conquest to the reformation.* Cambridge, 1918; 2nd ed., 1939. Reprinted New York, 1968. Still a masterly sketch, with forty illustrations added.
863   Dodds, Madeleine H. (ed.). *A history of Northumberland.* Vols. 12–15. Newcastle-upon-Tyne, 1926–40. Massive and valuable.
864   Ganshof, François L. *Feudalism.* London and New York, 1952. Includes a selective bibliography. A scholarly survey, especially of comparative institutions.
865   Goff, Jacques le. *La civilisation de l'occident médiéval.* Paris, 1964. A masterly synthesis of medieval civilization.
866   Grant, Isabel F. *The social and economic development of Scotland before 1603.* Edinburgh, 1930. A standard work.
867   Heers, Jacques. *L'Occident aux XIVe et XVe siècles: aspects économiques et sociaux.* "Nouvelle Clio": l'histoire et ses problèmes, 23 (1963). Contains classified bibliographies.
868   Hoskins, William G. *Local history in England.* 1959. Required preliminary reading for any serious student of local history.
869   Lyon, Bryce D. *From fief to indenture: the transition from feudal to non-feudal contract in Western Europe.* Cambridge, Mass., 1957. A valuable contribution to the whole question of feudal service, showing the significance of the *fief-rente* in the transition from a society based on status to one based on money.
870   Mackinnon, James. *The social and industrial history of Scotland.* Vol. 1. From the earliest times to the Union. 1920.
871   Poole, Austin L. (ed.). *Medieval England.* Oxford, 1958, 2 vols. A revision of H.W. Charles Davis' ed. of Barnard's *Companion to English history.* Invaluable for social and cultural history.
872   Pryde, George S. *et al. The burghs of Scotland.* 1965. Origin and status of 482 burghs.
873   Salzmann, Louis F. *English life in the Middle Ages.* Oxford, 1926. A popular but scholarly survey. See also Quennell, Marjorie and Charles H.B. *A history of everyday things in England.* Vol. 1, *1066–1499.* 4th ed., New York, 1966. Lively and scholarly book; the standard work.
874   Wagner, Anthony R. *English genealogy.* Oxford, 1960. A fascinating volume covering a large range of social history.

3 Monographs

875 Adler, Michael. *London.* Jewish Communities ser. Philadelphia Penna., 1930.

876 Altschul, Michael. *A baronial family in medieval England: the Clares, 1217–1314.* Baltimore, Md., 1965. An excellent study of an important family.

877 Anderson, Mary D. *A saint at stake: the strange death of William of Norwich 1144.* 1964. An episode in the growth of anti-semitism in England.

878 Ashdown, Charles H. *History of the worshipful company of glaziers of the city of London . . .* 1919.

879 Baildon, W. Percy. *Baildon and the Baildons: a history of a Yorkshire manor and family.* 1912–27, 3 vols.

880 Bellamy, John G. *Crime and public order in the later Middle Ages.* Toronto, 1973. Pioneer work; also 'The Coterel gang: an anatomy of a band of fourteenth-century criminals', *EHR*, 79 (1964), 598–717. Interesting analysis of criminals who later became pillars of local administration.

881 Billson, Charles J. *Medieval Leicester.* Leicester, 1920.

882 Bird, Ruth. *The turbulent London of Richard II.* 1949. Competent analysis.

883 Blackham, Robert J. *London livery companies.* 1931.

884 Blakeway, George S. *The city of Gloucestershire: its royal charters of liberties and varying fortunes.* Gloucester, 1924.

885 Boutruche, Robert. *La crise d'une société. Seigneurs et paysans du Bordelais pendant la Guerre de Cents Ans.* Paris, 1947. Extremely suggestive.

886 Bracken, Charles W. *A history of Plymouth and her neighbours.* 2nd ed., Plymouth, 1934. First published 1931.

887 Brewer, Derek S. *Chaucer in his times.* 1965. An account of how life looked and felt round about Chaucer.

888 Brooke, Iris. *English costume of the early Middle Ages, from the tenth to the thirteenth centuries; drawn and described.* 1936.

889 Chadwick, Dorothy. *Social life in the days of Piers Plowman.* Cambridge, 1922. Most useful summary.

890 Chambers, Edmund K. *Eynsham under the monks.* Oxford, 1936.

891 Clay, Rotha M. *The medieval hospitals of England.* 1909. Reprinted New York, 1966.

892 Clifford, Esther R. *A knight of great renown: the life and times of Othon de Granson.* Chicago, 1961. A Savoyard who served Edward I and Edward II. Contains information about the cosmopolitan society of the age.

893 Consitt, Frances. *The London weavers' company.* Vol. 1, *From the twelfth to the sixteenth century.* Oxford, 1933.

894 Coulton, George G. *Scottish abbeys and social life.* Cambridge, 1933.

895 Crow, Martin M. and Clair C. Olson (eds.). *Chaucer life-records.* Oxford, 1966. From materials compiled by John M. Manly and Edith Rickert. A contribution to biography and social and economic history even more than to literary study and criticism.

896 Curtis, Muriel E.A. *Some disputes between the city and cathedral authorities of Exeter.* Manchester, 1932.

897 Dawe, Donovan A. *XI Ironmonger Lane.* 1952. A good contribution to London history.

898 Denholm-Young, Noël. *Seignorial administration in England.* Oxford, 1937. Valuable and suggestive, but marred by inaccuracies.

899 ———— *History and heraldry, 1254–1310: a study of the historical value of the roll of arms.* Oxford, 1965. Has been described as a stimulating but irritating volume.

900 ———— *The country gentry in the fourteenth century, with special reference to the heraldic roll of arms.* Oxford, 1969.

901 Dobson, Richard B. *The Jews of medieval York and the massacre of 1190.* York, 1974.

902 Douglas, David C. *The social structure of medieval East Anglia.* Oxford, 1927. Brings the study of this structure up to date.

903 Du Boulay, Francis R.H. *The lordship of Canterbury. An essay on medieval society.* New York, 1966. An important contribution to Kentish social history.

904 Ekwall, B.O. Eilert. *Street names of the city of London.* Oxford, 1954.
905 —— *Studies on the population of medieval London.* Stockholm, 1956. Mainly a biographical dictionary of Londoners, *c.* 1270 to *c.* 1350. A valuable survey.
906 Evans, Cyril J.O. *Glamorgan: its history and topography.* 2nd ed. revised. Cardiff, 1943.
907 Farrer, William. *Honours and knights' fees.* Manchester, 1923—25, 3 vols.
908 Finberg, Herbert P.R. *Tavistock abbey: a study in the social and economic history of Devon.* Cambridge, 1951. An expert survey, full of valuable information.
909 —— (ed.). *Gloucestershire studies.* Leicester, 1957. Contains some important essays, especially by Finberg and Hilton.
910 Fox, Levi. *The administration of the honour of Leicester in the fourteenth century.* Leicester, 1940. Scholarly.
911 —— *Stratford-upon-Avon.* Stratford, 1953. A good general account.
912 —— and Percy Russell. *Leicester Forest.* Leicester, 1948. A careful study.
913 Friedman, Lee M. *Robert Grosseteste and the Jews.* Cambridge, Mass., 1934.
914 Furley, John S. *City government of Winchester from the records of the fourteenth and fifteenth centuries.* Oxford, 1923. Valuable. With documents photographed and transcribed.
915 Gardiner, Dorothy A. *The story of Lambeth palace: a historic survey.* 1930.
916 Gill, Conrad. *Studies in midland history.* Oxford, 1930. Late medieval social and economic structure.
917 Gunn, John and Marion I. Newbigin (eds.). *The city of Glasgow: its origin, growth, and development.* Edinburgh, 1921. Cf. Robert Renwick and John Lindsay, *History of Glasgow.* Vol. 1. Glasgow, 1921.
918 Hartopp, Henry. *Roll of the mayors of the borough and lord mayors of the city of Leicester, 1209—1935 . . .* Leicester, 1936.
919 Henderson, Charles G. *Essays on Cornish history.* ed. A. Leslie Rowse and Mary I. Henderson. Oxford, 1935.
920 Hill, Derek I. *The ancient hospitals and almshouses of Canterbury.* Canterbury Archaeological Society. 1969.
921 Hill, James W.F. *Medieval Lincoln.* Cambridge, 1965. First ed. Cambridge, 1948. A model survey.
922 Hilton, Rodney H. *A medieval society: the west midlands at the end of the thirteenth century.* 1967. By an important economic historian: a work of synthesis; looking from the bottom upward. Writing somewhat uneven.
923 —— *The decline of serfdom in medieval England.* 1969. A pamphlet of seventy-two pp.
924 Holmes, George A. *The estates of the higher nobility in fourteenth-century England.* Cambridge, 1957. Argues that the magnates acted from motives of dynastic aggrandisement and that these were the basis of political dispute.
925 Holmes, Urban T. *Daily living in the twelfth century.* Madison, Wis., 1952. An interesting and expert treatise, quoting extensively from Alexander Neckham's *De nominibus utensilium.*
926 Homans, George C. *English villagers of the thirteenth century.* Cambridge, Mass., 1941. A landmark in medieval English social history.
927 Hoskins, William G. *The midland peasant. The economic and social history of a Leicestershire village.* 1957. Scholarly popularization. Full of artistic observations.
928 —— and Herbert P.R. Finberg. *Devonshire studies.* 1952. Social, agrarian, economic.
929 Houston, Mary G. *A technical history of costume.* Vol. 3, *the thirteenth, fourteenth and fifteenth centuries.* 1939. See also Herbert Norris, *Costume and fashion.* Vol. 2. 1933.
930 Hübner, Gustave. *England und die Gesittungsgrundlage der europäischen Frühgeschichte, Studien zur Englandkunde.* Frankfurt-am-Main, 1930. Includes essays in the rise of standard English, witchcraft, and *Piers.*
931 Ingleby, Clement (ed.). *A supplement to Blomefield's Norfolk . . .* 1929. First published 1921. Introduction by Christopher Hussey.

932   Johnson, Arthur H. *The history of the worshipful company of the Drapers of London and her gilds up to the close of the XVth century.* Oxford, 1914—22, 5 vols.

933   Jones, Philip E. *The worshipful company of poulters of the City of London: a short history.* 2nd ed., 1965. First published 1939.

934   Kahl, William F. *The development of London livery companies.* Boston, 1960.

935   Keen, Maurice. *The outlaws of medieval England.* 1961. Breaking new ground. Questioned by James C. Holt in *PP*, 18 (1960), 89—107. See also *PP*, 14 (1958), 31—44; 19 (1961), 7—15; 20 (1961), 79; also *Yorks. Arch. J.*, 36 (1944), 4—46.

936   Kelly, Francis M. and Randolph Schwabe. *A short history of costume and armour chiefly in England, 1066—1800.* 1931, 2 vols. Illustrations.

937   Kermack, William R. *The Scottish highlands: a short history.* Edinburgh, 1957. The best guide up to date, in a brief compass, to the intricate evolution of Highland society.

938   Knight, Charles B. *A history of the city of York from the foundation of the Roman fortress of Eboracum, A.D. 71 to the close of the reign of Queen Victoria, A.D. 1901.* York, 1944.

939   Knoop, Douglas and Gwilym P. Jones. *The Scottish mason, and mason word.* Manchester, 1939.

940   Kramer, Stella. *The English craft gilds: studies in their progress and decline.* New York, 1927.

941   Labarge, Margaret W. *A baronial household of the thirteenth century.* 1965. Based on the household roll of Eleanor of Montfort. An unassuming but scholarly work.

942   Lincoln, F. Ashe. *The Starra, their effect on early English law and administration.* Oxford, 1939. Deals with legal and social position of the Jews before the expulsion.

943   Lipman, Vivian D. *The Jews of medieval Norwich.* Jewish Historical Society. 1967.

944   Lobel, Mary D. *The history of Dean and Chalford.* Oxford Record Society, 17 (1935).

945   —— *The borough of Bury St Edmund's: a study in the government and development of a monastic town.* Oxford, 1935. A scholarly survey with documents from the twelfth to the sixteenth century.

946   Lodge, Eleanor C. *Gascony under English rule.* 1926.

947   Mackenzie, William M. *The Scottish burghs.* Edinburgh, 1949. A learned, brief, discussion. See also John D. Mackie and George S. Pryde. *The estate of the burgesses in the Scots parliament.* St Andrews, 1923; David Murray. *Early burgh organisation in Scotland.* Glasgow, 1924, 1932, 2 vols.

948   Maitland, Frederic W. *Township and borough.* Cambridge, 1898. Reprinted Cambridge, 1964. Has been thought by some to have been his most brilliant work.

949   Majendie, Severne A. *The ancient hospital of St Katherine [London].* 1924. Small pamphlet with six illustrations and translation of Queen Eleanor's charter of 1273.

950   Mander, Charles H.W. *A descriptive and historical account of the guild of cordwainers of the city of London.* 1931.

951   Martin, Alexander F. and Robert W. (eds.). *The Oxford region: a scientific and historical survey.* Oxford, 1954.

952   Martin, Geoffrey H. *The early court roll of the borough of Ipswich.* University of Leicester, Department of English Local History Occasional Papers, no. 5 (1954). Critical analysis.

953   Mayer, Edward. *The curriers and the city of London.* 1968.

954   Miller, Edward. *The abbey and bishopric of Ely: the social history of an ecclesiastical estate from the tenth century to the early fourteenth century.* Cambridge, 1951. Detailed and scholarly.

955   Moore, John S. *Laughton: a study in the evolution of the Wealden landscape.* Leicester, 1965.

956   Moore, Norman. *The history of St Bartholomew's hospital.* 1918, 2 vols. Includes plates of charters and deeds.

957   Murray, Katherine M.E. *The constitutional history of the Cinque Ports.* University of Manchester Historical ser. 68 (1935). The best treatment up to date.

958   Oman, Charles W.C. *The great revolt of 1381.* 1906; 2nd ed. Oxford, 1969. New and scholarly Introduction and notes by Edmund B. Fryde.

959   Page, William. *St Albans.* 1920.

960   Pantin, William A. (ed.). *Survey of Oxford by H.E. Salter.* Oxford Historical Society, n.s., 14, 20 (1960, 1969), 2 vols.

961   Pape, Thomas. *Medieval Newcastle-under-Lyme.* Manchester, 1928. Careful and well documented.

962   Parks, George B. *The English traveller to Italy.* Vol. 1, *the Middle Ages (to 1525).* Stanford, Cal., 1954. Contains much information.

963   Pendrill, Charles. *London life in fourteenth century.* 1925; *Wanderings in medieval London,* 1928; *Old parish life in London.* Oxford, 1937.

964   Poole, Austin L. *Obligations of society in the XII and XIII centuries.* Oxford, 1946. An expert analysis.

965   Raine, Angelo. *Medieval York, a topographical survey based on original sources.* 1955. Excellent topographical guide, but inadequate on stages of development.

966   Redford, Arthur. *The history of local government in Manchester.* Vol. 1: *Manor and township.* 1939. Illustrations and maps. Still valuable.

967   Rees, William. *South Wales and the March, 1284–1415. A social and agrarian study.* 1924. A pioneer and uneven book.

968   Renouard, Yves. *Bordeaux sous les rois d'Angleterre (Histoire de Bordeaux III).* Bordeaux, 1965. A work of collaboration: places the city in the general setting of medieval urbanism and in relation to the English connection. See also Charles Bémont in *Revue historique,* 123 (1916), 1–53, 253–93.

969   Richardson, Harold. *The medieval fairs and markets of York.* St Anthony's Hall Publications, 20 (1961).

970   Richardson, Henry G. *The English Jewry under Angevin kings.* 1960. The standard work.

971   Robertson, David and Marguerite Wood. *Castle and town: chapters in the history of the royal burgh of Edinburgh.* Edinburgh, 1928.

972   Robertson, Durant W., Jr. *Chaucer's London.* New York, 1968. Contains some blemishes, but gives a clear picture of the lay-out of fourteenth-century London.

973   Robo, Etienne. *Medieval Farnham: Everyday life in an episcopal manor.* Farnham, 1935. Excellent local history.

974   Rosenthal, Joel T. *The purchase of paradise: gift giving and the aristocracy, 1307–1485.* Toronto, 1972.

975   Roth, Cecil. *The Jews of medieval Oxford.* Oxford Historical Society, n.s. 9 (1951); also *The intellectual activities of medieval English Jewry.* British Academy Pamphlet. 1949.

976   ——— *A history of the Jews in England.* 3rd ed., Oxford, 1964. First published 1941.

977   Russell, Josiah C. *British medieval population.* Albuquerque, N.M., 1948. By an expert.

978   Salisbury-Jones, Goronwy T. *Street life in medieval England.* Oxford, 1939.

979   Salter, Herbert E. *Map of medieval Oxford.* Oxford, 1934. Twelve pp. and five maps; and also *Medieval Oxford.* Oxford Historical Society, 100 (1936); and *Survey of Oxford.* Vol. 1 [ed. William Pantin]. Oxford Historical Society, n.s., 14 (1960).

980   Salzmann, Louis F. *English life in the middle ages.* 1926.

981   ——— *English trade in the middle ages.* New ed., 1964; *English industries in the middle ages.* 1913. 2nd ed., Oxford, 1923. New ed., 1964, enlarged. A scholarly popular survey.

982   Setton, Kenneth M. (ed.). *The age of chivalry.* Washington, D.C., 1969. Foreword by M.B. Grosvenor.

983   Sheehan, Michael M. *The will in medieval England from the conversion of the Anglo-Saxons to the end of the thirteenth century.* Toronto, 1963. Social history at its best. Suggests an important general change between the death of Henry I and that of John.

984   Sitwell, George R.T. *Tales of my native village, being studies of life, manners, art, minstrelsy, and religion in the form of short stories.* Oxford, 1933. Recreates atmosphere of Middle Ages.

985   Stenton, Frank M. *Norman London.* Historical Association Leaflets 93–4 (1934). A valuable essay. Included are a map of London under Henry II, and notes by E. Jeffries Davis.

986   ——— *The first century of English feudalism 1066–1166.* Oxford, 1932. 2nd ed., 1961. Authoritative and illuminating.

987   Tait, James. *The medieval English borough: studies in its origin and constitutional history.* Manchester, 1936. Reprinted Manchester, 1968. Still the standard work. See also 'The study of early municipal history in England', *PBA*, 10 (1921), 201–17. Important; also 'Liber burgus', *EPTT*, 79–97. Explains the sudden appearance of the term at the end of the twelfth century; 'The *firma burgi* and the commune in England, 1066–1191', *EHR*, 42 (1927), 321–60; Still authoritative; 'The origins of town councils in England', *EHR*, 44 (1929), 177–202, 399. First authoritative survey; 'The borough community in England', *EHR*, 45 (1930), 529–51. Definitive; 'The common council of the borough', *EHR*, 46 (1931), 1–29. Still the best account.

988   Thornton, Gladys A. *A short history of Clare, Suffolk.* Cambridge, 1930; 2nd ed., Brentwood, 1968. A good sketch.

989   Thrupp, Sylvia L. *A short history of the worshipful company of bakers of London.* 1933; and also *The merchant class of medieval London, 1300–1500.* Chicago, 1948. An authoritative pioneer work. See also Alice Beardwood. *Alien merchants in England, 1350–1377.* Cambridge, Mass., 1931.

990   Thuresson, Bertil. *Middle English occupational terms.* Lund studies in English, no. 19 (1950). Contains material for students of social life.

991   Tierney, Brian. *Medieval poor law: a sketch of canonical theory and its application in England.* Cambridge, 1959. Lively, acute, and learned discussion.

992   Tout, Thomas F. *Medieval town planning.* Manchester, 1917. Still a useful introduction; see also Charles Billson. *Wyke upon Hull in 1293.* Hull, 1929. On medieval town planning and borough development.

993   Trenholme, Norman M. *The English monastic boroughs.* University of Missouri Studies. 1927. A careful and valuable study.

994   Trevelyan, George M. *Illustrated English social history.* Vol. 1, *Chaucer's England and the early Tudors.* 1949. 176 plates (illustrations selected by Ruth C. Wright). Written with style and designed for the general reader.

995   Tupling, George H. (ed.). *South Lancashire in the reign of Edward II.* Chetham Society, ser. 3, 1 (1949).

996   Urry, William. *Canterbury under the Angevin kings.* 1967. A definitive work by a great archivist and antiquary.

997   Veale, Elspeth M. *The English fur trade in the later Middle Ages.* Oxford, 1966. English social history at its best.

998   Weinbaum, Martin. *Verfassungsgeschichte Londons, 1066–1263.* Stuttgart, 1929. See also Weinbaum's *London unter Eduart I und II.* Stuttgart, 1933, 2 vols, which contains a general review of the city to 1268, with valuable documents; also *The incorporation of boroughs.* Manchester, 1937.

999   Welch, Charles. *History of the cutlers' company of London.* 1916–23, 2 vols.

1000 Welsford, Enid. *The fool. His social and literary history.* 1935.

1001 West, John. *Village records.* 1962. As far as possible follows the documentary history of a single Worcestershire village.

1002 Westlake, Herbert F. *The parish gilds of medieval England.* 1919.

1003 Wettwer, Albrecht. *Englisher Sport im 14ten Jahrhundert.* Göttingen, 1933. A questionable reference to football. Cf. Francis P. Magoun. 'Football in medieval England and in middle English literature', *AHR*, 35 (1930), 33–45.

1004 Whitmore, Mary E. *Medieval English domestic life and amusements in the works of Chaucer.* Washington, D.C., 1937. Much information, but to be read with great caution.

1005 Wightman, Wilfred E. *The Lacy family in England and Normandy, 1066–1194.* Oxford, 1966.

1006 Wilkinson, Bertie and Ruth C. Easterling. *The medieval council of Exeter.* Exeter, 1931. Analyses the personnel and corrects Edward A. Freeman.

1007 Williams, Elijah. *Early Holborn and the legal quarter of London: a topographical survey of the beginnings* . . . 1927, 2 vols. Includes inns of court of chancery.

1008 Williams, Gwyn A. *Medieval London: from commune to capital.* 1963. The best general account of the period from 1215 to 1338: lively and polished.

1009 Ziegler, Philip. *The black death.* 1969. See Charles E. Boucher. 'The black death in Bristol', *Bristol and Gloucestershire Archaeological Society*, 60 (1939), 31–46; Elizabeth Carpentier. 'Autour de la peste noire: famines et epidémies dans l'histoire du XIVe siècle. *Annales, économies, sociétés, civilisations*, 17, 1062–92, a massive synthesis; John L. Fisher. 'The black death in Essex', *Essex Review*, 52 (1943), 13–20; Reginald S. France. 'A history of the plague in Lancashire', *LancsHistoric.*, [1938] (1940), 1–175; and also 'The black death in Wales', *TRHS*, ser. 4, 3 (1920), 115–35; Etienne Robo. 'The black death in the hundred of Farnham', *EHR*, 44 (1929), 560–72; John M.W. Bean. 'Plague, population and economic decline in the later middle ages', *EcHR*, ser. 2, 15 (1963), 423–37, an excellent discussion; Helen Robbins. 'A comparison of the effects of the black death on the economic organization of France and England', *Journal of Political Economy*, 36 (1928), 447–79; Ada E. Levett and Adolphus Ballard. *The black death on the estates of the see of Winchester.* Oxford, 1916; J. Ambrose Raftis. 'Changes in an English village after the black death', *MS*, 24 (1962), 349–68; Anna M. Campbell. *The black death and men of learning.* New York, 1931; Aubrey O. Gwynn. 'The black death in Ireland', *Studies*, 24 (1935), 25–42; John Saltmarsh. 'Plague and economic decline in England in the later Middle Ages', *CHJ*, 7 (1941), 23–41; Anthony Bridbury. 'The black death', *EcHR*, 26 (1973), 557–92.

4 Biographies

1010 Adler, Michael. 'Aaron of York', *Jewish Historical Society Transactions*, 13 (1936), 113–55. Important study, with documents. Reprinted 1936.

1011 Roth, Cecil. 'Elijah of London', *Jewish Historical Society Transactions*, 15 (1946), 29–62. Important study. Includes genealogical tree.

1012 Stones, Edward L.G. 'Sir Geoffrey le Scrope (*c.* 1280 to 1340), chief justice of the king's bench', *EHR*, 69 (1954), 1–17. Valuable preliminary study.

1013 Turner, Ralph V. 'William de Forz, count of Aumale: an early thirteenth-century English baron', *Proceedings of the American Philosophical Society*, 115 (1971), 221–47.

1014 Warren, Wilfred L. *Henry II.* Berkeley, Cal., 1973. An authoritative study.

5 Articles

1015 Ackerman, Robert W. 'The knighting ceremonies in the Middle English romances', *Speculum*, 19 (1944), 285–313. The romances in the main give an accurate description of the events.

1016 Ault, Warren O. 'Village by-laws by common consent', *Speculum*, 29 (1954), 378–94. Valuable comments on such common action.

1017 —— 'Village assemblies in medieval England', *Studies presented to the international commission for representative and parliamentary institutions*, 23, Louvain, 1960, 13–35. Important evidence on an obscure subject.

1018 Bailey, Stanley J. 'Warranties of land in the thirteenth century', *Cambridge Law Journal*, 8 (1944), 274–99; 9 (1945), 82–106.

1019 Baldwin, James F. 'Litigation in English society', in Christabel F. Fiske (ed.).

Medieval studies by members of the faculty of Vassar College. New Haven, Conn., 1923, 151—80.

1020 —— 'The household administration of Henry Lacy and Thomas of Lancaster', *EHR*, 42 (1927), 180—200. Thomas living far beyond his means.

1021 Ballard, Adolphus. 'The theory of the Scottish burgh', *SHR*, 13 (1915), 16—29.

1022 Barrow, Geoffrey W.S. 'The beginnings of feudalism in Scotland', *BIHR*, 29 (1956), 1—27. An important article; also 'Northern society in the early Middle Ages', *Northern History*, 4 (1969), 1—28.

1023 Baskervill, Charles R. 'Dramatic aspects of medieval folk festivals in England', *Studies in Philology*, 17 (1920), 18—87.

1024 Bassett, Marjory. 'Newgate prison in the Middle Ages', *Speculum*, 18 (1943), 233—46; also 'The Fleet prison in the Middle Ages', *University of Toronto Law Journal*, 5 (1944), 383—402.

1025 Beardwood, Alice. 'Mercantile antecedents of the English nationalization laws', *Med et Hum*, 16 (1964), 64—76.

1026 Bémont, Charles. 'Les institutions municipales de Bordeaux au moyen âge: la mairie et la jurade', *Revue historique*, 123 (1916), 1—53, 253—93. Of great value for students of Anglo-Gascon history.

1027 Bennett, Henry S. 'The reeve and the manor in the fourteenth century', *EHR*, 41 (1926), 358—65.

1028 Bennett, Josephine W. 'The medieval loveday', *Speculum*, 33 (1958), 351—70.

1029 Bertolino, Alberto. 'Idee e condizioni sociali dell' Inghilterra del trecento nel' opera di John Gower', *Studi in onore di Filippo Virgilii.* Rome, 1936, 242—92.

1030 Blair, Claude H.H. (ed.). 'Mayors of Newcastle-upon-Tyne 1216—1399', *Arch Ael*, 18 (1940), 1—57.

1031 Blake, John B. 'The medieval coal trade of northeast England: some fourteenth century evidence', *Northern History*, 2 (1967), 1—26.

1032 Brewer, Derek. 'Class distinction in Chaucer', *Speculum*, 43 (1968), 290—305. Reflecting society in change.

1033 Cahill, Edward. 'Norman French and English languages, in Ireland, 1170—1540', *Irish Ecclesiastical Record*, ser. 5, 51 (1938), 159—73.

1034 Carr, Antony D. 'An aristocracy in decline: the native Welsh lords after the Edwardian conquest', *WHR*, 5 (1970), 103—29.

1035 Carus-Wilson, Eleanora M. 'Origins and early development of the Merchant Adventurers': organization in London as shown in their own medieval records', *EcHR*, 4 (1932—34), 147—76.

1036 —— 'The first half century of the borough of Stratford-upon-Avon', *EcHR*, ser. 2, 18 (1965), 46—63. Illuminating study of foundation and growth in the twelfth and thirteenth centuries.

1037 Chew, Helena M. 'The office of escheator in the City of London during the Middle Ages', *EHR*, 58 (1943), 319—30; also 'Mortmain in medieval London', *EHR*, 60 (1945), 1—15.

1038 Cheyette, Frederic. 'Some notations on Mr Hollister's "irony" ', *JBS*, 5 (1965), 1—14. Discusses what is 'feudalism'.

1039 Cline, Ruth H. 'The influence of romances on tournaments in the Middle Ages', *Speculum*, 20 (1945), 204—11. Some interesting examples.

1040 Cohen, Sarah. 'The Oxford Jewry in the thirteenth century', *Jewish Historical Society Transactions*, 13 (1936), 293—322. Includes map of medieval Oxford.

1041 Coulton, George G. 'Nationalism in the Middle Ages', *CHJ*, 5 (1935—37), 15—40. Broad, stimulating discussion.

1042 Cronne, Henry A. 'The borough of Warwick in the Middle Ages', *Dugdale Society Occasional Papers*, 10 (1951) [in bound vol.].

1043 Davies, Robert R. 'The survival of the bloodfeud in medieval Wales', *History*, 54 (1969), 338—57. A re-appraisal of its value.

1044 Denholm-Young, Noël. 'The Yorkshire estates of Isabella De Fortibus', *Yorks. Arch.J.*, 31 (1934), 389—420.

1045 —— 'Feudal society in the thirteenth century: the knights', *History*, 29

(1944), 107—119. Discusses the shortage of knights; see also Denholm-Young's 'The tournament in the thirteenth century', *SPFP*, 240—68. Stresses the connection between the tournament and politics; Reginald F. Treharne. 'The knights in the period of reform and rebellion, 1258—67: a critical phase in the rise of a new class', *BIHR*, 21 (1946—48), 1—12. Shows how the responsibilities of the knights increased.

1046   Devlin, Mary Aquinas. 'An English knight of the garter in the Spanish chapel in Florence', *Speculum*, 4 (1929), 270—81. With plates.

1047   Dodd, Arthur H. 'Welsh and English in east Denbighshire; a historical retrospect', *Transactions of the Cymmrodorian Society* [for 1940] (1941), 34—65.

1048   Dodwell, Barbara. 'The free tenantry of the hundred rolls', *EcHR*, 14 (1944), 163—71. A large and heterogeneous group.

1049   Draper, John W. 'Chaucer's "wardrobe"?', *English Studies*, 60 (1926), 238—51.

1050   Du Boulay, Francis R.H. 'Gavelkind and knight's fees in medieval Kent', *EHR*, 77, 504—11. Important comments on Kentish social conditions.

1051   Fox, Levi. 'The honour and earldom of Leicester: origin and descent, 1066—1399', *EHR*, 54 (1939), 385—402.

1052   Fraser, Constance M. and Kenneth Emsley. 'Law and society in Northumberland and Durham, 1290—1350', *ArchAel*, ser. 4, 47 (1969), 47—70.

1053   Friedman, Albert B. 'Medieval popular satire in Matthew Paris', *Modern Language Notes*, 74 (1959), 673—78. Discusses two fragments of what are generally assumed to be twelfth-century English soldier songs.

1054   Furley, John S. 'Merchants' courts at Winchester', *EHR*, 35 (1920), 98—103.

1055   Galway, Margaret. 'Chaucer's shipman in real life', *Modern Language Review*, 34 (1939), 497—514.

1056   ———— 'Joan of Kent and the order of the garter', *UBHJ*, 1 (1947—48), 13—50. Much light on Edward III and Joan.

1057   Hallam, Herbert E. 'Some thirteenth century censuses', *EcHR*, ser. 2, 11 (1958), 340—61.

1058   Hamelins, Paul. 'The travels of Sir John Mandeville', *Quarterly Review*, 227 (1917), 331—52.

1059   Hamil, Frederick C. 'Wreck of the sea in medieval England', in Arthur E.R. Boak (ed.). *University of Michigan Historical Essays*. Ann Arbor, Mich., 1937, 1—24.

1060   Harrison, Edward. 'The court rolls and other records of the manor of Ightham as a contribution to local history', *ArchCam*, 43 (1936), 169—218; 44 (1937), 1—95.

1061   Hill, Mary C. 'Jack Faukes, king's messenger, and his journey to Avignon in 1343', *EHR*, 57 (1942), 19—30. Informative details.

1062   Hilton, Rodney H. 'Social structure of rural Warwickshire in the Middle Ages', *Dugdale Society Occasional Papers*, 9 (1950), [in bound volume].

1063   ———— 'Y eut-il une crise générale de la féodalité?', *Annales, économies, sociétés, civilisations*. (1951). Sees mixed elements.

1064   ———— 'Freedom and villeinage in England', *PP*, 31 (1965), 3—19.

1065   Homans, George C. 'Men and land in the Middle Ages', *Speculum*, 11 (1936), 338—51. Some wise things about custom and happiness in medieval farming.

1066   Honeybourne, Marjorie B. 'The leper hospitals of the London area: with an appendix on some other medieval hospitals of Middlesex', *Transactions of the London and Middlesex Archaeological Society*, n.s., 21 (1967), 1—61.

1067   Hulbert, James R. 'English in manorial documents of the thirteenth and fourteenth centuries', *Modern Philology*, 34 (1936), 37—61.

1068   Imray, Jean M. ' "Les bones gentes de la Mercerye de Londres" ', a study of the membership of the medieval mercers' company, in Albert E.J. Hollaender and William Kellaway (eds.). *Studies in London history presented to Philip Edmund Jones*. 1969, 155—78.

1069   Jack, R. Ian. 'Welsh and English in the medieval lordship of Ruthin', *Transactions of the Denbighshire Historical Society*, 18 (1969), 23—50.

1070 Johnson, Charles. 'London shipbuilding, A.D. 1295', *Antiquaries Journal*, 7 (1927), 424–37. Prints extracts.
1071 Jones, Glanville R.J. 'The distribution of medieval settlement in Anglesey', *AngAntiq*, (1955), 27–96. With the late Professor Thomas Jones-Pierce (his teacher) Glanville Jones is the foremost authority on medieval Welsh social history. Jones-Pierce and Jones disagreed, but all the work of both is important and interlinked; and their numerous regional studies add up to make a general picture [if one has the stamina].
1072 ——— 'The tribal system in Wales: a reassessment in the light of settlement studies', *WHR*, 1 (1961), 111–133.
1073 Jones, Thomas. 'Gerald the Welshman's "Itinerary through Wales" and "Description of Wales" ', *NLWJ*, 6 (1949–50), 117–148, 197–219; and Thomas Jones. *Gerald the Welshman.* Cardiff, 1947; also J. Conway Davies. 'Geraldus Cambrensis, 1146–96', *ArchCamb*, (1947), 85–108, 256–81; and Frederick M. Powicke. 'Gerald of Wales', *BJRL*, 12 (1928), 389–410; and Urban T. Holmes. 'Gerald the naturalist', *Speculum*, 11 (1936), 110–21; and 'The Cambriae Descriptio of Gerald the Welshman', *Med et Hum*, 1 (1976), 217–31; Michael Richter. 'Geraldus Cambrensis', *NLWJ*, 16 (1970), 193–252.
1074 Kellaway, William. 'The coroner in medieval London', in Albert E.J. Hollaender and William Kellaway (eds.). *Studies in London history presented to Philip Edmund Jones.* 1969, 75–91. Includes list beginning 10 Henry III.
1075 King, Edmund. 'Large and small landowners in thirteenth century England: the case of Peterborough abbey', *PP*, 47 (1970), 26–50.
1076 Kuhl, Ernest P. 'Chaucer's burgesses', *Transactions of the Wisconsin Academy*, 18 (1916), 632–75.
1077 Langmuir, Gavin J. 'The Jew and the archives of Angevin England: reflections on medieval anti-semitism', *Traditio*, 19 (1963), 183–244.
1078 Legge, Mary D. 'Anglo-Norman and the historian', *History*, 26 (1941), 163–75. An important article; also 'The French language and the English cloister', in Veronica Ruffer and Alfred J. Taylor (eds.). *Medieval studies presented to Rose Graham.* Oxford, 1950, 146–62. Interesting and important.
1079 Lennard, Reginald V. 'Early manorial juries', *EHR*, 77 (1962), 511–18.
1080 Levett, Ada E. 'Baronial councils and their relation to manorial courts', *Mélanges d'histoire offerts à Ferdinand Lot.* Paris, 1925, 421–41.
1081 Lobel, Mary D. 'A detailed account of the 1327 rising at Bury St Edmunds . . . ', *Proceedings of the Suffolk Archaeological Institute*, 21 (1934), 215–31.
1082 ——— 'Some Oxford borough customs', in *Miscellanea mediaevalia in memoriam Jan Frederick Niermeyer.* Groningen, 1967, 187–200.
1083 Lucas, Henry S. 'The great European famine of 1315, 1316, and 1317', *Speculum*, 5 (1930), 343–77. Includes much information on conditions in England.
1084 Lyon, Bryce D. 'The money fief under the English kings, 1066–1485', *EHR*, 66 (1951), 161–93; also 'The feudal antecedents of the indenture system', *Speculum*, 29 (1954), 503–11.
1085 McCutcheon, Kenneth L. 'Yorkshire fairs and markets to the end of the eighteenth century', *Thoresby Society*, 39 (1939), 1–177.
1086 Mace, Frances A. 'Devonshire ports in the fourteenth and fifteenth centuries', *TRHS*, ser. 4, 8 (1925), 98–126.
1087 McFarlane, Kenneth B. 'Bastard feudalism', *BIHR*, 20 (1943–45), 161–80. An important contribution.
1088 ——— 'The English nobility in the later Middle Ages', *Rapports, XIIᵉ congrès international des sciences historiques*, 1 (1965), 337–45.
1089 ——— 'Parliament and "bastard feudalism" ', in Richard W. Southern (ed.). *Essays in medieval history selected from the transactions of the Royal Historical Society on the occasion of its centenary.* 1968, 240–70; *TRHS*, ser. 4, 26 (1944), 53–79. Stresses interdependence of magnates and gentry.

1090   Mariella, Sister. 'The parson's tale and the marriage group', *Modern Language Notes*, 53 (1938), 251—56.

1091   Martin, Geoffrey H. 'The English borough in the thirteenth century', *TRHS*, 13 (1963), 123—44. Important discussion of sources.

1092   Masters, Betty. 'The mayor's household [London] before 1600', in Albert E.J. Hollaender and William Kellaway (ed.). *Studies in local history presented to Philip Edmund Jones*. 1969, 95—114.

1093   Moor, Charles. 'The Bygods, earls of Norfolk', *Yorks.Arch.J.*, 32 (1935), 172—213.

1094   Moorman, John R.H. 'Edward I at Lanercost priory, 1306—7', *EHR*, 67 (1952), 161—74. Details of expenditure.

1095   Murray, Katherine M.E. 'Faversham and the cinque ports', *TRHS*, 18 (1935), 53—84. Ingenious attempts by Faversham to join the ports so as to escape monastic and manorial jurisdictions.

1096   Myers, Alec R. 'The wealth of Richard Lyons', *EPBW*, 301—29. Throws new light on Richard and gives the first detailed inventory of a London merchant's house.

1097   Olson, Clair C. 'The minstrels at the court of Edward III', *Publications of the Modern Language Association*, 56 (1941), 601—11.

1098   Otway-Ruthven, A. Jocelyn. 'The medieval county of Kildare', *Irish Historical Studies*, 11 (1959), 181—99. Includes a map of Kildare *c.* 1300.

1099   Owen, Leonard V.D. 'The borough of Nottingham 1284—1485', *Thoroton Society*, 50 (1946), 25—35.

1100   Owst, Gerald R. 'The people's Sunday amusements in the preaching of medieval England', *Holborn Review*, 68 (1926), 32—45.

1101   ——— '*Sortilegium* in English homiletic literature of the fourteenth century', *SPHJ*, 272—303. Discusses the existence of witchcraft and magic.

1102   Painter, Sidney. 'The family and the feudal system in twelfth century England', *Speculum*, 35 (1960), 1—16. Shows how feudal custom gave the lord control over the acquisition of land by vassal families and over marriage alliances among them; also Jean V. Scammell. 'Freedom and marriage in medieval England', *EcHR*, 27 (1974), 523—37.

1103   Pelham, Reginald A. 'Fourteenth century England', in H. Clifford Darby (ed.). *Historical geography of England*. Cambridge, 1936, 230—66, 298—329.

1104   ——— 'The provisioning of the Lincoln parliament in 1301', *UBHJ*, 3 (1951—52), 16—32.

1105   Postan, Michael M. 'Some social consequences of the Hundred Years' War', *EcHR*, 12 (1942), 1—12. Gave rise to vigorous debate. See also Édouard Perroy. 'Gras profits et rançons pendant la Guerre de Cent Ans: l'affaire du comte Denia', in *Mélanges d'histoire du moyen âge . . . à . . . Louis Halphen*. Paris, 1951, 573—80; Michael M. Postan. 'The costs of the Hundred Years' War', *PP*, 27 (1964), 34—53; Kenneth B. McFarlane. 'War, the economy and social change. England and the Hundred Years' War', *PP*, 22 (1962), 3—18; Denis Hay. 'The division of the spoils of war in the fourteenth century', *TRHS*, ser. 5, 4 (1954), 91—109.

1106   Power, Eileen. 'English craft gilds in the Middle Ages', *History*, 4 (1920). 211—14. A historical revision.

1107   Powicke, Frederick M. 'Loretta, countess of Leicester', *EHJT*, 247—73. A lively insight into thirteenth-century aristocratic society.

1108   ——— 'Observations on the English freeholder in the thirteenth century', in *Wirtschaft und Kultur. Festschrift zum 70 Geburtstag von Alfons Dopsch*. Baden bei Wien, 1938, 382—93.

1109   ——— 'The oath of Bromholm', *EHR*, 56 (1941), 529—48.

1110   Prior, William H. 'Notes on the weights and measures of medieval England', *Bulletin du Cange*, 1 (1925), 77—141.

1111   Raftis, J. Ambrose. 'Social structures in five east midland villages', *EcHR*, ser. 2, 18 (1965), 83—100. A study of the possibilities in the use of court roll data; 'The concentration of responsibility in five villages', *MS*, 28 (1966), 92—118. Part of an illuminating investigation.

1112   Roderick, Arthur J. (ed.). *Wales through the ages*. Vol. 1. Aberystwyth, 1959.

See Thomas Jones-Pierce. 'The Wales of Gerald', pp. 105–12; 'The age of the two Llywelyns', pp. 113–19; 'The social scene in the fourteenth century', pp. 153–59. See also Thomas Jones-Pierce. 'Medieval Cardiganshire: a study in social origins', *Ceredigion*, 3 (1959), 265–84; and 'Social and historical aspects of the Welsh laws', *WHR*, special no. (1963), 33–51.

1113   Rothwell, William. 'The teaching of French in medieval England', *Modern Language Review*, 63 (1968), 37–46. See also Helen Suggett. 'The use of French in England in the later Middle Ages', in Richard W. Southern (ed.). *Essays in medieval history*. 1968, 213–39; Richard M. Wilson. 'English and French in England, 1100–1300', *History*, 28 (1943), 37–60; George E. Woodbine. 'The language of English law', *Speculum*, 18 (1943), 395–436. An important article, suggesting that the triumph in the law courts was a result of a French 'invasion' of the mid-thirteenth century; Basil Cottle. *The triumph of English 1350–1400*. 1969.

1114   Russell, Josiah C. 'The preplague population of England', *JBS*, 5 (1966), 1–21 (Cf. *EcHR*, ser. 2, 15 (1962–63, 138–44.) See also Russell's 'Length of life in England, 1250–1348', *Human Biology*, 9 (1937), 415–528; also Sylvia L. Thrupp. 'The problem of replacement rates in medieval English population', *EcHR*, ser. 2, 18 (1965), 101–19; Jan Z. Titow. 'Some evidence of the thirteenth century population increase', *EcHR*, ser. 2, 13 (1961–62), 218–23; John Krause. 'The medieval household; large or small?', *EcHR*, ser. 2, 9 (1955), 420–32. Rejects Russell's figure for average household; Michael M. Postan. 'Some economic evidence of declining population in the later Middle Ages', *EcHR*, ser. 2, 3 (1950), 221–46.

1115   Sabine, Ernest L. 'Butchering in medieval London', *Speculum*, 8 (1933), 335–53. Well worth writing about; 'Latrines and cesspools in medieval London', *Speculum*, 9 (1934), 303–21. A thorough survey; 'City cleaning in medieval London', *Speculum*, 12 (1937), 19–43. A scholarly analysis.

1116   Salter, Herbert E. 'The city of Oxford in the Middle Ages', *History*, 14 (1929), 97–105; also 'An Oxford mural mansion', *EHJT*, 299–305. Throws light on repair of walls of the city.

1117   Sanders, Ivor J. 'The boroughs of Aberystwyth and Cardigan in the early fourteenth century', *BBCS*, 15 (1954), 282–93.

1118   Savage, Henry L. 'Hunting in the Middle Ages', *Speculum*, 8 (1933), 30–41. Still standard.

1119   Sayles, George O. 'The dissolution of a gild at York in 1306', *EHR*, 55 (1940), 83–98.

1120   Scottish Motor Traction Company. 'The lowland families of Scotland', *Scottish Motor Traction Magazine*, 25 (1940), 28–108. Includes the Bruces, Douglasses, Erskines, etc.

1121   Sheehan, Michael M. 'The formation and marriage in fourteenth century England', *MS*, 33 (1971), 128–63.

1122   Somerville, Robert. 'The duchy and county palatine of Lancaster', *Lancs Historic*, 103 (1951), 59–67; also 'The Cowcher books of the duchy of Lancaster', *EHR*, 51 (1936), 598–615. Great cowchers contain records dating in the three centuries before 1400.

1123   Soto, Anthony. 'The structure of society according to Duns Scotus', *FS*, 11 (1951), 194–212.

1124   Stenton, Frank. 'The changing feudalism of the Middle Ages', *History*, 19 (1935), 289–301. Contains much that is still valuable.

1125   ——— 'The road systems of medieval England', *EcHR*, 7 (1936–37), 1–21. This is an important pioneer survey.

1126   Stewart-Brown, Ronald. 'The end of the Norman earldom of Chester', *EHR*, 35 (1920), 26–54.

1127   ——— 'The hospital of St John at Chester', *LancsHistoric*, 78 (1926), 66–106.

1128   Stillwell, Gardiner. 'John Gower and the last years of Edward III', *Studies in Philology*, 45 (1948), 454–72.

1129   Stones, Edward L.G. 'The Folvilles of Ashley-Folville, Leicestershire', *TRHS*, ser. 5, 7 (1957), 117–36. Illustrating the forces of disorder in the fourteenth century.

1130   Strayer, Joseph R. 'The laicization of French and English society in the four-teenth century', *Speculum*, 15 (1940), 76—86. Some important general-izations.

1131   Stretton, Grace. 'The travelling household in the Middle Ages', *JBAA*, n.s., 40 (1940), 75—103.

1132   Tease, G.E. 'The spicers and apothecaries in the royal household in the reigns of Henry III, Edward I and Edward III', *Nottingham Medieval Studies*, 3 (1959), 19—52.

1133   Thomas, Arthur H. 'Sidelights on medieval London life', *JBAA*, ser. 3, 2 (1937), 99—120; 'Life in medieval London', *JBAA*, n.s., 35 (1929), 122—47; *JBAA*, ser. 3 (1937), 99—120.

1134   Thorne, Samuel E. 'English feudalism and estates in land', *Cambridge Law Journal*, 23 (1959), 193—209. By the end of the twelfth century one who holds to himself and his heirs is no longer a life tenant but the real lord of the land.

1135   Thornley, Isobel D. 'Sanctuary in medieval London', *JBAA*, n.s. 38 (1932), 293—315.

1136   Thrupp, Sylvia L. 'Medieval gilds reconsidered', *Journal of Economic History*, 2 (1942), 164—73.

1137   —— 'Economy and society in medieval England', *JBS*, 2 (1962), 1—13. Comments on relations between economic and social history.

1138   Toms, Elsie. 'Medieval juries', *EHR*, 51 (1936), 268—70.

1139   Veale, Elspeth M. 'Craftsmen and economy of London in the fourteenth cen-tury', in Albert E.J. Hollaender and William Kellaway (eds.). *Studies in London history presented to Philip Edmund Jones*. 1969, 133—51.

1140   Wake, Joan. 'Communitas villae', *EHR*, 37 (1922), 406—13.

1141   Wedemeyer, Ellen. 'Social groupings at the fair of St Ives (1275—1302)', *MS*, 32 (1970), 27—59.

1142   Weinbaum, Martin. 'Stalhof und Deutsche Gildhalle zu London', *Hans.Gesch.*, 33 (1928), 45—65; see also Weinbaum's 'Zur Stellung des Fremden im Mittelalterlichen England', *Zeitschrift für vergleichende Rechtswisssen-schaft*, 46 (1931), 360—78.

1143   Westman, Barbara H. 'The peasant family and crime in fourteenth-century England', *JBS*, 13 (1974), 1—18.

1144   Willard, James F. 'Inland transportation in England during the fourteenth century', *Speculum*, 1 (1926), 361—74. Stresses the large amount of movement on roads and streams and the high degree of safety.

1145   —— 'The use of carts in the fourteenth century', *History*, 17 (1932), 246—50. The pack-horse was ubiquitous, but so also was the cart.

1146   Williams, Gwyn A. 'London and Edward I', *TRHS*, ser. 5, 11 (1961), 81—99. Argues that the reign was a watershed in the history of the city.

VII. ECONOMIC HISTORY

1 Printed Sources

1147   Bishop, Terence A.M. (ed.). 'The extents of the prebends of York [*c.* 1295], and extent of Monk Friston, 1320', *Yorks.Arch.Rec.*, 94 (1937), 1—72.

1148   Brown, R. Allen. *The memoranda roll for the tenth year of the reign of king John (1207—8)*. Pipe Roll Society, 31 (1957); also Brown *et al.* (eds.). *Miscellaneous contents. 1196—1216*. Pipe Roll Society, 69 (1957). Includes unpublished letters.

1149   Cannon, Henry L. (ed.). *The great roll of the pipe for the twenty-sixth year of king Henry III, A.D. 1242*. New Haven, Conn., 1918.

1150   Carter, William F. (trans. and ed.). *The lay subsidy roll for Warwickshire of King Edward III*. (1332). Dugdale Society, 6 (1926). Some inadequacies. An Appendix contains three early subsidy rolls for Stratford-upon-Avon and an extract from the assize roll of 1323.

1151   Carus-Wilson, Eleanora M. (ed.). *The overseas trade of Bristol in the later*

Middle Ages. Bristol, 1937. Reprinted New York, 1967. Various records, mainly fifteenth century. An important volume; also Carus-Wilson, with Olive and P. Coleman. *England's export trade, 1275—1547.* Oxford, 1963. Important statistical tables and graphs.

1152   Chibnall, Albert C. (ed.). *Early taxation returns, taxation of personal property in 1332 and later.* Buckinghamshire Record Society, 14 (1966).

1153   Chibnall, Marjorie M. (ed.). *Select documents of the English lands of the abbey of Bec.* Camden Society, ser. 3, 73 (1951). Charters and deeds, twelfth to thirteenth centuries, with thirteenth-century account rolls. Expertly edited.

1154   Churchill, Irene J. *et al.* (eds.). *Calendar of Kent feet of fines to the end of Henry III's reign.* Kent Archaeological Society Record Branch, 15 (1956). Introduction by Frank W. Jessup.

1155   Davies, Oliver and David B. Quinn (eds.). *The Irish pipe roll of 14 John, 1211—1212. Ulster Journal of Archaeology*, Supplement 4 (1941). Text and translation.

1156   Davis, Ralph H.C. (ed.). *The kalendar of abbot Samson of Bury St Edmunds and related documents.* Camden Society, ser. 3, 84 (1954). General inventory of revenues, 1182—1211.

1157   Dodwell, Barbara (ed.). *Feet of fines for the county of Norfolk, 1198—1202.* Pipe Roll Society, n.s., 27 (1952); also *Feet of fines for the county of Norfolk 1201—1214, for the county of Suffolk 1199—1214.* Pipe Roll Society, n.s., 32 (1958).

1158   Drucker, Lucy (ed.). *Warwickshire feet of fines abstracted from the originals in the Public Record Office,* Vol. 3, *19 Edw. III (1345)—24 Henry VII (1509).* Dugdale Society, 18 (1943).

1159   Erskine, Audrey M. (ed.). *The Devonshire lay subsidy of 1332.* Devon and Cornwall Record Society, n.s., 14 (1969).

1160   Essex Archaeological Society. *Feet of fines for Essex.* Pt. 19, *1—13. Edward III.* Colchester, 1929; Pt. 5 of Vol. 3 (*A.D. 1365—76*). Colchester, 1934.

1161   Fletcher, William G.D. (ed.). 'Shropshire feet of fines, A.D. 1218—1248', Shropshire Archaeological and Natural History Society, ser. 4, 6 (1916—17), 169—92.

1162   Fowler, G. Herbert and Michael W. Hughes. *A calendar of the pipe rolls of the reign of Richard I for Buckinghamshire and Bedfordshire 1189—1199. BedsRec,* 7 (1923).

1163   Fowler, Robert C. (ed.). *Feet of fines for Essex.* Vol. 3, *1327—1422.* Essex Archaeological Society, 3 (1949).

1164   Fraser, Constance M. *The Northumberland lay subsidy roll of 1296.* Newcastle-upon-Tyne, 1968.

1165   Fry, Edward A. *A calendar of feet of fines relating to the county of Wiltshire, 1195—72.* Wiltshire Archaeological Society. 1930.

1166   Fryde, Edmund B. *The wool accounts of William de la Pole, a study of some aspects of the English wool trade at the start of the Hundred Years' War.* St Anthony's Hall Publications, 25 (1964). Brief but valuable. Includes text of account for 1337.

1167   —— *Some business transactions of York merchants . . . 1336—1349.* St Anthony's Hall Publications, Borthwick Papers, 29 (1966). Brief pamphlet, but informative. Includes table of financial transactions 1338—40 and debts of Walter Chiriton.

1168   Gidden, Harry W. (ed.). *The book of remembrance of Southampton.* Vol. 2. Southampton, 1928. Errors in transcription.

1169   Griffin, Ralph H. *et al.* (eds.). *Kent feet of fines, Kent Records,* 15, Pt. 1. Kent Archaeological Society Records Branch, 1939. 1—144.

1170   Griffiths, John. 'Early accounts relating to North Wales, temp. Edward I', *BBCS,* 14, Pt. 3 (1951), 235—42; 15, Pt. 1 (1953), 126—57; 16, Pt. 2 (1955), 109—35.

1171   Gross, Charles *et al. Select cases concerning the law merchant, 1270—1638.* Selden Society, 23, 46, 49 (1908—32), 3 vols. Local and central courts.

1172   HMSO. *Calendar of liberate rolls preserved in the Public Record Office.* Vols. 1—6, *1226—75.* 1916—24; *Calendar of fine rolls.* Vols. 1—8. *1272—1377.*

1911—24; *Calendar of memoranda rolls* (exchequer) *Michaelmas 1326—Michaelmas 1327.* 1968; *Liber feodorum: the book of fees. Part I. 1198—1242.* 1922. Results of enquiries by the exchequer, 1198—1237.

1173　Hollings, Marjory (ed.). *The red book of Worcester containing surveys of the bishop's manors and other records chiefly of the twelfth and thirteenth centuries.* Pts. 1—3. Worcestershire Historical Society, 1934—35. Contains much information.

1174　Holt, James C. (ed.). *Praestitia roll, 14—18 John, roll of summonses of 1214. Scutage roll, 16 John.* Pipe Roll Society, 37 (1964).

1175　Hughes, Michael W. (ed.). *A calendar of feet of fines for the county of Buckingham, 7 Richard I to 44 Henry III.* Architectural and Archaeological Society for Buckinghamshire, Record Branch, 4 (1942).

1176　Jenkinson, C. Hilary (ed.). *Calendar of the plea rolls of the exchequer of the Jews preserved in the Public Record Office.* 3. Jewish Historical Society, 1929. For the years 1275—77.

1177　——— and Beryl E.R. Formoy (eds.). *Select cases in the exchequer of pleas.* Selden Society, 48 (1932). Valuable Introduction, with text and translations, 20 Henry III—33 Edward I.

1178　——— and James F. Willard and Montague S. Guiseppi (eds.). *Surrey Taxation Returns.* Surrey Record Society, 11 (1932). The 1332 assessment and subsequent assessments to 1623. See also Harold C. Johnson (ed.). *Surrey taxation returns; Part A. fifteenths and tenths the 1332 assessment: Part B. documents subsequent to 1332.* Surrey Record Society, 11 (1932). Important comments on system of taxation.

1179　Latham, Ronald E. *Calendar of memoranda rolls (exchequer). Michaelmas 1326—Michaelmas 1327.* 1968. HMSO.

1180　Lewis, Edward A. (ed.). 'The account roll of the chamberlain of North Wales, Mich. 1304—Mich. 1305', *BBCS*, 1 (1922), 256—75; also 'The account roll of the chamberlain of West Wales, Mich. 1301—Mich. 1302', *BBCS*, 2 (1923), 49—86.

1181　Lilburn, A.J. (ed.). 'The pipe roll of Ed. I', Pts. 1—2. *ArchAel*, 32 (1954), 323—40; 33 (1955), 163—75; 34 (1956), 176—95; 35 (1957), 144—62; 36 (1958), 277—95; 38 (1960), 179—91; 39 (1961), 327—43; 41 (1963), 107—22.

1182　Lister, John (ed.). *The early Yorkshire woollen trade. Extracts from the Hull customs roll and complete transcripts of the ulnagers' rolls. York.Arch. Rec.*, 64 (1924).

1183　Lunt, William E. 'The text of an ordinance of 1184 concerning an aid for the Holy Land', *EHR*, 37 (1922), 235—42.

1184　Lydon, James F. (ed.). 'Survey of the memoranda rolls of the Irish exchequers, 1294—1509', *Analecta Hibernica*, 23 (1966), 51—134. Checking and amplifying the calendar of rolls lost in 1922.

1185　Mander, Gerald P. (ed.). 'Ancient deeds preserved at the Wodehouse Wombourne', *Collections for a history of Staffordshire ed. by the staff of the Staff. Rec. Soc.* (1928). Kendal, 1930, 3—134.

1186　Maxwell-Lyte, Henry C. *et al.* (eds.). *Inquisitions and assessments relating to feudal aids, 1284—1431.* 1920. HMSO.

1187　——— and Charles G. Crump (eds.). *The book of fees commonly called testa de Nevill.* 1920—31, 3 vols. Compare the actual with the possible proceeds of an aid.

1188　Midgley, L. Margaret (ed.). *Minister's accounts of the earldom Cornwall 1296—1297,* Camden Society, ser. 3, 66, 68 (1942) (1945).

1189　Mills, Mabel H., with co-operation of C. Hilary Jenkinson and Montague S. Guiseppi (eds.). *The pipe roll for 1295. Surrey membrane.* Surrey Record Society, 7 (1924). Text and translations. Long technical Introduction; Mabel H. Mills and Ronald Stewart-Brown (eds.). *Cheshire in the pipe rolls, 1158—1301.* Lancashire and Cheshire Record Society, 92 (1938).

1190　Northumberland. *Feet of fines, Northumberland A.D. 1273—A.D. 1346.* Newcastle-upon-Tyne, Records Committee, Record ser. 11 (1934).

1191　Oresme, Nicholas of. *The "De Moneta" of Nicholas Oresme and English mint documents*, ed. and trans. Charles Johnson. 1956. The most celebrated monetary tract of the Middle Ages.

1192   Parker, John B. (ed.). 'Lay subsidy rolls, 1 Edward III. North Riding, Yorks., and the city of York', *Yorks.Arch.Rec.*, 74 (1929). *Miscellanea*, 2 106–71.

1193   —— *Feet of fines for the county of York from 1218–1272. Yorks.Arch. Rec.*, 62, 67, 82 (1921–32).

1194   PRO. *Liber feodorum*. 1920–31, 3 vols. Vol. 3 is an index to the previous two vols. dealing with an inquest made by Edward I in connection with an aid *pour fille marier* in 1302.

1195   Pugh, Ralph B. (ed.). *Abstracts of the feet of fines relating to Wiltshire for the reigns of Edward I and Edward II.* Devizes, 1939.

1196   Reichel, Oswald J. and Francis B. Prideaux (eds.). *Devon feet of fines.* Vol. 2, *1 Ed. I–43 Ed. III.* Devon and Cornwall Record Society, 46 (1939), 453–94.

1197   Rhys, Myvanwy. *Ministers account for west Wales, 1277 to 1306.* Cymmrodorion Record ser. 13 (1936). For 1352–53 see Myvanwy Rhys, *BBCS*, 10 (1939–40), 60–83, 139–56, 256–71. See also William H. Waters (ed.). 'Account of the sheriff of Caernarvon for 1303–4', *BBCS*, 7 (1934), 143–53.

1198   Richardson, Henry G. *The memoranda roll for the Michaelmas term of the first year of king John, 1199–1200.* Pipe Roll Society, n.s., 21 (1943).

1199   Robinson, Chalfont (ed.). *The memoranda roll of the king's remembrancer for Michaelmas 1230–Trinity 1231.* Princeton, N.J., 1933. There is a useful Introduction.

1200   Roper, M. (ed.). *Feet of fines for the county of York from 1300 to 1314. Yorks.Arch.Rec.*, 127 (1965).

1201   Rouquette, R.P.R. (ed.). 'Comptes du guardien Henry de Cobham pour l'années 1294–95 (le plus ancien document conservé dans l'île)', *Bulletin annuel de la société jersiaise*, 13 (1936), 19–32.

1202   Salter, Herbert E. (ed.). *The feet of fines for Oxfordshire, 1195–1291.* Oxford Record Society, 41 (1930).

1203   Slingsby, Francis H. (ed.). *Feet of fines for the county of York from 1272 to 1300. Yorks.Arch.Rec.*, 121 (1956).

1204   Stenton, Doris M. (ed.). *The chancellor's roll 8 Richard I, Michaelmas, 1196.* Pipe Roll Society, 42 (1930); Doris M. Stenton *et al.* (eds.). *The great roll of the pipe 31 Henry II (1187–88)–14 Henry III (Mich. 1230).* Pipe Roll Society, n.s., 1 (1925); n.s., 4 (1927); n.s., 39 (1964, 1972).

1205   Walker, Margaret S. (ed.). *Feet of fines for the county of Lincoln, 1199–1216.* Pipe Roll Society, 29 (1954).

2 General Surveys

1206   Beresford, Maurice W. and John K.S. St Joseph. *Medieval England: an aerial survey.* Cambridge, 1958. Valuable comments.

1207   Brentano, Lujo. *Eine Geschichte der wirtschaftlichen Entwicklung Englands.* Vol. 1, *Von den Anfängen bis gegen Ende 15 Jahrhunderts.* New York, 1968. First published in Jena, 1927.

1208   Grant, Isabel F. *The economic history of Scotland.* 1934. The best short account at that time.

1209   Hodgen, Margaret T. *Change and history: a study of the dated distribution of technological innovations in England.* New York, 1952. A major contribution to economic history; a new approach to the subject.

1210   Jamis, Margery K. *Studies in the medieval wine trade.* Oxford, 1971.

1211   Mitchell, Sydney K. *Taxation in medieval England*, ed. Sidney Painter. New Haven, 1951. Deals with machinery of taxation mainly in thirteenth century, especially with the problem of consent, but not very satisfactorily.

1212   Nolan, Patrick. *A monetary history of England.* Vol. 2. 1928. From the Anglo-Norman invasion to the death of Elizabeth.

1213   Postan, Michael M. *The medieval economy and society: an economic history* of Britain, 1100–1500. Berkeley, Cal., 1972; *Essays on medieval agriculture and general problems of the medieval economy*. Cambridge, 1973. *Medieval trade and finance*. New York, 1973. All authoritative. And, with Edwin E. Rich *et al.* (eds.). *The Cambridge economic history*. Vols. 2 and 3. A standard work. Includes a comparative study of France and England by Edward E. Miller, and analyses of public credit by Edmund B. and Michael M. Fryde.

1214   Ramsay, James H. *A history of the revenues of the kings of England, 1066–1399*. Oxford, 1925, 2 vols. Criticised in Anthony Steel. 'Some aspects of English finance in 14th century', *History*, 12 (1928), 298–309.

1215   Stewart, Ian H. *The Scottish coinage*. 1915. With plates.

3 Monographs

1216   Barnes, Patricia and Cecil F. Slade (eds.). *A medieval miscellany for Doris May Stenton*. Pipe Roll Society, n.s., 36 (1962). A group of excellent essays, including several on the twelfth and thirteenth centuries.

1217   Beresford, Maurice W. *Lay subsidies and poll taxes*. Bridge Place near Canterbury, 1963. Deals with the lay subsidies of 1290–1334 and the poll taxes of 1377, 1379 and 1381.

1218   Bridbury, Anthony R. *England and the salt trade in the later Middle Ages*. Oxford, 1955. Scholarly, though a little uneven.

1219   Brooke, George C. *English coins from the seventh century to the present day*. 3rd ed. 1950. See also Charles W.C. Oman. *The coinage of England*. Oxford, 1931; N.J. Mayhew. 'Numismatic evidence of falling prices in the fourteenth century', *EcHR*, ser. 2, 27 (1974), 1–15.

1220   Carus-Wilson, Eleanora M. *The overseas trade of Bristol in the later Middle Ages*. Bristol, 1937. Valuable. See also Eleanora M. Carus-Wilson. *Medieval merchant venturers: collected studies*. 1967. First published 1954. Includes: 'An industrial revolution, XIII c.'; 'Eng. cloth industry in the XII and XIII centuries'; 'Trends in the export of English woollens in the XIV c.'; 'Effects of acquisition and loss of Gascony on Eng. wine trade'. See also Edward E. Miller. 'The fortunes of the English textile industry during the thirteenth century', *EcHR*, ser. 2, 18 (1965), 64–82.

1221   Chibnall, Albert C. *Taxation of personal property in 1332 and later*. 1969.

1222   Crump, William B. and S. Gertrude Ghorbal. *History of the Huddersfield woollen industry*. Huddersfield, 1935; also Herbert Heaton. *Yorkshire woollen and worsted industries from the earliest times up to the industrial revolution*. 2nd ed. 1966. First published 1920; Ephraim Lipson. *The history of the woollen and worsted industries*. 1921.

1223   Davidson, John and Alexander Gray. *The Scottish staple at Veere*. 1920. Has a good introductory chapter.

1224   Gras, Norman S.B. *The early English customs system: a documentary study of the institutional and economic history of the customs from the thirteenth to the sixteenth century*. Cambridge, Mass., 1918. Includes much original material. Still a standard work.

1225   Hewitt, Herbert J. *Medieval Chester. An economic and social history of Cheshire in the reign of the three Edwards*. Chetham Society, n.s., 88 (1929). A scholarly survey.

1226   Jenkins, James T. *The herring and the herring fisheries*. 1927.

1227   Kershaw, Ian. *Bolton priory: the economy of a northern monastery, 1286–1325*. New York, 1973.

1228   O'Sullivan, Mary D. *Italian merchant bankers in Ireland in the thirteenth century*. Dublin, 1962. A pioneer study. See also Armando Sapori. *Le compagnia mercantili dei Bardi e dei Peruzzi in Inghilterra nei secoli xiii e xiv*. Florence, 1926; and Armando Sapori. *La compagnia dei Frescobaldi in Inghilterra*. Florence, 1947. Also 'Le compagni dei Bardi e dei Peruzzi in Inghilterra', *Archivio Storico Italiano*, 80 (1922), 5–63; and see Alice Beardwood. 'Alien merchants and the English crown in the later fourteenth century', *EcHR*, 2 (1929–30), 229–60. Discusses the final settlement with the Bardi; Alwyn A. Ruddock. *Italian merchants and shipping* in Southampton, 1270—1600. Oxford, 1951; 'The Flanders galleys', *History*, n.s., 24 (1944), 192—202; 'Italian trading fleets in medieval England', *History*, n.s., 29 (1944), 192—202; 'The trade of Southampton with the Mediterranean in the Middle Ages', *BIHR*, 20 (1943—45), 43—45; 'Alien merchants in Southampton in the later Middle Ages', *EHR*, 61 (1946), 1—17; see also Ephraim Russell. 'The societies of Bardi and Peruzzi and their dealings with Edward III, 1327—45', in George Unwin. *Finance and trade under Edward III*. Manchester, 1918, 93—135; George A. Holmes. 'Florentine merchants in England, 1345—1436', *EcHR*, ser. 2, 13 (1960—61), 193—208; Hugh G. Rawlinson. 'The Flanders galley: some notes on seaborne trade between Venice and England, 1327—1532', *Mariner's Mirror*, 12 (1926), 145—68; W. Stanford Reid. 'Frescobaldi in Guyenne (1307—12)', *Archivio Storico Italiano*, 122 (1964), 459—70. Describes their activities as bankers of the English king; Richard W. Kaeuper. *Bankers to the crown: the Riccardi of Lucca and Edward I*. Princeton, N.J., 1973.

1229 Perry, Reginald. 'The Gloucestershire woollen industry 1100—1690', Bristol and Gloucestershire Archaeological Society, 66 (1945), 49—137.

1230 Power, Eileen. *Wool trade in English medieval history*. Oxford, 1941. Ford lectures by a great expert.

1231 Steel, Anthony. *The receipt of the exchequer*. 1954; also 'The marginalia of the treasurer's receipt rolls, 1349—99', *BIHR*, 7 (1930), 67—84, 133—43, and *BIHR*, 8 (1931), 1—13.

1232 Sturler, Jean V. de. *L'étape des laines anglaises en Brabant et l'Angleterre au moyen âge . . .* Paris, 1936.

1233 Unwin, George (ed.). *Finance and trade under Edward III*. Manchester, 1918. Still valuable: its appearance marked a clear advance in the study of the period.

1234 —— *The gilds and companies of London*. New York, 1964. Reprint of a classic. New Introduction by William F. Kahl.

1235 Willard, James F. *Parliamentary taxes on personal property, 1290 to 1334*. Cambridge, Mass., 1934. A thoroughly documented and illuminating study.

4 Articles

1236 Ames, Edward. 'The sterling crisis of 1337—39', *Journal of Economic History*, 25 (1965), 496—522.

1237 Ault, Warren O. 'Manors and temporalities', *EGAW*, 3, 3—34.

1238 Baker, Robert L. 'The establishment of the English wool staple in 1313', *Speculum*, 31 (1956), 444—53. Suggests it was a concession to English merchants by the king.

1239 —— 'English customs service, 1307—43. A study of medieval administration', *Transactions of the American Philosophical Society*, 51, Pt. 6 (1961), 3—51.

1240 Beardwood, Alice. 'Bishop Langton's use of statute merchant recognizances', *Med et Hum*, 9 (1955), 54—70.

1241 Berben, Henri. 'Une guerre économique au moyen âge. L'embargo sur l'exportation des laines anglaises, 1270—74', *in Études d'histoire dédiées à la mémoire de Henri Pirenne*. Brussels, 1926, 1—17. See also Elizabeth von Roon-Bassermann. 'Die Handelssperre Englands gegen Flandern 1270—1274 und die lizenzierte englische Wollensfuhr', *Vierteljahrschrift für Sozial-und Wirtschaftsgeschichte*, 50 (1963), 71—82.

1242 Beveridge, William H. 'Wages in the Winchester manors', *EcHR*, 7 (1936—37), 22—43; and Beveridge's 'Westminster wages in the manorial era', *EcHR*, 8 (1955—56), 18—35. Shows that there was variety and change in the management of affairs. See also E.H. Phelps Brown and Sheila V. Hopkins. 'Seven centuries of the price of consumables compared with the builders' wage-rates', *Economica*, n.s., 23 (1956), 293—314; and 'Seven centuries of wages and prices: some earlier estimates', *Economica*, n.s., 28 (1961), 30—36; David L. Farmer. 'Some price fluctuations in Angevin England',

EcHR, ser. 2, 9 (1956), 34—43; 'Some grain price movements in thirteenth century England', *EcHR*, ser. 2, 10 (1957—58), 207—20; 'Some livestock price movements in thirteenth century England', *EcHR*, ser. 2, 22 (1969), 1—16.

1243 Bigwood, Georges. 'Un marché de matières premières: laines d'Angleterre et marchands italiens vers la fin du XIIIe siècle', *Annales, économies, sociétés, civilisations*, 2 (1930), 193—209.

1244 Blake, John B. 'Medieval smuggling in the North-East; some fourteenth-century evidence', *ArchAel*, ser. 4, 43 (1965), 243—60.

1245 Bryant, William N. 'The financial dealings of Edward III with the county communities, 1330—1360', *EHR*, 83 (1968), 760—71. Interesting experiments in taxation outside of parliament.

1246 Carus-Wilson, Eleanora M. 'The aulnage accounts: a criticism', *EcHR*, 14 (1944), 114—23. Shows unreliability; 'The English cloth industry in the late twelfth and early thirteenth centuries', *EcHR*, 14 (1944), 32—50; 'The effects of acquisition and the loss of Gascony on the English wine trade', *BIHR*, 21 (1946—48), 145—54. Late twelfth and early thirteenth centuries saw a complete revolution in the source of English imported wine; 'The medieval trade of the ports of the Wash', *Medieval Archaeology*, 6—7 (1962—63), 182—201. An important discussion.

1247 Cazel, Fred A. 'The tax of 1185 in aid of the Holy Land', *Speculum*, 30 (1955), 385—92. Paid by laity and clergy with the common assent of the bishops and barons of England and of France; also 'The fifteenth of 1225', *BIHR*, 34 (1961), 67—81. The tax brought in only about two-thirds of the amount usually received. Prints relevant documents. See also Margaret Curtis. 'The London lay subsidy of 1332', in George Unwin (ed.). *Finance and trade under Edward III*. Manchester, 1918, 35—60.

1248 Chew, Helena M. 'Scutage under Edward I', *EHR*, 37 (1922), 321—36; 'Scutage in the fourteenth century', *EHR*, 38 (1923), 19—41; 'A Jewish aid to marry, A.D. 1221', *Jewish Historical Society Transactions*, 11 (1928), 92—111. Prints extracts from Receipt roll, E 401/4.

1249 Colvin, Howard M. 'Holme Lacy: an episcopal manor and its tenants in the twelfth and thirteenth centuries', in Veronica Ruffer and Alfred J. Taylor (eds.). *Medieval studies presented to Rose Graham*. Oxford, 1950, 15—40. Prints documents.

1250 Cowley, F.G. 'The Cistercian economy in Glamorgan 1130—1349', *Morgannwg*, 11 (1967), 5—27.

1251 Darby, H. Clifford. 'The economic geography of England, A.D. 1000—1250', in H. Clifford Darby (ed.). *Historical geography of England*. Cambridge, 1936.

1252 Davies, J. Conway. 'An assembly of wool merchants in 1332', *EHR*, 31 (1916), 596—606. Prints record of the assembly; also 'Shipping and trade in Newcastle-upon-Tyne 1294—1296', *ArchAel*, ser. 4, 31 (1953), 175—204. Throws light on growth and on trade with Baltic; 'The wool accounts for Newcastle-upon-Tyne for the reign of Edward I', *ArchAel*, ser. 4, 32 (1954), 220—308.

1253 ———— 'The memoranda rolls of the exchequer in 1332', *SPHJ*, 97—154.

1254 Deighton, Herbert S. 'Clerical taxation by consent', *EHR*, 68 (1953), 161—92. Decline in practice of consent by clergy.

1255 Denholm-Young, Noël. 'The negotiation of wardrobe debentures in the fourteenth century', *EHR*, 44 (1929), 439—53. Prints records.

1256 Dept, Gaston. 'Les marchands flamands et le roi d'Angleterre 1154—1215', *Revue du Nord*, 12 (1926), 303—24.

1257 Deroisy, Armand. 'Les routes terrestres des laines anglaises vers la Lombardie', *Revue du Nord*, 25 (1939), 40—60.

1258 Donnelly, James S. 'Changes in the grange economy of English and Welsh Cistercian abbeys, 1300—1540', *Traditio*, 10 (1954), 399—458.

1259 Du Boulay, Francis R.H. 'A rentier economy in the later Middle Ages: the archbishopric of Canterbury', *EcHR*, ser. 2, 16 (1963), 427—38. Income increased by about 38% between 1291 and 1422.

1260 Elman, Peter. 'The economic causes of the expulsion of the Jews in 1290',

EcHR, 7 (1937), 145—54; also 'Jewish trade in thirteenth century England', *Historia Judaica*, 1 (1939), 91—104. Little evidence of large-scale trading operations.

1261   Fox, Levi. 'Ministers' accounts of the honor of Leicester (1322—24)', *Leicestershire Archaeological Society*, 19 (1938), 199—273; 20 (1938), 77—158.

1262   Fraser, Constance M. 'Medieval trading restrictions in the North-east', *Arch Ael*, ser. 4, 39 (1961), 135—50; 'The pattern of trade in the North-east of England, 1265—1350', *Northern History*, 4 (1969), 44—66.

1263   Fryde, Edmund. 'Materials for the study of Edward III's credit operations, 1327—48', *BIHR*, 22 (1949), 105—38; 23 (1950), 1—30. Expertly discusses the king's loans, including administrative processes; 'The deposits of Hugh Despenser the younger with Italian bankers', *EcHR*, ser. 2, 3 (1950—51), 344—62. An aspect of the expansion of Italian merchants in England; 'Dismissal of Robert de Wodehouse from the office of treasurer, December 1338', *EHR*, 67 (1952), 74—78. Throws light on relations between Edward III abroad and his ministers at home; 'Edward III's wool monopoly of 1337; a fourteenth century royal trading venture', *History*, 37 (1952), 8—24; 'The English farmers of the customs, 1343—51', *TRHS*, ser. 5, 9 (1959), 1—17. Profited only a small group of businessmen at the expense of most other economic interests in England; 'The last trials of Sir William de la Pole', *EcHR*, ser. 2, 15 (1962—63), 17—30. The dampening effect on loans to the crown; 'Financial resources of Edward III in the Netherlands, 1337—40: main problems and some comparisons', *Revue Belge*, 40 (1962), 1168—87; 45 (1967), 1142—1216. Detailed analysis.

1264   Galbraith, Vivian H. 'The tower as an exchequer record office in the reign of Edward II', *EPTT*, 231—47. Prints records.

1265   Gras, Norman S.B. 'English customs revenue up to 1275', *American Historical Association Annual Report for 1917*, 1920, 295—301.

1266   Gray, Howard L. 'The production and exportation of English woollens in the fourteenth century', *EHR*, 39 (1924), 13—35. Valuable: includes also the manufacture of cloth.

1267   Harris, Brian E. 'King John and the sheriffs' farms', *EHR*, 79 (1964), 532—42. King John imposed increments on the farms.

1268   Harriss, Gerald L. 'Preference at the medieval exchequer', *BIHR*, 30 (1957), 17—40. Surveys government borrowing in the fourteenth and fifteenth centuries; also 'Aids, loans and benevolencies', *Historical Journal*, 6 (1963), 1—19. Goes back to 1297.

1269   Herbruck, Wendell. 'Forestalling, regrating and engrossing', *Michigan Law Review*, 27 (1929), 365—88.

1270   Hewitt, Herbert J. 'The trade of Chester in the reigns of the three Edwards', *Journal of the Chester Architectural and Archaeological Society*, 26 (1925), 43—73.

1271   Hyams, Paul R. 'The origins of a peasant land market in England', *EcHR*, ser. 2, 23 (1970), 18—31.

1272   Jenkinson, C. Hilary. 'Financial records of the reign of king John', in Henry E. Malden (ed.). *Magna carta commemoration essays*. For the Royal Society, 1917, 244—300; also 'A money-lender's bonds of the twelfth century', *EPRP*, 190—210. Eight new documents printed (William Cade) with expert comments.

1273   Knoop, Douglas and Gwilym P. Jones. 'Masons and apprenticeship in medieval England', *EcHR*, 3 (1931—32), 346—66; also 'The impressment of masons in the Middle Ages', *EcHR*, 8 (1937—38), 57—67; and 'The English medieval quarry', *EcHR*, 9 (1938—39), 17—37. See also Ernest Neaverson. 'Medieval quarrying in North-Eastern Wales', *Flintshire Historical Society*, 14 (1954), 1—21. Shows much technical knowledge.

1274   Lennard, Reginald V. 'The demesnes of Glastonbury abbey in the eleventh and twelfth century', *EcHR*, ser. 2, 8 (1955—56), 354—63.

1275   Levett, Ada E. 'The courts and court rolls of St Albans abbey', *TRHS*, 7 (1924), 52—76.

1276 —— 'The financial organization of the manor', *EcHR*, 1 (1927—28), 65—86. Discusses methods of accounting.

1277 Lydon, James F. 'Edward II and the revenues of Ireland', *Irish Historical Studies*, 14 (1964), 39—57. Prints documents and gives list of revenues.

1278 McCusker, John J., Jr. 'The wine press and medieval mercantile shipping', *Speculum*, 41 (1966), 279—96. Discusses the development of the *ceol* and *hulc*.

1279 Meekings, Cecil A.F. 'The pipe roll order of 12 February 1270', in J. Conway Davies (ed.). *Studies presented to Sir Hilary Jenkinson*. 1957, 222—53.

1280 Miller, Edward E. 'The English economy in the thirteenth century: implications of recent research', *PP*, 28 (1964), 21—40. A learned and balanced survey; 'England in the twelfth and thirteenth century: an economic contrast', *EcHR*, 24 (1971), 1—14; see also Clyde G. Reed and Terry L. Anderson, 'An economic explanation of English agricultural organization in the twelfth and thirteenth centuries', *EcHR*, 26 (1973), 134—37; and rejoinder by Edward Miller, *EcHR*, 26 (1973), 138—40.

1281 Mills, Mabel H. 'Adventus vicecomitum', *EHR*, 36 (1921), 481—96; 38 (1923), 331—54. Examines affairs at exchequer, 1258—1307; also 'The reforms at the exchequer, 1232—42', *TRHS*, ser. 4, 10 (1927), 111—33; 'The collectors of customs', *EGAW*, 2, 168—200; 'Experiments in exchequer procedure (1200—1232)', in Richard W. Southern (ed.). *Essays in medieval history selected from the 'transactions' of the Royal Historical Society on the occasion of its centenary*. 1968, 129—45. From *TRHS*, 8 (1925), 151—70. Insights into exchequer development.

1282 Miskimin, Harry A. 'Monetary movements and market structure; forces for contraction in fourteenth and fifteenth-century England', *Journal of Economic History*, 24 (1964), 470—95.

1283 Oschinsky, Dorothea. 'Notes on the Lancaster estates in the thirteenth and fourteenth centuries', *Lancs.Historic.*, 100 (1949), 9—32.

1284 O'Sullivan, Mary D. 'Italian merchant bankers and the collection of the customs in Ireland, 1275—1311', *SPAG*, 168—202.

1285 Pelham, Reginald A. 'The early wool trade in Warwickshire and the rise of the merchant middle class', *Birmingham Archaeological Society Transactions and Proceedings*, 63 (1944), 41—62.

1286 —— 'The cloth markets of Warwickshire during the later Middle Ages', *Birmingham Archaeological Society Transactions and Proceedings*, 66 (1945—46), 131—41.

1287 Poole, Austin L. 'Live stock prices in the twelfth century', *EHR*, 55 (1940), 284—95.

1288 Postan, Michael M. 'Private financial instruments in medieval England', *Vierteljahrschrift für Sozial-und Wirtschaftsgeschichte*, 23 (1930), 26—75; also 'The rise of a money economy', *EcHR*, 14 (1944), 123—34. 'The rise of a money economy does not mean the rise of money'; 'Partnership in English medieval commerce', *Studi in onore di Armando Sapori*. Milan, 1958, 521—49; Michael Postan and Jan Z. Titow. 'Heriots and prices on Winchester manors', *EcHR*, ser. 2, 11 (1958—59), 392—411; 12 (1959—60), 77—78; Shows that failure of harvests in the thirteenth and fourteenth centuries resulted in large increase in deaths, indicating a society balanced on the edge of subsistence. See also, for a criticism, Barbara F. Harvey. 'The population trend in England between 1300 and 1348', *TRHS*, ser. 5, 16 (1966), 23—42; and Rodney H. Hilton. 'L'Angleterre économique et sociale des XIVe et XVe siècles', *Annales, économies, sociétés, civilisations*, 13 (1958), 541—63. Also a notable volume by Anthony R. Bridbury, *Economic growth: England in the later Middle Ages*. 1962, which is very convincing; and Paul D.A. Harvey. *A medieval Oxfordshire village: Cuxham. 1240—1400*. Oxford, 1965—, a notable volume; Michael M. Postan. *Rapports, Congrès international des sciences historiques*. Vol. 1. Paris, 1950, 225—41.

1289 Pugh, Ralph B. 'Some medieval moneylenders', *Speculum*, 43 (1968), 274—89. Lending by king's clerks.

1290 Putnam, Bertha H. 'Records of the courts of common law, especially of the sessions of the justices of the peace: sources for the economic history of England in the fourteenth and fifteenth centuries', *Proceedings of the American Philosophical Society*, 19 (1947), 258—73.

1291 Reid, W. Stanford. 'The Scots and the Staple ordinance of 1313', *Speculum*, 34 (1959), 598—610. Discusses reasons for the ordinance.

1292 Rich, Edwin E. 'The mayors of the staples', *CHJ*, 4 (1932), 120—42.

1293 Richardson, Henry G. 'Richard Fizneal and the Dialogus de Scaccario', *EHR*, 43 (1928), 161—71, 321—40; 'An early fine: its causes and consequences', *LQR*, 48 (1932), 415—21. Discusses the early system (twelfth century); see also Richardson and George O. Sayles. 'Irish revenue 1278—1384', *Proceedings of the Irish Academy*, 62 (1961—62), Sec. C, 87—100. Gives table of receipts by treasurers.

1294 Sagher, Henri E. de. 'L'immigration des tisserands flamands et brabançons en Angleterre sous Édouard III', *Études d'histoire dédiées à la mémoire de Henri Pirenne*. Brussels, 1926, 109—26.

1295 Sandys, Agnes. 'The financial and administrative importance of the London Temple in the thirteenth century', *EPTT*, 147—62. A royal 'treasury and bank'.

1296 Sayles, George O. 'The "English company" of 1343 and a merchant's oath', *Speculum*, 6 (1931), 177—205. Prints oath taken by William de la Pole, whose reputation is brought into question.

1297 Stein, Walter. 'Die Hanse und England beim Ausgang des hundert-jährigen Krieges', *Hans.Gesch.*, 26 (1921), 27—126.

1298 Stephenson, Carl. 'The aids of the English boroughs', *EHR*, 34 (1919), 457—75. The decline of arbitrary impositions.

1299 Stone, Edward. 'Profit-and-loss accountancy at Norwich cathedral priory', *TRHS*, ser. 5, 12 (1962), 25—48. A major change following 1289.

1300 Sturler, Jean V. de. 'Le port de Londres au XIIe siècle', *Revue de l'Université de Bruxelles*, 1 (1936), 61—77.

1301 Tout, Thomas F. and Dorothy M. Broome. 'A national balance sheet for 1362—3, with documents subsidiary thereto', *EHR*, 39 (1924), 404—19. Important figures and discussion of technicalities.

1302 Trabut-Cussac, Jean-Paul. 'Le financement de la croisade anglaise de 1272', *Bibliothèque de l'école de chartes*, 119 (1962), 113—40.

1303 Tupling, George H. 'Markets and fairs in medieval Lancashire', *EHJT*, 345—57. Especially thirteenth century; and also 'The origins of markets and fairs in medieval Lancashire and their tolls', *Lancs.Antiq.*, 49 (1933), 75—94; 50 (1934—35), 107—37; 51 (1936), 86—110.

1304 Veale, Elspeth M. 'Craftsmen and the economy of London in the fourteenth century', in Albert E.J. Hollaender and William Kellaway (eds.). *Studies in local history presented to Philip Edmund Jones*. 1969, 133—61. Impact of war with France: a preliminary study; and Martin Weinbaum. 'Das Londoner Iter von 1341', *EHJT*, 399—405. Discusses impact of war.

1305 Ward, Grace F. 'The early history of the merchant staplers', *EHR*, 33 (1918), 297—318. Supplements Charles Gross. *The gild merchant*. Oxford, 1890.

1306 Weinbaum, Martin. 'Beiträge zur älteren englischen Gewerbe- und Handelsgeschichte', *Vierteljahrschrift für Sozial-und Wirtschaftsgeschichte*, 18 (1925), 277—311.

1307 ——— 'Stalhof und Deutsche Gildhalle zu London', *Hans.Gesch.*, 33 (1928), 45—65.

1308 Whiting, Charles E. 'The Durham trade gilds', *Architectural and Archaeological Society of Durham and Northumberland Transactions*, 9 (1942—44), 143—262, 265—416.

1309 Willard, James F. 'The assessment of lay subsidies, 1290—1332', *American Historical Association Annual Report for 1917* (1920), 283—92; also 'An early exchequer tally', *BJRL*, 7 (1923), 269—78. Illustration (1293). Conjectures that their use in the system of drawing on the tax collector was an innovation of the first decade of the fourteenth century; 'The memoranda rolls and remembrancers, 1282—1350', *EPTT*, 215—29; 'A brief guide to the records dealing with the tax on movables, 1290—1350', *American Historical Association Annual report for 1922*. Vol. 3 (1926),

27–37; 'The crown and its creditors, 1327–1333', *EHR*, 42 (1927), 12–19; 'An exchequer reform under Edward I', in Louis J. Paetow (ed.). *The crusades and other historical essays presented to Dana C. Munro* ... New York, 1928, 225–44; 'The treasurer's issue roll and the clerk of the treasurer, Edward I–Edward III', *BIHR*, 8 (1931), 129–35.

VIII. AGRICULTURAL HISTORY

1 Printed Sources

1310 Ault, Warren O. (ed.). *Court rolls of the abbey of Ramsey and of the honor of Clare.* New Haven, Conn., 1928. Mainly from the late thirteenth and early fourteenth centuries. Uneven editing.

1311 Bannister, Arthur T. (ed.). *A transcript of 'the red book' of the bishopric of Hereford.* Royal Historical Society. Camden Miscellany, 15 (1929).

1312 Barley, Maurice W. (ed.). *Documents relating to the manor and soke of Newark-on-Trent.* Thoroton Society, 16 (1956). Important discussion of agrarian questions.

1313 Bishop, Terrence A.M. (ed.). 'An extent of Barton in Richmondshire, 1309', *Yorks.Arch.J.*, 32 (1934), 86–97.

1314 Boulton, Helen E. (ed.). *The Sherwood Forest book.* Thoroton Society, 23 (1965). Prints earliest extant forest book; late fourteenth or early fifteenth century.

1315 Brett-James, Norman G. 'Some extents and surveys of Hendon', *Transactions of the London and Middlesex Archaeological Society*, n.s., 6 [1929–33] (1933), 547–78. Hendon survey of 1321.

1316 Brooke, Christopher N.L. and Michael M. Postan (eds.). *Carte nativorum. A Peterborough abbey cartulary of the fourteenth century.* Northants Record Society, 20 (1960). Interesting collection of charters recording buying and selling of land, chiefly by villeins.

1317 Cripps-Day, Francis H. (ed.). *The manor farm. To which are added reprint-facsimiles of 'The Boke of Husbandry'... by Walter of Henley... and 'The Boke of Thrift'...* 1931.

1318 Dale, Marion R. (ed. and trans.). *Court roll of Chalgrave manor, 1278–1313. BedsRec*, 28 (1950).

1319 Farr, Michael W. (ed.). *Accounts and surveys of the Wiltshire lands of Adam of Stratton.* Wiltshire Archaeological Survey, 14 (1959). Late thirteenth century. Of great interest to the economic historian. See also Ralph B. Pugh (ed.). *Court rolls of the Wiltshire manors of Adam de Stratton.* Wiltshire Archaeological Society, 24 (1968). Late thirteenth century.

1320 Hardy, William Le. 'Harefield deeds. Tarleton family documents', *Transactions of the London and Middlesex Archaeological Society*, n.s., 10 [1947–51] (1951), 244–51. Prints agreement as to enclosure of land, 1316, text, translation, and plate.

1321 Hilton, Rodney H. (ed.). *The Stoneleigh leger book.* Dugdale Society, 24 (1960). Contains varied material including charters and other records. Valuable Introduction.

1322 Hunt, Timothy J. (ed.). *The medieval customs of the manors of Taunton and Bradford on Tone.* Somerset Record Society Publications, 66 (1962). Includes an extent of Taunton, 1243–52 and a customal of Bradford, 1353. Illustrates growth of population.

1323 Jenkinson, C. Hilary and Helen M. Briggs (eds.). *Surrey manorial accounts.* Surrey Record Society, 37 (1935). Introduction of fifty-five pp. dealing especially with methods of accounting.

1324 *Legal and manorial formularies edited from originals at the B.M. and the P.R.O., in memory of Julius P. Gilson.* Oxford, 1933.

1325 Lister, John and John W. Walker (eds.). *Court rolls of the manor of Wakefield.* Vols. 3–5, 1313–31. *Yorks.Arch.Rec.*, 57–109 (1917–45).

1326 Morris, Lawrence E. (ed.). 'A customal of Ruislip', *Transactions of London and Middlesex Archaeological Society*, 19 (1958), 22—33. Dates from the thirteenth century, *c.* 1288. There is a translation from a transcript by Marjorie Chibnall.

1327 Neilson, G. Nellie (ed.). 'A terrier of Fleet, Lincolnshire', in *Records of the social and economic history of England and Wales*. Vol. 4. British Academy, 1920.

1328 —— *The cartulary and terrier of the priory of Bilsington, Kent.* 1928. Documents belong mainly to the thirteenth and fourteenth centuries.

1329 Oschinsky, Dorothea (ed.). *Walter of Henley and other treatises on estate management and accounting.* Oxford, 1971. A new, standard text.

1330 Page, Frances M. (ed.). *Wellingborough manorial accounts, 1258—1323, from the account rolls of Crowland abbey.* Northants Record Society, 8 (1936). Reprinted Northampton, 1968 by Trevor H. Aston with a note on the dating of the rolls. Valuable.

1331 Redstone, Lillian J. 'Westminster abbey muniments: some Hendon farm accounts', *Transactions of the London and Middlesex Archaeological Society*, n.s., 7 (1934), 71—90.

1332 Salzmann, Louis F. (ed.). *Minister's accounts of the manor of Petworth, 1347—53.* Sussex Record Society, 55 (1955). In English translation only, but by a fine scholar. Gives material for effects of Black Death.

1333 Stitt, Frederick B. (ed.). *London priory estate accounts 1296 to 1298.* Thoroton Society, 19 (1959). Introduction discusses agrarian and economic questions.

1334 Willis, Dorothy (ed.). *The estate book of Henry de Bray of Harleston.* Camden Society, ser. 3, 27 (1916). Henry died about 1340. His book gives many details of the parish of Harleston near Northampton.

2 Surveys

1335 Ault, Warren O. *Open-field farming in medieval England: a study of village by-laws.* New York, 1972. In effect a new ed. of *Open-field husbandry and the village community.* Philadelphia, Penna., 1965.

1336 Bennett, Henry S. *Life on the English manor. A study of peasant conditions, 1150—1400.* Cambridge, 1937; see also George G. Coulton on the village, no. 1350; Albert C. Chibnall. *Sherington: fiefs and fields of a Buckinghamshire village.* Cambridge, 1965. An excellent study; J. Ambrose Raftis. *Tenure and mobility: studies in the social history of the medieval English village.* Studies and Texts, no. 8. Toronto, 1964. A fine pioneer work; Arthur G. Rushton and Denis Witney. *Hooton Pagnell, the agricultural evolution of a Yorkshire village.* 1934; Maurice W. Beresford. *The lost villages of England.* 1954; 4th ed., 1963, with corrections. A very significant study; Maurice W. Beresford and John G. Hurst. *Studies in medieval villages.* 1971. Keith J. Allison *et al. The deserted villages of Oxfordshire,* and *The deserted villages of Northamptonshire.* University of Leicester, Department of English Local History Occasional Papers, no. 17 (1965) and no. 18 (1966); Norman S.B. and Ethel C. Gras. *The economic and social history of an English village (Crawley, Hampshire) A.D. 909—1928.* Cambridge, Mass., 1930.

1337 Duby, Georges. *L'économie rurale et la vie des campagnes dans l'Occident médiéval.* Paris, 1962. Trans. C. Postan as *Rural economy and country life in the medieval West.* New York, 1968. See also Duby's 'Les campagnes anglaises au moyen âge', *Annales, économies, sociétés, civilisations*, 15 (1966), 549—55.

1338 Ernle, Lord [Rowland G. Prothero]. *English farming past and present.* ed. Alfred D. Hall. 6th ed., 1936. Contains new Introduction by George E. Fussell and Oliver R. McGregor.

1339 Hodgett, Gerald A.J. *Agrarian England in the later Middle Ages.* 1966.

1340 Hoskins, William G. *The making of the English landscape.* 1955. An authoritative and sometimes poetic survey.

1341 Jones, Eric L. *Seasons and prices. The role of the weather in English agricultural history.* 1964.

1342　Orwin, Charles S. *A history of English farming*. 1949. A valuable survey.
1343　―――― and Christabel S. Orwin. *The open fields*. Oxford, 1938; 2nd ed., Oxford, 1954. Breaks much new ground. Second ed. contains important changes.
1344　Sylvester, Dorothy. *The rural landscape of the Welsh borderland: a study in historical geography*. New York, 1969.
1345　Thirsk, Joan (ed.). *The agrarian history of England and Wales*. Vol. 4. Cambridge, 1967.
1346　Titow, Jan Z. *English rural society 1200–1350*. 1969. A good introduction for students.
1347　Vinogradoff, Paul. *Villeinage in England: essays in English medieval history*. New York, 1968. First ed. Oxford, 1892; see also Rodney H. Hilton. 'Freedom and villeinage in England', *PP*, 31 (1965), 3–19.

3 Monographs

1348　Clark, George N. *Open fields and enclosures at Marston near Oxford*. 1924. A small pamphlet, but represents a well-digested piece of historical research.
1349　Cook, Arthur R. *A manor through four centuries*. Oxford, 1938.
1350　Coulton, George G. *The medieval village*. Cambridge, 1925. Valuable, but suffers from its wide geographical and chronological range.
1351　Curtler, William H.R. *The enclosure and redistribution of our land*. Oxford, 1920.
1352　Darby, H. Clifford. *The medieval Fenland*. Cambridge, 1940. From early times to end of fifteenth century. The standard work.
1353　Eland, George. *At the courts of Great Canfield*. Oxford, 1949. Contributes to the stock of material available for manorial history.
1354　Emmison, Frederick G. *Types of open-field parishes in the Midlands*. Historical Association Pamphlet, no. 108 (1937). Has three maps.
1355　Finberg, Herbert P.R. *The making of the English landscape: Gloucestershire*. 1955. A good general survey.
1356　Hallam, Herbert E. *Settlement and society: a study of the early agrarian history of South Lincolnshire*. Cambridge, 1965. Covers the period 1086– *c.* 1250. An important pioneer work.
1357　Hatcher, John. *Rural economy and society in the duchy of Cornwall, 1300– 1500*. Oxford, 1970.
1358　Hilton, Rodney H. *Economic development of some Leicestershire estates in the 14th and 15th centuries*. Oxford, 1947. By an outstanding authority.
1359　Hockey, Stanley F. *Quarr abbey and its lands, 1132–1631*. Leicester, 1970.
1360　Hoskins, William G. *Midland England*. 1949. Survey of country between Chiltern and Trent. Seminal.
1361　―――― (ed.). *Studies in Leicestershire agrarian history*. Leicestershire Archaeological Society. 1948. Includes paper by Rodney H. Hilton (manor of Kebworth Harcourt).
1362　Kosminsky, Eugeny A. *Studies in the agrarian history of England in the thirteenth century*, ed. Rodney H. Hilton. Oxford, 1956. The most comprehensive and expert study of English rural society in the middle ages since Vinogradoff's *Villeinage in England*. Translation is by Rodney H. Hilton and R. English. See comments by Trevor Aston. 'The English manor', *PP*, 10 (1956), 6–14; see also Eugeny Kosminsky. 'Services and money rents in the thirteenth century', *EcHR*, 5–6 (1935), 24–45; 'The evolution of feudal rent in England from the XIth to the XVth centuries', *PP*, 7 (1955), 12–36; 'The hundred rolls of 1279–80 as a source for English agrarian history', *EcHR*, 3 (1931–32), 16–44. See also Charles S. Orwin. 'Observations on the open fields', *EcHR*, 8 (1938), 125–35; Joan Thirsk. 'The common fields', *PP*, 29 (1964), 3–25. Argues for crucial developments in the twelfth and thirteenth centuries. Criticized in Jan Z. Titow. 'Medieval England and the open-field system', *PP*, 32 (1965), 86–102. Lively and convincing comments. See also Titow's 'Some differences between manors and their effects on the condition of

the peasant in the thirteenth century', in Walter E. Minchinton (ed.). *Essays in agrarian history*. Vol. 1. Newton Abbot, 1968. Supports the view of overpopulation, thirteenth century, and the benefits brought by disasters of 1315–17 and the Black Death. See also Edmund King. *Peterborough abbey, 1086–1310: a study in the land market*. New York, 1973.

1363 Levett, Ada E. *Studies in manorial history*, ed. Helen M. Cam, Mary Coate, and Lucy S. Sutherland. Oxford, 1938. Valuable studies published posthumously.

1364 Newton, Kenneth C. (ed.). *Thaxted in the fourteenth century*. Chelmsford, 1960. Translations of related documents. Microfilm of originals available.

1365 Page, Frances M. *The estates of Crowland abbey*. Cambridge, 1934. From mid-thirteenth century until 1529. A valuable book, throwing much light on manorial economy.

1366 Postan, Michael M. *The famulus, the estate labourer in the twelfth and thirteenth centuries*. Cambridge, 1954. An important analysis of the mixed forms of labour on the estates of the period.

1367 Raftis, J. Ambrose. *The estates of Ramsey abbey: a study in economic growth and organization*. Toronto, 1957. An original approach to agrarian history. Of first-rate importance.

1368 Waites, Bryan. *Moorland and vale-land farming in north-east Yorkshire: the monastic contribution in the thirteenth and fourteenth centuries*. St Anthony's Hall, Borthwick Papers, 32 (1967).

4 Articles

1369 Ault, Warren O. 'Some village by-laws', *EHR*, 45 (1930), 208–31. Early by-laws proceeded from the farming community rather than from the lord of the manor.

1370 Baker, Alan R.H. 'Field system in the vale of Holmesdale', *AgHR*, 14 (1966), 1–24.

1371 ——— 'Evidence in the "Nonarum Inquisitiones" of contracting arable lands in England during the early fourteenth century', *EcHR*, ser. 2, 19 (1966), 518–32.

1372 Barrow, Geoffrey W.S. 'Rural settlement in central and eastern Scotland: the medieval evidence', *Scottish Studies*, 6 (1962), 123–44.

1373 Beecham, Helen A. 'The review of the balks as strip boundaries in open fields', *AgHR*, 4 (1956), 22–44. A convincing criticism of Eric Kerridge. 'Ridge and furrow in agrarian history', *EcHR*, ser. 2, 4 (1951–52), 14–36; there is a reply in *AgHR*, 4 (1956), 121–22. See also Charles S. Orwin. 'Observations on the open fields', *AgHR*, 8 (1938), 125–35.

1374 Bennett, Merrill K. 'British wheat yield per acre for seven centuries', *Economic History*, 3 (1935), 12–29; also William H. Beveridge. 'The yield and price of corn in the Middle Ages', *Economic History*, 1 (1927), 155–67; 'Wheat measures in the Winchester rolls', *Economic History*, 2 (1930), 19–44.

1375 Birrell, Jean R. 'The forest economy of the honour of Tutbury in the fourteenth and fifteenth centuries', *UBHJ*, 8 (1962), 114–34; 'Peasant craftsmen in the medieval forest', *AgHR*, 17 (1969), 91–107.

1376 Bishop, Terence A.M. 'The distribution of manorial demesne in the vale of Yorkshire', *EHR*, 49 (1934), 386–406; and 'Monastic granges in Yorkshire', *EHR*, 51 (1936), 193–214, 758; 'Assarting and the growth of the open fields', *EcHR*, 6 (1935–36), 13–29. Special reference to central and east Yorkshire; also 'The rotation of crops at Westerham, 1297–1350', *EcHR*, 9 (1938–39), 38–44.

1377 Britnell, R.N. 'Production for the market on a small fourteenth-century estate', *EcHR*, ser. 2, 19 (1966), 380–87.

1378 Curwen, E. Cecil. *Air-photography and the evolution of the cornfield*. Economic History Society Bibliographies and Pamphlets, no. 2 (1938). Second ed. Illustrations.

1379 Denoon, D.G. and Trelawny Roberts. 'The extent of Edgware, A.D. 1277',

Transactions of the London and Middlesex Archaeological Society, n.s., 7 (1934), 158–74.

1380 Donkin, Robert A. 'A disposal of Cistercian wool in England and Wales during the 12th and 13th centuries', *Citeaux in de Nederlanden*, 8 (1957), 109–31, 181–96; also 'Settlement and depopulation on Cistercian estates during the twelfth and thirteenth centuries, especially in Yorkshire', *BIHR*, 33 (1960), 141–57. By 1300 the vigour of the High Middle Ages was spent, and settlement was tending to recede; 'Cattle on the estates of medieval Cistercian monasteries in England and Wales', *EcHR*, ser. 2, 15 (1962–63), 31–53. New light on Cistercian farming.

1381 Dyer, Christopher. 'Population and agriculture on a Warwickshire manor in the late Middle Ages', *UBHJ*, 11 (1968), 113–27.

1382 Eyre, Samuel R. 'The curving plough-strip and its historical implications', *AgHR*, 3 (1955), 80–94.

1383 Gowland, Tom S. 'The manors and liberties of Ripon', *Yorks.Arch.J.*, 32 (1934), 43–85.

1384 Grundy, George B. 'The ancient woodland of Wiltshire', *Wiltshire Archaeological and Natural History Magazine*, 48 (1939), 530–98.

1385 Halcrow, Elizabeth M. 'The decline of demesne farming on the estates of Durham cathedral priory', *EcHR*, ser. 2, 7 (1954–55), 345–56. Detects four phases in period thirteenth to fifteenth century.

1386 Hall, Hubert. 'Walter of Henley and the gospel of husbandry', *Contemporary Review*, 145 (1934), 573–81; also Hall and Frieda J. Nicholas. 'Manorial accounts of the priory of Canterbury, 1260–1420', *BIHR*, 8 (1931), 137–56.

1387 Hallam, Herbert E. 'The agrarian economy of medieval Lincolnshire before the Black Death', *Historical Studies, Australia and New Zealand*, 11 (1964), 163–69.

1388 Harley, John B. 'Population trends and agricultural developments from the Warwickshire hundred rolls of 1279', *EcHR*, ser. 2, 22 (1969), 17–27. Leasing not always to peasants, but rather often to 'gentry'.

1389 Hatcher, John. 'A diversified economy: later medieval Cornwall', *EcHR*, ser. 22 (1969), 208–27. Demographic decline did not create a slump in demand for land.

1390 Hilton, Rodney H. 'Peasant movements in England before 1381', *EcHR*, ser. 2, 2 (1949), 117–36. Emphasizes peasant discontents from early thirteenth century.

1391 ——— 'Gloucester abbey leases of the late 13th century', *EcHR*, ser. 2 (1953–54), 1–17. Includes transcripts of some leases. See also Barbara Harvey. 'The leasing of the abbot of Westminster's demesnes in the later Middle Ages', *EcHR*, ser. 2, 22 (1969), 17–27. Leasing not always to peasants, but rather often to gentry.

1392 ——— 'The content and sources of English agrarian history before 1500', *AgHR*, 3 (1957), 3–19. Good bibliographical survey.

1393 ——— 'Winchcombe abbey and the manor of Sherborne', in Herbert P.R. Finberg (ed.). *Gloucestershire studies*. Leicester, 1957, 89–113; 'Old enclosures in the west Midlands: a hypothesis about their late medieval developments', *Annales de l'Est mémoire no. 21: géographie et histoire agraires*. Nancy, 1959, 272–83.

1394 Homans, George C. 'Man and land in the Middle Ages', *Speculum*, 11 (1936), 338–51; 'Partible inheritance of villagers' holdings', *EcHR*, 8 (1937–38), 48–56; 'The explanation of English regional differences', *PP*, 42 (1969), 18–34. Fascinating and authoritative. For comments, see Rosamund J. Faith. 'Peasant families and inheritance customs in medieval England', *AgHR*, 14 (1966), 77–95; David Roden. 'Inheritance customs and succession to land in the Chiltern hills in the thirteenth and early fourteenth centuries', *JBS*, 7 (1967), 1–11.

1395 Jones, Glanville R.J. 'Some medieval rural settlements in North Wales', *Institute of British Geographers, Transactions*, 19 (1954), 51–72; also 'Medieval open fields and associated patterns in north-west Wales', *Annales de l'Est mémoire no. 21: géographie et histoire agraires*. Nancy,

1959, 313—28; 'The pattern of settlement on the Welsh border', *AgHR*, 8 (1960), 66—81.

1396 Jones-Pierce, Thomas. 'Some tendencies in the agrarian history of Caernarvonshire during the later Middle Ages', *Transactions of the Caernarvonshire Historical Society*, 1 (1939), 18—36.

1397 ——— 'The growth of commutation in Gwynedd during the thirteenth century', *BBCS*, 10 (1941), 309—32. Most important controversial discussion of North Welsh settlement patterns, using the post-Conquest enquiries of Edward I; 'Medieval settlement in Anglesey', *AngAntiq*, 21—23 (1951), 1—33.

1398 Joüon des Longrais, Frédéric. 'Le vilainage anglais et le servage réel et personnel, quelques remarques sur la période 1066—1485', *Recueil de la société Jean Bodin*. 1937, 199—242.

1399 Kershaw, Ian. 'The great famine and agrarian crisis in England, 1315—22', *PP*, 59 (1973), 3—50.

1400 Lennard, Reginald V. 'What is a manorial extent?', *EHR*, 44 (1929), 256—63; also 'Statistics of corn yields in medieval England: some critical questions', *Economic History*, 3 (1936), 173—92; 'Statistics of sheep in medieval England, a question of interpretation', *AgHR*, 6—7 (1959), 75—81. Calculation should be by 'hundred' meaning five score; 'Early manorial juries', *EHR*, 77 (1962), 511—18. Appeared in the second half of the twelfth century on ecclesiastical estates, for surveys and custumals; 'Agrarian history: some vistas and pitfalls', *AgHR*, 12 (1964), 83—98. Devastating criticisms by an expert.

1401 Miller, Edward E. 'The estates of the abbey of St Albans', *St Albans and Hertfordshire Architectural and Archaeological Society Transactions*, n.s., 5 (1939), 285—300.

1402 Otway-Ruthven, A. Jocelyn. 'The organization of Anglo-Irish agriculture in the Middle Ages', *Journal of the Royal Society of Antiquaries of Ireland*, 81 (1951), 1—13.

1403 Pelham, Reginald A. 'Studies in the historical geography of medieval Sussex', *Sussex Archaeological Collections*, 72 (1931), 157—84.

1404 Postan, Michael M. 'Village livestock in the thirteenth century', *EcHR*, ser. 2, 15 (1962—63), 219—49. Population increase in the thirteenth century caused pasture to decline and crops to increase; also 'The chronology of labour services', in Walter E. Minchinton (ed.). *Essays in agrarian history*. Vol. 1. Newton Abbot, 1968, 75—91. Reprinted after revision from *TRHS*, ser. 4, 20 (1937), 169—93. Suggests typical sequence from labour services to complete commutation and then back again to partial or complete labour services.

1405 Raftis, J. Ambrose. 'Marc Bloch's comparative method and the rural history of medieval England', *MS*, 24 (1962), 349—68; also 'The structure of commutation in a fourteenth century village', *EPBW*, 282—300. Investigates the complexities of commutation in the fourteenth century, breaking new ground. Part of a broad investigation.

1406 Richardson, Henry G. 'The medieval plough team', *History*, 26 (1942), 287—96. Important comments.

1407 Roberts, B.K. 'A study of medieval colonization in the forest of Arden, Warwickshire', *AgHR*, 16 (1968), 101—113; see also Eleanor C. Vollans. 'The evolution of farm lands in the central Chilterns in the twelfth and thirteenth centuries', *Transactions of the Institute of British Geographers*, 26 (1959), 197—241.

1408 Saltmarsh, John and H. Clifford Darby. 'The infield-outfield system on a Norfolk manor', *Economic History*, 3 (1935), 30—44.

1409 Smith, Reginald A.L. 'High farming on the Canterbury estates: a study in medieval agriculture', *Canterbury Catholic Chronicle*, 35 (1940), 10—15.

1410 Thomas, Colin. 'Thirteenth-century farm economies in north Wales', *AgHR*, 16 (1968), 1—14.

1411 Ugawa, Kaoru. 'The economic development of some Devon manors in the thirteenth century', *Transactions of the Devon Association*, 94 (1962), 630—83.

1412   Waites, Bryan. 'The monastic grange as a factor in the settlement of north-
        east Yorkshire', *Yorks.Arch.J.*, 40 (1962), 627—56.
1413   Watts, David G. 'A model for the early fourteenth century', *EcHR*, ser. 2, 20
        (1967), 543—47. Shows boom in peasant landmarket in early fourteenth
        century. Questions Postan's view of fourteenth century.
1414   Wilkinson, Bertie. 'The peasants' revolt of 1381', *Speculum*, 15 (1940), 12—
        35. Re-examines causes and motives. See also Edmund B. Fryde. 'British
        parliament and the peasants' revolt of 1381', in *Liber memorialis Georges
        de Lagarde. Études présentés à la commission international pour l'histoire
        des assemblées d'états*, 38. Louvain, 1970 [1969], 73—88.
1415   Wretts-Smith, Mildred. 'Organization of farming at Croyland abbey, 1257—
        1321', *Journal of Economic and Business History*, 4 (1932), 168—92.
1416   Yates, Edward M. 'Medieval assessments in north-west Sussex', *Transactions
        of the Institute of British Geographers*, 20 (1954), 75—92.

IX. SCIENCE AND TECHNOLOGY

1 Printed Sources

1417   Bacon, Roger. *Opera haectenus inedita Rogeri Baconi, Fac. IX, De Ratar-
        datione accidentium senectutis cum aliis opusculis de rebus medicinalibus*,
        ed. Andrew G. Little and Edward Withington. Oxford, 1928.
1418   ——— 'An unnoticed treatise of Roger Bacon on time and motion', ed. S.
        Harrison Thomson, *Isis*, 27 (1937), 219—24.
1419   Chaucer, Geoffrey. *Chaucer and Messahalla on the astrolabe. Now printed in
        full for the first time with the original illustrations*, ed. Robert W.T.
        Gunther. Oxford, 1929. Vol. 5 of *Early Science in Oxford*, 1920—32, 9
        vols.
1420   ——— *Chaucer's treatise on the astrolabe. MS. 4862—4869 of the royal
        library in Brussels*, ed. P. Pintelon. Antwerp, 1940.
1421   Grosseteste, Robert. *On Light (De Luce)*, trans. Clare C. Reidl. Milwaukee,
        Wis., 1942.
1422   ——— *Roberti Gresseteste episcopi Lincolniensis commentarius in VII libros
        physicorum Aristotelis*. Richard C. Dales. Boulder, Colo., 1963. An
        important addition to our knowledge about Robert.
1423   ——— 'Robert Grosseteste's treatise "De Finitate Motus et Temporis" ', ed.
        Richard C. Dales, *Traditio*, 19 (1963), 245—66.
1424   ——— 'The text of Robert Grosseteste's *Questio de fluxu et refluxu maris*',
        ed. Richard C. Dales, *Isis*, 57 (1966), 455—74.
1425   Ockham. William of. 'The prologue of Ockham's exposition of the physics of
        Aristotle', ed. Gaudens E. Mohun, *FS*, n.s., 5 (1945), 235—46.

2 Surveys

1426   Sarton, George. *Introduction to the history of science*. Vols. 2 and 3. Balti-
        more, Md., 1931—48. A survey of intellectual life in the thirteenth and
        fourteenth centuries that throws light on practically every problem that
        troubles the student of the period.
1427   Singer, Charles *et al.* (eds.). *A history of technology*. Vols. 2—5. Oxford,
        1956—58. Vol. 2 covers *c.* 700 B.C. to *c.* 1500 A.D. more in the form of
        annals than history proper, but authoritative.
1428   Talbot, Charles H. *Medicine in medieval England*. 1967. A scholarly, com-
        prehensive survey.

3 Monographs

1429   Aguirre y Respaldiza, Andrés. *La ciencia positiva en el siglo XIII. Rogerio
        Bacon*. Barcelona, 1935; also David C. Lindberg. 'Roger Bacon's theory
        of the rainbow: progress or regress?', *Isis*, 57 (1966), 235—48; and

Edward Rosen. 'Did Roger Bacon invent eyeglasses?', *Archives internationales d'histoire des sciences*, 7 (1954), 3—15; Clement C.J. Webb. 'Roger Bacon on Alphonse of Poitiers', *EPRP*, 290—300.

1430　Batten, Marjorie and David Smith. *English windmills.* 1932, 2 vols.

1431　Creighton, Charles. *A history of epidemics in Britain: from A.D. 664 to the extinction of the plague.* Cambridge, 1891, 2 vols. 2nd ed., 1965. Second ed. contains material by David E.C. Eversley, E. Ashworth Underwood, and Lynda Overnall.

1432　Crombie, Alistair C. *Oxford's contribution to the origins of modern science.* Oxford, 1954. Paper read to British Association for Advancement of Science.

1433　Crosby, Henry L., Jr. *Thomas of Bradwardine, his 'Tractatus de Proportionibus': its significance for the development of mathematical physics.* Madison, Wis., 1955.

1434　Effler, Roy R. *John Duns Scotus and the principle of 'omnes quod movetur ab alio movetur'.* New York, 1962.

1435　Fox, John C. *The medieval sciences in the works of John Gower.* Princeton, N.J., 1931.

1436　Gaselle, Stephan. 'Natural science in England at the end of the twelfth century', *Royal Institute of Great Britain*, 29 (1937), 397—417.

1437　Gunther, Robert W.T. *Early science in Oxford*, 1937. Vol. 11 of *Oxford colleges and their men of science.*

1438　Taylor, Eva G.R. *Ideas on the shape, size and movements of the earth.* Historical Association Pamphlet, no. 126 (1943).

1439　Taylor, Frank S. *The alchemists: founders of modern chemistry.* Baltimore, Md., 1948.

1440　Wedel, Theodore O. *The medieval attitude toward astrology, particularly in England.* New Haven, Conn., 1920. A valuable survey.

1441　Wilson, Curtis. *William Heytesbury, medieval logic and the rise of mathematical physics.* Madison, Wis., 1956. A valuable addition to works on fourteenth century.

4 Biographies

1442　Crombie, Alistair C. *Robert Grosseteste and the origins of experimental science 1100—1700.* Oxford, 1953. Broad sweep of a master.

1443　Curry, Walter C. *Chaucer and the medieval sciences.* New York, 1960. New ed. revised and enlarged.

1444　Easton, Stewart. *Roger Bacon and his search for a universal science.* Oxford, 1952. Valuable analysis: Bacon's limitations only serve to enhance his real greatness.

1445　Read, John. 'Michael Scot: a Scottish pioneer of science', *Scientia*, 64 (1938), 190—97.

5 Articles

1446　Aiken, Pauline. 'Vincent of Beauvais and Chaucer's knowledge of alchemy', *Studies in Philology*, 41 (1944), 371—89. See Edgar H. Duncan. 'The literature of alchemy and Chaucer's canon's yeoman's tale: framework, theme, and characters', *Speculum*, 43 (1968), 638—56; and Bruce L. Greenberg. 'The canon's yeoman's tale: Boethian wisdom and the alchemists', *Chaucer Review*, 1 (1966), 37—54; John D. North. 'Kalenderes enlumyned ben they: some astronomical themes in Chaucer', *Review of English Studies*, n.s., 20 (1969), 129—54, 257—83, 418—44; Hamilton M. Smyser. 'A view of Chaucer's astronomy', *Speculum*, 45 (1970), 359—73; John J. O'Connor. 'The astrological background of the miller's tale', *Speculum*, 31 (1956), 120—25.

1447　Bullough, Vern L. 'Medical study at medieval Oxford', *Speculum*, 36 (1961), 600—12. Traces evidence from the thirteenth to the fifteenth centuries.

1448　———— 'The medical school at Cambridge', *MS*, 24 (1962), 161—68.

1449　Cule, John. 'The court mediciner and medicine in the laws of Wales', *Journal of the History of Medicine*, 21 (1966), 213—36.

1450   Eastwood, Bruce C. 'Robert Grosseteste's theory of the rainbow. A chapter in the history of experimental science', *Archives internationales d'histoire des sciences*, 77 (1966), 313–32; also 'Grosseteste's quantitative law of refraction: a chapter in the history of non-experimental science', *Journal of the History of Ideas*, 28 (1967), 415–22; 'Medieval empiricism: the case of Grosseteste's optics', *Speculum*, 43 (1968), 306–21; also Alistair C. Crombie. 'Robert Grosseteste's position in the history of science', in Daniel A.P. Callus (ed.). *Robert Grosseteste scholar and bishop*. Oxford, 1955, 98–120. Includes an Appendix 'On the heat of the sun'; also Richard C. Dales. 'Robert Grosseteste's scientific works', *Isis*, 52 (1961), 381–402; and 'Robert Grosseteste's views on astrology', *MS*, 29 (1967), 357–63; and Colin M. Turbayne. 'Grosseteste and an ancient optical principle', *Isis*, 50 (1959), 467–72.

1451   Flemming, Percy. 'The medical aspect of the medieval monastery in England', *Proceedings of the Royal Society of Medicine*, 22 (1928), 771–82.

1452   Garbáty, Thomas J. 'The summoner's occupational disease', *Medical History*, 7 (1963), 348–58.

1453   Hammond, Eugene A. 'Physicians in medieval English religious houses', *Bulletin of the History of Medicine*, 32 (1958), 105–20.

1454   —— 'The Westminster abbey infirmarer's rolls as a source of medical history', *Bulletin of the History of Medicine*, 39 (1965), 261–76.

1455   Harting, Edward F. 'Medical education in the 12th century', *Medical Life*, 41 (1934), 20–31.

1456   Hill, Boyd H., Jr. 'The grain and the spirit in medieval anatomy', *Speculum*, 40 (1965), 63–73. Includes some observations on Chaucer.

1457   Lennox, William G. 'John Gaddesden on epilepsy', *Annals of Medical History*, ser. 3 (1939), 283–307. John was an English physician, 1280–1361.

1458   MacKinney, Loren C. and Harry Bober. 'A thirteenth century medical case history in miniature', *Speculum*, 35 (1960), 251–59.

1459   Mayer, Claudius F. 'A medieval English leechbook and its XIVth century poem on bloodletting', *Institute of History of Medicine Bulletin*, 7 (1939), 381–91.

1460   Russell, Josiah C. 'Hereford and Arabic science in England about 1175–1200', *Isis*, 18 (1932), 14–25.

1461   —— 'Medical writers of thirteenth-century England', *Annals of medical history*, n.s., 7 (1935), 327–40.

1462   Sharp, Dorothea E. 'The *De ortu scientiarum* of Robert Kilwardby', *New Scholasticism*, 8 (1934), 1–30.

1463   Thorndike, Lynn. 'A new work by Robert Holkot (Corpus Christi college, Oxford, MS. 138)', *Archives internationales d'histoire des sciences*, 40 (1957), 227–235. A scientific treatise.

1464   Vogt, Berard. 'The "Forma corporeitatis" of Duns Scotus and modern science', *FS*, n.s., 3 (1943), 47–62.

X. MILITARY AND NAVAL HISTORY

1 Printed Sources

1465   Coopland, George W. (ed.). *The tree of battles on Honoré Bonet*. Cambridge, Mass., 1952. A comprehensive guide to the laws of chivalry; a fourteenth-century bestseller. Text in translation only. Throws light on medieval law of nations and of war.

1466   Fryde, Edmund B. (ed.). *Book of prests of the king's wardrobe for 1294–5.* [Presented to John Goronwy Edwards.] Oxford, 1962. Illuminating and scholarly examination of Welsh war and its financing.

1467   Jones, Evan J. (ed.). *Medieval heraldry: some fourteenth century heraldic works.* Cardiff, 1943. With English translation, an Introduction by Jones and foreword by Anthony R. Wagner.

2 Surveys

1468   Blair, Claude. *European armour circa 1066 to circa 1700.* New York, 1957.
First general survey in English for fifty years. Will become a standard
work.
1469   Brown, R. Allen. *English medieval castles.* 1955. The best account up to date.
Excellent illustrations.
1470   Keen, Maurice H. *The laws of war in the late Middle Ages.* 1965. Wide-ranging
and important.
1471   Marcus, Geoffrey J. *Naval history of England.* Vol. 1. Boston, 1961.
1472   Oman, Charles W.C. *The art of war in the Middle Ages, A.D. 578—1515,* ed.
and revised by John H. Beeler. Ithaca, N.Y., 1953. Corrects some con-
spicuous errors in the original (1885); also John H. Beeler. *Warfare in
England 1066—1189.* Ithaca, N.Y., 1966. A most stimulating volume,
though it has to be handled with care. Discusses strategy and tactics of
military operations.
1473   Sanders, Ivor J. *Feudal military service in England: a study of the constitutional and military power of the barons in medieval England.* 1955.
Important but uneven; also *English baronies: a study of their origin and
descent.* Oxford, 1960. An alphabetical directory to the baronies with
information about military duties.
1474   Toy, Sidney. *The castles of Great Britain.* 1953. A fine survey, with photographs and measured drawings.

3 Monographs

1475   Allmand, Christopher T. (ed.). *Society at war: the experience of England and
France during the Hundred Years' War.* New York, 1973.
1476   Barron, Evan M. *The Scottish war of independence: a critical study.* 2nd ed.,
Inverness, 1934. Written from the Celtic point of view.
1477   Brooks, Frederick W. *The English naval forces, 1199—1272.* 1932. See also
Romola and Roger C. Anderson. *The sailing ships.* 1926. A standard work.
1478   Burne, Alfred H. *The Crécy war: military history of the Hundred Years' war
from 1337 to the peace of Brétigny, 1360.* 1955. Vivid, but somewhat
uneven.
1479   Chew, Helena M. *The ecclesiastical tenants-in-chief and knight service
especially in the thirteenth and fourteenth centuries.* 1932. A good book.
Discusses the spread of scutage and the problem of the decline of
feudalism.
1480   Clapham, R.C. *The tournament, its periods and phases.* 1919.
1481   Cripps-Day, Francis H. *The history of the tournament in England and France.*
1918. Illustrated.
1482   Denquin, Marcel. *Calais sous la domination anglaise, 1347—1558.* Calais,
1939.
1483   Hewitt, Herbert J. *The Black Prince's expedition of 1351—1357.* 1958. The
best study of English warfare in France in these years. See also Hewitt's
The organization of war under Edward III. Manchester, 1966. Much
scholarly detail.
1484   Hope, William H. St J. *A grammar of English heraldry,* ed. and revised
Anthony R. Wagner. Cambridge, 1953. Wagner is the outstanding authority.
1485   Leask, Harold G. *Irish castles and castellated houses.* Dundalk, 1941; 2nd ed.,
1946. William M. Mackenzie. *The medieval castle in Scotland.* 1927.
Scholarly; illustrated.
1486   Levi, Camille B. *La bataille de Bouvines (dimanche, 27 Juillet 1214).*
Bayonne, 1934.
1487   Mackenzie, William M. *The Bannockburn myth.* Edinburgh, 1932; and see
also Thomas Miller. *The site of the battle of Bannockburn: new evidence
and reply to Dr Mackenzie.* Stirling, 1933.
1488   Mann, James G. *An outline of arms and armour in England.* 1960.

1489   Miller, Edward E. *War in the North: the Anglo-Scottish wars of the Middle Ages*. University of Hull Publications. 1960. Excellent.
1490   Morris, John E. *The Welsh wars of Edward I*. Oxford, 1901; Reprinted 1968. The standard work; still invaluable.
1491   O'Neil, Bryan H. St J. *Castles and cannon. A study of early fortifications in England*. Oxford, 1960.
1492   Painter, Sidney. *Studies in the history of the English feudal barony*. Baltimore, Md., 1943. Important for changes in the twelfth and thirteenth centuries. Argues that the body provided for in clause 14, Magna carta, was an abortive innovation.
1493   Powicke, Michael R. *Military obligation in medieval England: a study in liberty and duty*. Oxford, 1962. A good, clear survey, with an attractive theme.
1494   Prestwich, Michael C. *War, politics and finance under Edward I*. Totowa, N.J., 1972. Authoritative; also 'A new account of the Welsh campaign of 1294–5', *WHR*, 6 (1972), 89–94.
1495   Sandberger, Dietrich. *Studien über das Rittertum in England vornehmlich während des 14 Jahrhunderts*. Berlin, 1937.
1496   Schlight, John. *Monarchs and mercenaries: a reappraisal of the importance of knight service in Norman and early Angevin England*. Bridgeport, Conn., 1968. Justly emphasizes the importance of mercenaries but exaggerates their role.
1497   Timbal, Pierre C.M.J. *et al. La guerre de Cent Ans vue à traves les registres du parlement, 1337–1369*. Paris, 1961. A study of the conduct of war. Half the volume consists of transcripts from the registers. Preface by André Chamson.
1498   Tremlett, John D. (ed.). *Rolls of arms of Henry III: the Matthew Paris shields; c. 1244–59*. 1967. Includes Glover's roll *c.* 1253–58 and Walford's roll *c.* 1273.
1499   Turner, Hilary L. *Town defences in England and Wales*. 1971.
1500   Wagner, Anthony R. *Historic heraldry of Britain. An illustrated series of British historical arms, with notes, glossary and introduction to heraldry*. Oxford, 1939. By a leading expert. With 142 illustrations; also John D. Tremlett (ed.). *Aspilogia, a catalogue of English medieval rolls of arms*. 2nd ed., 1967, 2 vols. First published Oxford, 1952. Tremlett's ed. includes additions and corrections to Vol. 1. Invaluable. See also *The records and collections of the College of Arms*. 1952; *Heralds of England: A history of the office and college of arms*. 1967. HMSO. A standard work; Anthony Wagner *et al. Royal and princely heraldry in Wales*. 1969. Contains English as well as Welsh heraldry.

4 Articles

1501   Allmand, Christopher T. 'War and profit in the late Middle Ages', *History Today*, 15 (1965), 762–69.
1502   Barnes, Patricia and Geoffrey W.S. Barrow. 'The movements of Robert Bruce between September 1307 and May 1308', *SHR*, 49 (1970), 46–59. The real turning point in Bruce's fortunes. Prints two unpublished letters.
1503   Beeler, John H. 'Towards a revaluation of medieval English generalship', *JBS*, 3 (1963), 1–10.
1504   Blair, Claude H.H. 'The early castles of Northumberland', *ArchAel*, ser. 4, 22 (1944), 116–68.
1505   ———— 'Knights of Durham who fought at Lewes 14 May, 1264', *ArchAel*, ser. 4, 24 (1946), 183–216.
1506   Brooks, Frederick W. 'William de Wrotham and the office of keeper of the king's ports and galleys', *EHR*, 40 (1925), 570–79. In the time of John: William performed functions later pertaining to the office of admiral; 'The king's ships and galleys mainly under John and Henry III', *Mariner's Mirror*, 15 (1929), 15–48. Enlargement under John and Henry III; 'The Cinq ports in the 12th and 13th centuries', *Mariner's Mirror*, 15 (1929), 148–208. Prints the charter of 1278 and compares raising the armies and

fleets; 'The battle of Damme, 1213', *Mariner's Mirror*, 16 (1930), 263–71. Connected with the idea of wider potentialities of the English fleet; 'The Cinque ports' feud with Yarmouth in the thirteenth century', *Mariner's Mirror*, 19 (1933), 27–51. The struggle of Yarmouth against the privileges of the barons of the Cinque ports and its influence on maritime organization.

1507 Brown, R. Allen. 'A list of castles, 1154–1216', *EHR*, 74 (1959), 249–80. A valuable compilation, with good Introduction.

1508 Burne, Alfred H. 'The battle of Poitiers', *EHR*, 53 (1938), 21–52. Reconstruction of events. Strongly questioned by Vivian H. Galbraith in 'The battle of Poitiers', *EHR*, 54 (1939), 473–75.

1509 Carr, Antony D. 'Welshmen and the Hundred Years' War', *WHR*, 4 (1968–69), 21–46. Gives very interesting details.

1510 Contamine, Philippe. 'La guerre de Cent Ans en France: une approche économique', *BIHR*, 47 (1947), 125–49.

1511 Dimmock, H.L.F. 'Some musings on the battle of Lewes, A.D. 1264', *Royal Artillery Journal*, 61 (1934), 258–67.

1512 Edwards, J. Goronwy. 'The battle of Maes Madog and the Welsh war of 1294–5', *EHR*, 39 (1924), 1–12. Revises the accepted view of the battle.

1513 ——— 'The site of the battle of Meismeidoc, 1295', *EHR*, 46 (1931), 262–65.

1514 ——— 'Edward I's castle-building in Wales', [Sir John Rhys Memorial Lecture] *PBA*, 32 (1946), 15–81. Includes estimate of the cost of these building operations.

1515 ——— 'Henry II and the fight at Coleshill: some further reflections', *WHR*, 3 (1966–67), 251–63. Questions some conclusions by David J.C. King in *WHR*, 2 (1964–65), 367–73.

1516 Freeman, Alvin Z. 'The king's penny: the headquarters paymasters under Edward I, 1295–1307', *JBS*, 6 (1966), 1–22. Explains the smooth supply of supplies and money to Edward's armies.

1517 ——— 'A moat defensive: the coast defence scheme of 1295', *Speculum*, 42 (1967), 442–62. A good analysis, showing the thoroughness of preparations.

1518 Herben, Stephen H.J., Jr. 'Arms and armour in Chaucer', *Speculum*, 12 (1937), 474–87. Valuable. Includes references to cannon; also Oliver G.F. Hogg. 'English artillery in the fourteenth century', *Royal Artillery Journal*, 71 (1944), 27–39.

1519 Keen, Maurice H. 'Brotherhood in arms', *History*, 47 (1962), 1–17. The compact of brothers-in-arms and its relation to chivalry.

1520 Keeney, Barnaby C. 'Military service and the development of nationalism, 1272–1327', *Speculum*, 22 (1947), 534–49. The importance of the community of the realm in the development of national monarchy and of national feeling.

1521 Lewis, Norman B. 'The English forces in Flanders, August–November 1297', *SPFP*, 310–18.

1522 ——— 'The recruitment and organization of a contract army, May to November, 1337', *BIHR*, 37 (1964), 1–19. Experiments in recruiting a volunteer army. A very significant essay.

1523 ——— 'The organization of indentured routines in fourteenth-century England', in Richard Southern (ed.). *Essays in medieval history selected from the 'transactions' of the Royal Historical Society on the occasion of its century.* 1968, 200–12. The indentured retinue a steadying influence in society. A sound view opposed to those of many modern writers.

1524 ——— 'The summons of the English feudal levy, 5 April 1327', *EPBW*, 236–49.

1525 Lydon, James F. 'The Bruce invasion of Ireland', *Historical Studies*, 4 (1963), 111–25.

1526 ——— 'Irish levies in the Scottish wars 1296–1302', *Historical Studies*, 5 (1963), 207–17.

1527 Moor, Charles. 'Knights of Edward I', *Harleian Society*, 80–84 (1929–32). Intended as a preliminary study of knightly family about temp. Edward I.

See also Eric St J. Brooks. *Knights fees in the counties of Wexford, Carlow and Kilkenny (13th–15th century)*. Dublin, 1950; Sally Harvey. 'The knight and the knight's fee in England', *PP*, 49 (1970), 3–43.

1528   Nicholson, Ranald. 'The siege of Berwick, 1333', *SHR*, 40 (1961), 19–42.

1529   —— 'The last campaign of Robert Bruce', *EHR*, 77 (1962), 233–46. Emphasises the importance of the military events of 1327.

1530   —— 'An Irish invasion of Scotland in 1335', *Irish Historical Studies*, 13 (1963), 197–211.

1531   Painter, Sidney. 'Castle-guard', *AHR*, 40 (1935), 450–59.

1532   —— 'English castles in the early Middle Ages: their number location, and legal position', *Speculum*, 10 (1935), 321–32. Still illuminating.

1533   Powicke, Michael R. 'Distraint of knighthood and military obligation under Henry III', *Speculum*, 25 (1950), 457–70. A careful analysis: shows that the purpose was military as well as financial; see also John S. Critchley. 'Summonses to military service early in the reign of Henry III', *EHR*, 86 (1971), 79–95.

1534   —— 'The general obligation to cavalry service under Edward I', *Speculum*, 28 (1953), 814–33. Edward reinforced the feudal force with a paid, national army.

1535   —— 'Edward II and military obligation', *Speculum*, 31 (1956), 83–119. An important analysis of the attitude of king and barons towards service in the militia.

1536   —— 'The English commons in Scotland in 1322 and the deposition of Edward II', *Speculum*, 35 (1960), 556–62.

1537   Prestwich, Michael. 'A new account of the Welsh campaign of 1294–95', *WHR*, 6 (1972), 89–94.

1538   Prince, Albert E.M. 'A letter of the Black Prince describing the battle of Nágara in 1367', *EHR*, 41 (1926), 415–18.

1539   —— 'The indenture system under Edward III', *EHJT*, 283–99. An important pioneer work on the subject.

1540   —— 'The importance of the campaign of 1327', *EHJT*, 299–302. Shows evidence of guns and uniforms.

1541   —— 'The payment of army wages in Edward III's reign', *Speculum*, 19 (1944), 137–60. Argues that the indenture system was a potent factor in the passing of the feudal system and wardrobe financing. Good pioneer study.

1542   —— 'The strength of the English armies in the reign of Edward III', *EHR*, 46 (1931), 353–71. Prints an indenture of 1346. Prince laid solid foundations for the later study of military service.

1543   —— 'The army and navy', *EGAW*, 1, 332–93. Still a most valuable contribution to the subject.

1544   Reid, W. Stanford. 'Sea power in the Anglo-Scottish war, 1296–1328', *Mariner's Mirror*, 46 (1960), 7–23. The part played by sea power under Edward I and Edward II was of great importance.

1545   Searle, Eleanor and Robert Burghart. 'The defence of England and the Peasants' revolt', *Viator*, 3 (1972), 365–88.

1546   Sherborne, James W. 'Indentured retinues and English expeditions to France, 1369–1380', *EHR*, 79 (1964), 718–46.

1547   —— 'The Hundred Years' War: the English navy, shipping, and manpower', *PP*, 37 (1967), 163–75.

1548   —— 'The battle of La Rochelle and the war at sea, 1372–5', *BIHR*, 42 (1969), 17–29. La Rochelle was not the naval disaster it has been thought to have been.

1549   Simpson, W. Douglas. 'Bodian castle', *Edinburgh Review*, 243 (1926), 355–64; 'James de Sancto Georgio', *AngAntiq*. The builder of several of the Edwardian castles in Wales; 'Castles of "livery and maintenance" ', *JBAA*, ser. 3, 4 (1939), 39–54. Compares Britain with France, and with Teutonic Order; 'The Warkworth donjon and its architect', *ArchAel*, 19 (1941), 93–103; ' "Bastard Feudalism" and the later castles', *Antiquaries Journal*, 26 (1946), 145–71.

1550   Treharne, Reginald F. 'The battle of Northampton, 5 April, 1264',

Northampton past and present. Northants Record Society, 2 (1955), 13–30. Discusses the strategic and political importance of Northampton in the barons' war of 1264–5.

1551   Viard, Jules. 'Le siège de Calais 4 Septembre 1346–4 Août 1347', *Le moyen âge*, 29–30 (1928–9), 129–89.

1552   Whiting, B. Jere. 'The vows of the heron', *Speculum*, 20 (1945), 261–78. The story of the vows of the heron convincingly described as 'a grimly satirical document', reflecting opposition to Edward III's war in the Low Countries.

XI. RELIGIOUS HISTORY

1 Printed Sources

1553   Adam, abbot of Eynsham. *Magna vita sancti Hugonis. The life of St Hugh of Lincoln*, ed. Decima L. Douie and Hugh Farmer. Edinburgh, 1961–62, 2 vols. Written soon after 1212. This is an excellent ed., but with one or two dubious translations.

1554   Ailred of Rievaulx. *De anima*, ed. Charles H. Talbot. 1952. Introduction mainly on Ailred's intellectual background and capacities.

1555   Barnes, Patricia M. and W. Raymond Powell (eds.). *Interdict documents.* Pipe Roll Society, 34 (1960). Royal surveys of lands made during the interdict of John's reign, and texts concerning the administration of Christ Church Canterbury.

1556   Baugh, Albert C. (ed.). *The English text of the Ancrene Riwle, Brit. Mus. MS. Royal 8 C.I.* Early English Text Society. Oxford, 1956; Mary S. Salu. (trans.). *The Ancrene Riwle (the corpus MS): Ancrene Wisse.* Notre Dame, Ind., 1955. Introduction by Gerard Sitwell. Preface by John R.R. Tolkien; William H. Trethewey. *The French text of the Ancrene Riwle.* Early English Text Society, 240 (1958); Geoffrey Shepherd (ed.). *Ancrene Wisse.* Parts six and seven. 1959. With an explanation of what the work meant to the thirteenth-century author and audience; E.J. Dobson. 'The date and composition of Ancrene Wisse', *PBA*, 52 (1966), 181–208.

1557   Bishop, Terance A.M. (ed.). 'Extents of the prebends of York (*c.* 1295)', *Yorks.Arch.Rec.*, 93 (1937), 175–89.

1558   Bosham, Herbert of. 'The Arras of MS. of Herbert of Bosham', ed. Theodore Craib, *EHR*, 35 (1920), 218–23. Prints pp. missing from the life of St Thomas of Canterbury.

1559   Brakelond, Jocelin of. *The chronicle of Jocelin of Brakelond concerning the acts of Samson, abbot of the monastery of St Edmund*, ed. and trans. H.E. Baker. Oxford, 1949. One of the richest sources of material for the monastic life at the end of the twelfth and the beginning of the thirteenth century.

1560   Brinton, Thomas. *The sermons of Thomas Brinton, bishop of Rochester (1373–1389)*, ed. Mary Aquinas Devlin. Camden Society, ser. 3, 85, 86 (1954), 2 vols. The editing has been subject to criticism.

1561   Brooks, Eric St John (ed.). *The register of the hospital of St John the Baptist without the New Gate, Dublin, transcribed and edited from the Bodleian MS. Rawl. B. 498.* Dublin, 1936. Stationery Office; *The Irish cartularies of Llanthony prima and secunda.* Dublin, 1953. Stationery Office. Of much value for thirteenth- and fourteenth-century conditions.

1562   Brown, William N. (ed.). *Registers of John le Romeyn and Henry of Newark, archbishops of York, 1286–1299.* Surtees Society, 123 (1913); 128 (1917), 2 vols.

1563   ——— and A. Hamilton Thompson (eds.). *The register of William Greenfield, lord architects of York, 1306–1315.* Pts. 1–5. Surtees Society, 145, 149, 151, 152, 153 (1931–40), 5 vols.

1564   Brundage, James A. 'The crusade of Richard I: two cannonical Quaestiones', *Speculum*, 38 (1963), 443–52.

1565   Bund, John W. (ed.). *The register of William de Geynesburgh, bishop of Worcestershire.* Oxford, 1907. [for the Worcestershire Historical Society] 1929. With an Introduction by Rowland A. Wilson. Includes a list of holders of benefices.

1566   Burns, Charles (ed.). 'Bagimond's roll for the diocese of Moray', *Publications of the Scottish Historical Society*, ser. 4, 2 (1965), 3–9; see also Annie I. Cameron (ed.). 'Bagimond's roll for the archdeaconry of Teviotdale, from a thirteenth century transcript in the Vatican archives', *Publications of the Scottish Historical Society*, 21 (1933), 79–106; Annie I. Dunlop (ed.). 'Bagimond's roll: statement of the tenths of the kingdom of Scotland', *Publications of the Scottish Historical Society*, ser. 3, 33 (1939), 3–77. Assessment by Baimundus de Vitia appointed 20 September 1274 to collect tenth for relief of the Holy Land.

1567   Butler, Constance M. and John M. Bernard (eds.). *The charters of the Cistercian abbey of Duiske in the county of Kilkenny.* Proceedings of the Royal Irish Academy, 35 (c) (1918). Mainly thirteenth century.

1568   Carter, Edward H. (ed.). *Studies in Norwich cathedral history. An episcopal visitation . . . in 1308 . . .* Norwich, 1935.

1569   Cheney, Christopher R. and William H. Semple (eds.). *Selected letters of pope Innocent III concerning England (1192–1216).* 1953. A collection of rare quality, with a fine Introduction; Christopher R. and Mary G. Cheney (eds.). *The letters of pope Innocent III (1198–1216) concerning England and Wales*: a calendar with an appendix of texts. Oxford, 1967. An exemplary ed.

1570   Chew, Helena M. (ed.). *Hemingby's register.* Wiltshire Archaeological and Natural History Society, 18 [1962] (1963). Important Introduction, including the Salisbury chapter 1329–49: personnel and methods of recruitment.

1571   Chibnall, Marjorie M. (ed.). 'Inventories of three alien priories', *JBAA*, ser. 3, 4 (1939), 141–49.

1572   Clarke, Maude V. (ed.). *Register of the priory of the Blessed Virgin Mary at Tristernaugh.* Dublin, 1941.

1573   Cobham, Thomas de. *Thomas de Cobham summa confessorum*, ed. F. Broomfield, *Analecta Medievalia Namurcensia*, 25 (1968).

1574   Cricklade, Robert of. 'A reconstruction of Robert Cricklade's *Vita et Miracula S. Thomas Cantauriensis*', ed. Margaret Orme, *Analecta Bollandiana*, 84 (1966), 379–98.

1575   Dalton, John M. (ed.). *The collegiate church of Ottery St Mary being the Ordinacio de Statuta ecclesie Sancta Marie de Ottery Exon. Diocesis A.D. 1338–9.* Cambridge, 1917. Gives the history in great detail.

1576   Daniel, Walter. *The life of Ailred of Rievaulx*, trans. Frederick M. Powicke. 1950. Long and illuminating introductory essay. Walter's 'life' is an important source for the beginnings of the Cistercian movement in England.

1577   Darlington, Reginald R. (ed.). *The cartulary of Worcester cathedral priory (register 1).* Pipe Roll Society, n.s., 38 (1968). A scholarly and important ed., including plates.

1578   Davies, J. Conway (ed.). *Episcopal acts relating to Welsh dioceses 1066–1272.* Historical Society of the Church in Wales Publications. 1, 3–4 (1946–53), 2 vols. The main collections of published records for Welsh medieval ecclesiastical history.

1579   Davis, Francis N. *et al.* (eds.). *The register of John Pecham archbishop of Canterbury 1279–1292.* Vols. 1 and 2. Canterbury and York Society, 64, 65 (1968–69), 2 vols.

1580   —— *et al.* (eds.). *Rotuli Ricardi Gravesend diocesis Lincolniensis.* Canterbury and York Society, 31 (1925). Introduction by A. Hamilton Thompson. Covers 1258–79.

1581   Deedes, Cecil (ed.). *Registrum Iohannis de Pontissara, 1282–1304.* [bishop of Winchester]. Canterbury and York Society, 19, 30 (1913–24). One of the most interesting registers the society has produced.

1582   Denholm-Young, Noël (ed.). *Cartulary of the medieval archives of Christ*

Church. Oxford, 1931. The volume is really a calendar of the documents.

1583 —— *Liber epistolaris of Richard de Bury.* Roxburghe Club. 1950.

1584 Dunning, Patrick J. 'The letters of Innocent III to Ireland', *Traditio*, 18 (1962), 229–53. Gives calendar of letters.

1585 Dunning, Robert W. (ed.). *The Hylle cartulary.* Somerset Record Society, 68 (1968).

1586 Duns Scotus, John. *Ioannis Duns Scoti Theologiae elementa,* ed. Charles Balić. Sibenik, Yugoslavia, 1933; *Les commentaires de Jean Duns Scotus sur les quatre livres des sentences,* ed. Charles Balić. Louvain, 1927; *A treatise on God as first principle: De primo principio,* ed. Allan B. Wolter. Chicago, 1966.

1587 Eccleston, Thomas. *Fratis Thomae vulgo dicti de Eccleston, Tractatus de adventu Fratrum Minorum in Angliam,* ed. Andrew G. Little. Manchester, 1951. A scholarly and standard ed. The French ed. is out of print.

1588 Edwards, Kathleen *et al.* (eds.). *The registers of Roger Martival bishop of Salisbury 1315–1330.* Canterbury and York Society, 55, 56, 57, 58 (1959–72), 4 vols.

1589 Evans, Cyril J.O. (ed.). 'Ely chapter ordinances and visitation records: 1241–1515', *Camden Miscellany,* 17. Camden Society, ser. 3, 64 (1940), v–xx, 1–67.

1590 Farmer, Hugh (ed.). *The monk of Farne.* 1961. Meditations of a fourteenth-century Durham monk who ended his life as a solitary on Inner Farne.

1591 Feltoe, Charles L. (ed.). *Vetus liber archidiaconi Eliensis.* Cambridge, 1917. Apparently drawn up in 1277: list of books and ornaments in various churches.

1592 Finberg, Herbert P.R. 'Church and state in XIIth century Devon: some documentary illustrations', *Devon Association Reports and Transactions for 1943,* 75 (1944), 245–57.

1593 —— 'Some early Tavistock charters', *EHR,* 62 (1947), 352–77. From a cartulary of the abbey, compiled mostly in the fourteenth and fifteenth centuries. Prints 52 documents.

1594 Fitzmaurice, Edward B. and Andrew G. Little (eds.). *Materials for the history of the Franciscan province of Ireland, A.D. 1294–1313.* Manchester, 1920.

1595 Flower, Cyril T. and Michael C.B. Dawes (eds.). *Registrum Simonis de Gandavo diocesis Saresbiriensis, A.D. 1297–1315.* Canterbury and York Society, 40, 41 (1934), 2 vols. Includes life and itinerary of Simon.

1596 Foliot, Gilbert. *The letters and charters of Gilbert Foliot, abbot of Gloucester (1139–48) and of London (1163–87),* ed. Adrian Morey and Christopher N.L. Brooke. Cambridge, 1967. A valuable contribution of the history of the twelfth century. The authors temper David Knowles' judgement on Gilbert.

1597 Foreville, Raymonde. 'Lettres "extravagantes" de Thomas Becket, archevêque de Canterbury', in *Mélanges d'histoire du moyen âge ... à ... Louis Halphen.* Paris, 1951, 225–38.

1598 Foster, Charles W. and Kathleen Major (eds.). *The registrum antiquissium of the cathedral church of Lincoln.* Lincoln Record Society, 27 (1931–68). Of major importance. Vol. 11 (1968) includes memoir of Sir Frank Stenton.

1599 Fowler, Robert C. (ed.). *Registrum Simonis de Sudbiria diocesis Londoniensis, A.D. 1362–1375.* Canterbury and York Society, 34, 38 (1927, 1938). Vol. 2 has a valuable Introduction by Claude Jenkins.

1600 Fraser, Constance M. (ed.). *Records of Antony Bek, bishop and patriarch, 1283–1311.* Surtees Society, 162 (193).

1601 Galbraith, Vivian H. 'Articles laid before the parliament of 1371', *EHR,* 34 (1919), 579–82. More evidence of anti-clericalism.

1602 Gibbs, Marion (ed.). *Early charters of the cathedral church of St Paul.* Camden Society, ser. 3, 58 (1939). Inadequate editing.

1603 Godber, Joyce (ed.). *The cartulary of Newnham priory.* Pts. 1 and 2. *Beds Rec,* 43 (1963–64). Compiled in early fifteenth century from material mostly thirteenth century.

1604 Goodman, Arthur W. (ed.). *Registrum Henrici Woodlock diocesis Winton-iensis, A.D. 1305—1316.* Canterbury and York Society, 43, 44 (1940—41). 2 vols. Includes Introduction on life and itinerary.

1605 Graham, Rose (ed.). *Registrum Roberti Cantauriensis archiepiscopi, A.D. 1294—1313.* Canterbury and York Society, 55—114 (1917—42). Introduction, itinerary, text, and precis. [Robert Winchelsey].

1606 Gransden, Antonia (ed.). *The Customary of the Benedictine abbey of Eynsham in Oxfordshire.* Corpus consuentudium monasticarum. 2. Siegberg, Germany, 1963. Gives a vivid and detailed picture of daily life.

1607 —— *The letter-book of William of Hoo, sacrist of Bury St Edmunds, 1280—1294.* Ipswich, 1963. The only known letter-book of an obientiary.

1608 —— *Chronica Buriensis 1212—1301 (The chronicle of Bury St Edmunds, 1212—1301).* 1964. More than a record of events in the abbey. The volume gives for the first time a complete text.

1609 Graves, Edgar B. 'Circumspecte agatis', *EHR*, 43 (1928), 1—20. Prints a revised text and offers what is now the accepted interpretation.

1610 Grosseteste, Robert. 'The summa theologiae of Robert Grosseteste', ed. Daniel A.P. Callus, *SPFP*, 180—208. Edits four quaestiones.

1611 Gwynn, Aubrey O. (ed.). 'Provincial and diocesan decrees of the diocese of Dublin during the Anglo-Norman period', *Archivium Hibernicum*, 11 (1944), 31—117.

1612 Haines, Roy M. (ed.). *A calendar of the register of Wolfstan de Bransford, bishop of Worcester (1339—49).* Worcestershire Historical Society, n.s., 4 (1966). Introduction contains a discussion of officers and *familia.*

1613 Harris, Mary D. (ed.). *The register of the guild of the Holy Trinity, St Mary, St John the Baptist and St Katherine of Coventry.* Dugdale Society, 13 (1935).

1614 Harvey, Barbara F. (ed.). *Documents illustrating the rule of Walter de Wenlock abbot of Westminster, 1283—1307.* Camden Society, ser. 2, 4 (1965).

1615 Hervey, Francis (ed.). *The Pinchbeck register.* Oxford, 1925. A register of the abbey of Bury St Edmunds kept by a monk named Walter of Pinchbeck in the middle of the fourteenth century.

1616 Hill, Rosalind M.T. (ed.). *The rolls and register of bishop Oliver Sutton, 1280—1299.* Lincoln Record Society, 39, 43, 48, 52, 60, 64 (1948—69), 6 vols.

1617 HMSO. *Calendar of the entries in the papal registers relating Great Britain and Ireland (1362—1492).* 1902—61, 11 vols.

1618 Hodgson, Phyllis (ed.). *The Cloud of unknowing and the book of privy counselling.* 1955; see also Justin McCann (ed.). *The cloud of unknowing and other treatises by an English mystic of the fourteenth century.* 1924; 2nd ed., 1936.

1619 Holdsworth, Christopher J. (ed.). 'John of Ford and the interdict', *EHR*, 78 (1963), 705—14. Edits a sermon by John, possibly *c.* 1210.

1620 Holt, Neville R. (ed.). *The pipe roll of the bishopric of Winchester 1210—1211 (P.R.O. Eccl. 2—22—1592.70B.).* Manchester, 1964. Introduction is specially interested in administration.

1621 Holzmann, Walther (ed.). *Papsturkunden in England.* Berlin and Göttingen, 1930—52. Invaluable; and Eric W. Kemp (eds.). *Papal decretals relating to the diocese of Lincoln in the twelfth century.* Lincoln Record Society, 47 (1954). An exemplary ed.

1622 Hope, William St J. (ed.). *The history of the London Charterhouse from its foundation until the suppression of the monastery.* 1925. S.P.C.K. Contains a register of the Charterhouse and an account by an unknown monk of the founding and the building of the monastery.

1623 Hugh Candidus. *The chronicle of Hugh Candidus, with La Geste de Burch,* ed. William T. Mellows. Oxford, 1948. The chronicle, written in the late twelfth century, deals with the early history of the monastery of Peterborough.

1624 Huygens, Robert B.C. 'Dialogus inter regem Henricum secundum et abbatem Bonevallis. Un écrit de Pierre de Blois réédité', *Revue bénédictine*, 68

(1958), 87—112. Dialogue composed by Peter in 1188: the editor suggests a basis of fact.

1625 Johnson, Charles (ed.). *Registrum Hamonis Hethe diocesis Roffensis A.D. 1319—1352.* Canterbury and York Society, 48, 49 (1914—48). Absorbing picture of life of a fourteenth-century prelate.

1626 Kilwardby, Robert. *Robert Kilwardby O.P.R. De natura theologiae; opuscula et textus, historiam ecclesiae eiusque vitam atque doctrinam illustrantia,* ed. Friedrich Stegmüller. Series Scholastica, fasc. 17 (1935); also 'Der Traktat des Robert Kilwardby, O.P. De imagine et vestigio Trinitatis', *Archives d'histoire doctrinale et littéraire du moyen âge.* 1936, 324—407.

1627 Knight, Ione K. (ed.). *Wimbeldon's sermon 'Redde rationem villicationis tue': a middle English sermon of the fourteenth century.* Louvain, 1967.

1628 Koch, Josef (ed.). 'Neue Aktenstücke zu dem gegen Wilhelm Ockham in Avignon geführten Prozess', *Recherches de théologie ancienne et médiévale,* 7 (1935), 353—80.

1629 Lancaster, Henry of. *'Le livre de seyntz medicines'. The unpublished devotional treatise of Henry of Lancaster,* ed. Émile J.F. Arnould. Oxford, 1940. A famous and unique treatise by a great magnate. See also Arnould. 'Henry of Lancaster and his *Livre des seintes medicines'*, *BJRL,* 21 (1937), 352—86; and Émile J.F. Arnould (ed.). *Le manuel des péchés: étude de littérature réligieuse anglo-normande.* Paris, 1940. Probably written in England between 1260 and 1270.

1630 Lees, Beatrice A. (ed.). *Records of the Templars in England in the twelfth century.* British Academy Records of Social and Economic History, 9 (1935). Impeccably edited: includes an important inquest of 1185; see also Thomas W. Parker. *The Knights Templars in England.* Tucson, Ariz., 1963. In spite of some weaknesses, a solid contribution to our knowledge of medieval religious institutions.

1631 Legg, J. Wickham (ed.). *The Sarum missal.* Oxford, 1916. Approximate date 1264.

1632 Little, Andrew and Franz Pelster (eds.). *Oxford theology and theologians, circa 1282—1302.* Oxford Historical Society, 94 (1934). Sermons preached at Oxford, adding greatly to our knowledge of theological studies and theologians at this period.

1633 London, Vera C.M. *The cartulary of the Canonsleigh abbey (Harleian MS. no. 3360: a calendar.* Devon and Cornwall Record Society, n.s., 8 (1965). House of Augustinian canonesses, founded in 1284.

1634 Lunt, William E. (ed.). *The valuation of Norwich.* Oxford, 1926. The first assessment of English and Welsh clerical incomes, completed in 1254. Valuable Introduction; also *Financial relations of the papacy with England to 1327.* Cambridge, Mass., 1939. A massive and scholarly volume of wide-ranging interest; *Financial relations of the papacy with England, 1327—1534.* Cambridge, Mass., 1962; Lunt and Edgar B. Graves (eds.). *Accounts rendered by papal collectors in England, 1317—1378.* Philadelphia, Penna., 1968.

1635 McNeill, Charles. *Register of chapter acts of the hospital of Saint John of Jerusalem in Ireland, 1326—1339.* Dublin, n.d. Stationery Office; also *Calendar of archbishop Alen's register, ca. 1172—1534.* Dublin, 1950. A valuable source for the administration of the Irish archdiocese of Dublin.

1636 McNulty, Joseph (ed.). *Thomas Southeron v. Cockersand abbey. A suit as to the advowson of Mitton church, 1369—70.* Chetham Society, 100. misc. n.s., 7 (1939), 1—147.

1637 Major, Kathleen (ed.). *Acta Stephani Langton Cantuariensis archiepiscopi A.D. 1207—1228.* Canterbury and York Society, 50 (1950). Introduction has a scholarly essay on diplomatics.

1638 Mander, Gerald P. 'The priory of the Black Ladies of Brewood', *Collections for a history of Staffordshire edited by the Staff. Rec. Soc.* [1939] Kendal, 1940, 177—220. Discovered in 1938.

1639 Mayr-Harting, Henry (ed.). *The acta of the bishops of Chichester 1075—1207.* Canterbury and York Society, 130 (1964). Good Introduction. The *acta* were compiled from eighteen repositaries.

1640   Mercati, Angelo. 'La prima relazione del cardinale Nicolò de Romanis sulla sua legazione in Inghilterra (1213)', *EPRP*, 274—89. Gives text of a report by a legate of Innocent III.

1641   Moore, Norman (ed.). *The book of the foundation of St Bartholomew's church in London.* Early English Text Society. 1929. Probably the only Latin 'life' composed under Henry II. English version *c.* 1400.

1642   Morris, T.J. 'The liber pontificalis Ariani of Bangor', *AngAntiq* (1962), 55—86.

1643   Newburgh, William of. *Explanatio sacri epithalami in matrem sponsi.* ed. John C. Gorman. Fribourg, 1960. Shows developing devotion to Mary in late twelfth century.

1644   Ockham, William of. *Gulielmi de Ockham. Epistola ad fratres minores.* ed. Charles K. Brampton. Oxford, 1929; also *Le tractatus de principiis theologiae attribué à G. d'Occam.* [Edition critique] ed. Léon Baudry. Paris, 1936; *The tractatus praedestatione et de praescientia Dei et de futuris contingientibus.* ed. Philotheus H. Boehner [with a study on the medieval problem of a three-valued logic]. New York, 1945; *Guillelmi de Ockham, scriptum in librum primum sententiarum ordinatio. Prologus et distinctio prima*, ed. Gedeon Gál and Stephen N. Brown. St Bonaventure, N.Y., 1967. The first of projected vols. giving a critical ed. of all Ockham's theological and philosophical writings. The series will be invaluable for students of medieval philosophy and theology.

1645   Offer, Clifford J. (ed.). *The bishop's register.* 1930. S.P.C.K. A collection of extracts (translated) designed to illustrate the nature of these records and of the bishops' activities.

1646   Pantin, William A. *Documents illustrating the activities of the general and provincial chapters of the Black monks.* Camden Society, ser. 3, 45, 47, 54 (1931, 1933, 1937), 3 vols. A fine ed.

1647   Pearce, Ernest H. (ed.). *The register of Thomas de Cobham bishop of Worcester 1317—1327.* Worcestershire Historical Society. 1930.

1648   Pecham, John. *Tractus de anima Ioannis Pecham*, ed. Gaudentius Melani. Florence, 1948. See also 'John Pecham's *Jerarchie*', ed. Mary D. Legge, *Medium Aevum*, 11 (1942), 77—84.

1649   Powicke, Frederick M. and Christopher R. Cheney (eds.). *Councils and synods, with other documents relating to the English church.* Vol. 2 (A.D. 1205—1313) [in two Pts.]. Oxford, 1964. A monument of historical scholarship.

1650   Purvis, John S. (ed.). *Monastic chancery proceedings, Yorkshire.* YorksArch Rec., 88 (1934). Ranging from the fourteenth century to 1540.

1651   Reading, abbot Hugh of. 'An unpublished letter of abbot Hugh II of Reading concerning archbishop Hubert Walter', ed. Giles Constable, *EPBW*, 17—31. Modifies the judgment of Stubbs on Hubert Walter's relations with the monks of Canterbury. Prints the letter of Hugh to Celestine III.

1652   Rolle, Richard of Hampole. *The 'incendium amoris' of Richard Rolle of Hampole*, ed. Margaret Deansley. Manchester, 1915.

1653   —— *Richard Rolle's 'Meditatio de passions Domini' according to MS Uppsala c. 494*, ed. Harold Lindkvist. Upsala, 1917.

1654   —— *Selected works of Richard Rolle, hermit*, ed. George C. Heseltine. 1930.

1655   —— *English writings of Richard Rolle hermit of Hampole*, ed. Hope E. Allen. Oxford, 1931; *The 'Melos Amoris' of Richard Rolle of Hampole*, ed. Émile J.F. Arnould. Oxford, 1957. Offers some corrections.

1656   Ross, Charles D. *The cartulary of Cirencester abbey, Gloucestershire.* 1964, 2 vols. Includes an important series of royal charters after the foundation of Henry I.

1657   Roth, Francis X. (ed.). *The English Austin friars, 1249—1538: 2 sources.* New York, 1961.

1658   Salisbury, John of. *Iohannis Saresberiensis historiae pontificalis quae supersunt*, ed. Reginald L. Poole. Oxford, 1927. Valuable Preface.

1659   —— *Ioannis Saresberiensis episcopi Carnotensis Metalogicon, libri III*, ed. Clement C.J. Webb. Oxford, 1929. Corrections in *Medieval and Renaissance Studies.* 1 (1941).

1660 ——— *The letters of John of Salisbury.* Vol. 1, *The early letters (1153–1161)*, ed. W.J. Miller *et al.* Shed much light on the history of the English church in the mid-twelfth century.

1661 ——— *John of Salisbury's memoirs of the papal court (Historia Pontificalis)*, trans. and ed. Marjorie M. Chibnall. 1956. An excellent Introduction. Takes issue on some points with Christopher N.L. Brooke.

1662 Salter, Herbert E. (ed.). *Chapters of the Augustinian canons.* 1922. Canterbury and York Society, 29 (1922). From 1216 on. Helpful Introduction.

1663 Saltman, Avrom (ed.). *The cartulary of Dale abbey.* 1967. HMSO. The abbey was founded *c.* 1200: the volume also includes documents from other sources.

1664 Savage, Henry L. (ed.). *The great register of Lichfield cathedral known as the Magnum Reistrum Album.* William Salt Archaeological Society, 48 (1926). Compiled between 1317 and 1328. Includes the Lichfield chronicle to 1322.

1665 Searle, Eleanor and Barbara Ross (eds.). *Accounts of the cellarers of Battle abbey, 1275–1513.* Sydney, 1967; also *The cellarers' rolls of Battle abbey, 1275–1513.* Sussex Record Society, 65 (1967).

1666 Sheehy, Maurice P. (ed.). *Pontifica Hibernica: medieval papal chancery documents concerning Ireland, 640–1261.* Dublin, 1962–65, 2 vols.

1667 Stenton, Frank M. (ed.). *Transcripts of charters relating to Gilbertine houses.* Lincoln Record Society, 18 (1922). Important for diplomatic and for social and agrarian history.

1668 Surtees Society. *The registers of John le Romeyn lord archbishop of York 1286–1296, Part 2, and of Henry of Newark, lord archbishop of York 1296–1299.* Surtees Society, 128 (1917). [editor unidentified].

1669 Thompson, A. Hamilton (ed.). *Visitations of religious houses in the diocese of Lincoln.* Vols. 1 and 2. Canterbury and York Society, 17, 23 (1917–); Vol. 3. Lincoln Record Society, 21 (1929), 3 vols.

1670 ——— *The register of William Greenfield, lord archbishop of York, 1306–15.* Surtees Society, 145, 149, 151, 152, 153 (1931–38), 5 vols.

1671 ——— and William N. Brown (eds.). *The register of Thomas of Corbridge lord archbishop of York 1300–1304.* Surtees Society, 138, 141 (1925–28), 2 vols.

1672 Thompson, E. Maunde. 'A fragment of a Witham charterhouse chronicle and Adam of Dryburgh, Premonstratensian and Carthusian of Witham', *BJRL*, 16 (1932), 482–506. Biography of a little-known Carthusian by Adam of Dryburgh, printed in full.

1673 Thorne, William. *William Thorne chronicle of St Augustine's abbey, Canterbury*, ed. Alfred H. Davis. Oxford, 1934. English translation. Covers years 578–1397.

1674 Tolhurst, John B.L. (ed.). *The monastic breviary of Hyde abbey, Winchester.* Henry Bradshaw Society, 69–80 (1932–42), 6 vols. A rare type MS., written possibly *c.* 1292–1304. Vol. 6 is an introduction to English monastic breviaries.

1675 ——— *The customary of the cathedral church of Norwich.* Henry Bradshaw Society, 82 (1948). Covers 1279–1288.

1676 Toms, Elsie and C. Hilary Jenkinson (eds.). *Chertsey abbey court rolls abstract, being a calendar of Lansdowns MS. no. 434 in the British Museum.* Surrey Record Society, 21 (1954). The rolls run from 1 through 21 Edward I.

1677 Turner, George J. and Herbert E. Salter (eds.). *The register of abbey commonly called the Black Book.* 1915–24, 2 vols.

1678 Walberg, Emmanuel (ed.). *La vie de Saint Thomas Becket par Guernes de Pont Sainte Maxence.* Paris, 1936.

1679 Watkin, Aelred. *Inventory of church goods, temp. Edward III.* Norfolk Record Society, 19, Pts. 1 and 2 (1947–48). Transcripts of visitations of the archdeacon of Norwich, *c.* 1368.

1680 Webb, Arthur N. (ed.). *An edition of the cartulary of Burscough priory.* Chetham Society, ser. 3, 18 (1970).

1681   Webb, Edward A. (ed.). *The records of St Bartholomew the Great, West Smithfield.* Oxford, 1921, 2 vols. Detailed study, good plates.
1682   West, James R. (ed.). *St Benet of Holme 1020—1210. The eleventh and twelfth century sections of Cott. MS. Galba, E.ii, the register of the abbey of St Benet of Holme.* Norfolk Record Society, 2 (1932).
1683   White, Newport B. (ed.). *Irish monastic and episcopal deeds, A.D. 1200—1600.* Dublin, 1936. Irish Manuscripts Commission; also *The 'Dignitas Decani' of St Patrick's cathedral, Dublin.* Dublin, 1957. Introduction by Aubrey O. Gwynn. Documents from last decade of twelfth century: an important source of Irish church history.
1684   Wickwane, William. 'Letters of William Wickwane, chancellor of York, 1266—1268', ed. Christopher R. Cheney, *EHR,* 47 (1932), 626—42.
1685   Wilson, James M. (ed.). *The 'Liber Albus' of the priory of Worcester: glimpses of life in a great Benedictine monastery of the fourteenth century.* Worcester Historical Society, 1919. Includes letter-book kept by the priors from 1301 to the mid-fifteenth century.
1686   Wilson, Rowland A. (ed.). *The register of Walter Reynolds bishop of Worcester 1308—1313.* 1927. For the Worcestershire Historical Society.
1687   Wood, Alfred C. *Registrum Simonis Langham Cantuariensis Archiespiscopi.* Canterbury and York Society, 53 (1956).
1688   Wyclif, John. *Johannis Wyclif tractatus de mandatis divinis, accedit tractatus de statu innocencie. de differentia inter peccatum moratale et veniale.* ed. Johann Loserth and Frederick D. Matthew. 1922. Reprinted New York, 1966; also *Johannis Wyclif Summa de ente libri primi, tractatus primus et secundus,* ed. S. Harrison Thomson. Oxford, 1930; and 'The Vatican manuscript Borghese 29 and the tractate "de Versuciis Anti-Christ" ', ed. I.H. Stein, *EHR,* 47 (1932), 95—103. Attributed to John Wyclif; also by I.H. Stein. 'The Latin text of Wyclif's *Complaint*', ed. *Speculum,* 7 (1932), 87—94; and *Johannis Wyclif Tractatus de Trinitate.* ed. Allen du Pont Breck. Boulder, Colo., 1962. Edition is marred by slips, but with valuable observations; also a detailed study, Wyclif's 'Bibelkommentar', ed. Gustave A. Benrath. Berlin, 1966, which stresses the traditional character of Wyclif's approach; and Michael Hurley's *'Scriptura sola': Wyclif and his critics.* New York, 1960, re-examining Wyclif's attitude towards the scriptures; also in *Traditio,* 16 (1960), 299—304; S. Harrison Thomson. 'Unnoticed MSS. and works of Wyclif', *Journal of Theological Studies,* 38 (1937), 24—36, 139—48; and also 'Three unprinted opuscula of John Wyclif', *Speculum,* 3 (1928), 248—53.

2 Surveys

1689   Baldwin, Marshal W. *The medieval church.* Ithaca, N.Y., 1953. Excellent introduction to subject.
1690   Barraclough, Geoffrey. *Papal provisions. Aspects of church history, constitutional, legal and administrative, in the later middle ages.* Oxford, 1935. The standard work; see also his essay *The medieval papacy.* New York, 1968. The best treatment written for a long time.
1691   Benson, Robert L. *The bishop-elect: a study in medieval ecclesiastical office.* Princeton, N.J., 1968. An important survey of a neglected subject.
1692   Chenu, Marie-Dominique. *Nature, man, and society in the twelfth century: essays in new theological perspectives in the Latin West,* ed. and trans. Jerome Taylor and Lester K. Little. Chicago, 1968. Preface by Etienne Gilson; also *L'éveil de la conscience dans la civilisation médiévale.* Paris, 1969.
1693   Coulton, George G. *Five centuries of religion.* Cambridge, 1923—50, 4 vols. Deep scholarship, but somewhat partisan interpretation of medieval monasticism and clergy.
1694   Duke, John A. *History of the church of Scotland to the Reformation.* Edinburgh, 1937.
1695   Easson, David E. *Medieval religious houses: Scotland.* 1957. The most

important contribution to ecclesiastical history of Scotland since the beginning of the twentieth century. Foreword by David Knowles.

1696   Emden, Alfred B. *A survey of Dominicans in England, based on the ordination lists in episcopal registers (1268 to 1538).* Rome, 1967.

1697   Fliche, Augustin. *Histoire de l'église depuis les origines jusqu'à nos jours.* Paris, 1934–, 22 vols. Vols. 4–15 deal with Middle Ages. A work of fundamental significance.

1698   Godfrey, John. *The English parish 600–1300.* 1969.

1699   Gwynn, Aubrey O. *A history of Irish catholicism.* Vol. 2. Dublin, 1968. Includes 'The church in the English lordship 1216–1307' (1–43) and 'Anglo-Irish church life: fourteenth and fifteenth centuries' (1–76). Authoritative surveys; also Gwynn and Richard N. Hadcock. *Medieval religious houses: Ireland.* 1970. List and comments.

1700   Hadcock, Richard N. *Map of monastic Ireland.* Ordnance Survey. Dublin, 1959; also *Map of monastic Britain.* Ordinance Survey. 2nd ed., Chessington, 1955.

1701   Knowles, David. *The monastic order in England: a history of its development from the times of St Dunstan to the fourth Lateran council, 943–1216.* Cambridge, 1940; 2nd ed., 1963.

1702   —— *The religious orders in England (1216–c. 1340).* Cambridge, 1948.

1703   —— *The end of the Middle Ages.* Cambridge, 1955. The three vols. form a general survey marked by fine scholarship and understanding. Indispensable for all students of religious life in the period.

1704   —— *From Pachomius to Ignatius: A study in the constitutional history of the religious orders.* Oxford, 1966.

1705   —— and Richard N. Hadcock. *Medieval religious houses: England and Wales.* 1953. Revised ed., New York, 1972. A standard work: a mine of information. Supplement in *EHR*, 72 (1957), 60–87.

1706   Lawrence, C. Hugh (ed.). *The English church and the papacy in the Middle Ages.* 1965. Includes chs. by Charles Duggan, C. Hugh Lawrence, and William A. Pantin on the period 1066–1400.

1707   Moorman, John R.H. *History of the church in England.* 1953.

1708   —— *History of the Franciscan order from its origins to the year 1517.* Oxford, 1916. A judicious and erudite survey.

1709   Powicke, Frederick M. *The Christian life in the Middle Ages and other essays.* Oxford, 1935. Eight papers, six published before. Includes 'Gerald of Wales', 'Stephen Langton', 'Loretta, countess of Leicester'. An outstanding series.

1710   Williams, Glanmor. *The Welsh church from the Conquest to the Reformation.* Cardiff, 1962. A masterful synthesis.

1711   Walberg, Emmanuel F.G. *La tradition hagiographique de Saint Thomas Becket avant la fin du XIIe siècle.* Paris, 1929. Indispensable to student of English ecclesiastical literature of the later twelfth century.

3 Monographs

1712   Allen, Hope E. *The writings ascribed to Richard Rolle, hermit of Hampole, and materials for his biography.* Modern Language Association. New York, 1927. A study of permanent value. See also Francis M.M. Comper. *The life of Richard Rolle, together with an edition of his English lyrics.* New York, 1969.

1713   Andrieu-Guitrancourt, Pierre. *Essai sur l'évolution de décanat rural en Angleterre d'après les counciles des XIIe, XIIIe, and XIVe siècles.* Paris, 1935.

1714   Ashley, Anne. *The church in the Isle of Man.* St Anthony's Hall Publications, 13 (1958), A short scholarly sketch.

1715   Bannister, Arthur T. *The cathedral church of Hereford: its history and constitution.* 1924.

1716   Barlow, Frank. *Durham juridictional peculiars.* Oxford, 1950. Sound contribution to ecclesiastical organization.

1717   Barnardiston, Katherine W. *Clare priory.* Cambridge, 1962.

1718   Bennett, Ralph F. *The early Dominicans. Studies in thirteenth-century Dominican history.* Cambridge, 1937.

1719   Boggis, Robert J.E. *A history of the diocese of Exeter.* 1922.

1720   Bourdillon, Anne F.C. *The order of minoresses in England.* British Society of Franciscan Studies, 12 (1926); also Mary Byrne. *The tradition of the nun in medieval England.* Washington, D.C., 1932; Eileen E. Power. *Medieval English nunneries, c. 1275 to 1535.* Cambridge, 1922.

1721   Brentano, Robert. *York metropolitan jurisdiction and papal judges delegate 1279–1296.* Berkeley, Cal., 1959. An illuminating study: includes fifteen appendices of documents; also Brentano's *Two churches: England and Italy in the thirteenth century.* Princeton, N.J., 1968. A learned attempt to high-light the character and ethos of the two churches.

1722   Brooke, Zachary N. *The English church and the papacy from the Conquest to the reign of John.* Cambridge, 1931; reprinted Cambridge, 1968. Still most valuable.

1723   Burne, Richard V.H. *The monks of Chester: the history of St Werburg's abbey.* 1962. A sober and scholarly study.

1724   Cheney, Christopher R. *Episcopal visitations of monasteries in the thirteenth century.* Manchester, 1931. Indispensable for all students of monastic history; also *English synodalia of the thirteenth century.* Oxford, 1941. New ed. with new Introduction, Oxford, 1968. Examines critically the composition and origin of synodal statutes. Texts to follow; *English bishops' chanceries, 1100–1250.* Manchester, 1950. An important book on a new subject; *From Becket to Langton: English church government, 1170–1213.* Manchester, 1956. An important analysis by a foremost authority.

1725   Churchill, Irene J. *Canterbury administration: the administrative machinery of the archbishopric of Canterbury illustrated from original records.* 1933, 2 vols. A landmark in this sphere of administrative history.

1726   Clay, Charles T. *The hermits and anchorites of England.* 1914. Reissued Detroit, 1968; Francis D.S. Darwin. *The English medieval recluse.* 1944. S.P.C.K. A useful introduction to subject; and Hubert Dauphin. 'L'érémitsme en Engleterre au XIe et XIIe siècles', in *L'eremitismo in Occidente nei secoli XIe et XIIe* Pubblicazioni del l'Università Cattolica del Sacro Cuore, Contributi, ser. 3. 1965; Rotha M. Clay. 'Some northern anchorites', *ArchAel*, ser. 4, 33 (1955), 202–17.

1727   —— *York minster fasti, being notes on the dignitaries, archdeacons and prebendaries in the church of York prior to the year 1307. Yorks. Arch. Rec.*, 123, 124 (1958–9), 2 vols.

1728   Colvin, Howard M. *The White canons in England.* Oxford, 1951. Thorough and scholarly.

1729   Cook, George H. *Medieval chantries and chantry chapels.* 1948; *The English medieval parish church*, 1954; *English monasteries of the Middle Ages.* 1961. But see 1700–02 above.

1730   Cotton, Charles. *The Grey friars of Canterbury, 1224 to 1538.* British Society of Franciscan Studies. 1924. Describes the arrival of friars on the occasion of the seventh hundred anniversary; Victor G. Green. *The Franciscans in medieval English life. FS*, 20 (1939); Edward Hutton. *The Franciscans in England, 1224–1538.* Boston, 1926. Relies heavily on Thomas Eccleston.

1731   Coulton, George G. *Studies in medieval thought.* 1940. Includes the universities and John Wyclif.

1732   Cranage, David H.S. *The home of the monk. An account of English monastic life and buildings in the Middle Ages.* 3rd ed., Cambridge, 1934.

1733   Crossley, Frederick H. *The English abbey: its life and work in the Middle Ages.* 1935; 3rd ed., 1949. Helpful survey with good photographs.

1734   Dawson, Christopher. *Medieval essays.* New York, 1954. A distinguished Roman Catholic interpretation. Contains an essay on the Vision of Piers Plowman.

1735   Deansley, Margaret. *The Lollard bible and other medieval biblical versions.*

Cambridge, 1920; there is an argument against one of her conclusions, Hugh Pope. 'The Lollard bible', *Dublin Review*, 168 (1921), 60—72.

1736   Dickinson, John C. *The origins of the Austin canons and their introduction into England.* 1950. Learned and attractive: deals with a neglected field; see also Dickinson's *The shrine of our lady Walsingham.* Cambridge, 1956. A small but scholarly book. Illustrations; and Dickinson. *Monastic life in medieval England.* 1961. Good introduction to the subject. But see 1700 above.

1737   Douie, Decima L. *Archbishop Geoffrey Plantagenet and the chapter of York.* Borthwick Institute, St Anthony's Hall Publications, 18 (1960). Brief, but scholarly pamphlet.

1738   Duggan, Charles. *Twelfth-century decretal collections and their importance in English history.* University of London, Historical Studies, 12 (1963). Scholarly and important.

1739   Edwards, Kathleen. *The English secular cathedrals in the Middle Ages: a constitutional study with special references to the fourteenth century.* 2nd ed., Manchester, 1967; first published in 1949. The best book on the subject.

1740   Ellis, John T. *Anti-papal legislation in medieval England, (1066—1377).* Washington, D.C., 1930. A doctoral dissertation with faults.

1741   Foreville, Raymonde. *Un procès de canonisation à l'aube de XIIIe siècle (1201—2). Le livre de Saint Gilbert de Sempringham.* Paris, 1943; also *L'église et la royauté en Angleterre sous Henri II Plantagenet (1154—1189).* Paris, 1943; *Le jubilé de saint Thomas Becket: du XIIIe au XVe siècle (1220—1470).* Paris, 1958. Fits the jubilees of 1220, 1270, 1320, and 1370 into the fabric of papal policy and English public life.

1742   Gabel, Leona C. *Benefit of clergy in England in the later Middle Ages.* Smith College Studies in History, 14 (1928—29).

1743   Galbraith, Georgina R. *The constitution of the Dominican order, 1216—1360.* Manchester, 1925. Thorough and lasting work. Reproduces original documents.

1744   Gibbs, Marion and Jane Lang. *Bishops and reform, 1215—1272, with special reference to the Lateran council of 1215.* 1934. A scholarly and important book.

1745   Gilbert, B. *Agnellus and the English Grey friars.* 1937.

1746   Graham, Rose. *English ecclesiastical studies, being some essays in research in medieval history.* 1929. Includes essays on ecclesiastical finance, an interdict imposed on Dover by archbishop Winchelsey, and a visitation of the diocese of Worcester by the same, in 1301. Also an essay on the civic position of women at common law before 1800.

1747   Gumbley, Walter. *The Cambridge Dominicans.* Oxford, 1938. A preliminary sketch.

1748   Gwynn, Aubrey O. *The English Austin friars in the time of Wyclif.* Oxford, 1940. An important study.

1749   ———— *The medieval province of Armagh.* Dundalk, 1946. A pioneer study of Irish ecclesiastical organization in the later Middle Ages.

1750   Haines, Roy M. *The administration of the diocese of Worcester in the first half of the fourteenth century.* 1965. A careful, scholarly book.

1751   Hallier, Amédée. *Un éducateur monastique.* Paris, 1959. An intelligent and sympathetic analysis of Ailred of Rievaulx's training of young monks.

1752   Hamman, Adalbert. *La doctrine de l'église et de l'état chez Occam.* Paris, 1942.

1753   Hartridge, Reginald A.R. *A history of vicarages in the Middle Ages.* Cambridge, 1930. Reprinted New York, 1968. Mainly concerned with appropriations; written by a disciple of George G. Coulton.

1754   Hays, Rhys W. *The history of the abbey of Aberconway 1186—1537.* Cardiff, 1963. An important Cistercian abbey.

1755   Hearnshaw, Fossey J.C. (ed.). *The social and political ideas of some great medieval thinkers.* 1937. Includes 'Wycliffe and divine dominion'.

1756   Heath, Peter. *Medieval clerical accounts.* St Anthony's Hall Publications, 26 (1964).

1757   Herkless, John and Robert K. Hannay. *The archbishops of St Andrews.* Edinburgh, 1907—15, 5 vols. Embodied much new material.

1758   Heseltine, George C. *William of Wykeham: a commentary.* 1932.

1759   Hill, Bennett D. *British Cistercian monasteries and their patrons in the twelfth century.* Urbana, Ill., 1968. A lucid study into the decline of an ideal.

1760   Hill, Rosalind M.T. *The labourer in the vineyard. The visitations of archbishop Melton in the archdeaconry of Richmond.* Borthwick Institute, St Anthony's Hall Publications, 35 (1968).

1761   Hinnebusch, William A. *The early English friar preachers.* Rome, 1951. Surveys every aspect of the movement. Partly supersedes Bede Jarret. *The English Dominicans. Studies in thirteenth-century Dominican history.* Cambridge, 1937; also no. 1718 above.

1762   Hodgson, Phyllis. *'The Orchard of Syon' and the English mystical tradition.* 1965; also *Three 14th century mystics.* 1967; Eric Colledge. *Medieval mystics of England.* New York, 1961; Greta Hoyt. *Sense and thought. A study in mysticism.* 1936. Deals with 'the cloud of unknowing'; *Piers Plowman and contemporary religious thought.* 1937; David Knowles. *The English mystics.* 1927; also David Knowles. *The English mystical tradition.* 1961; Joseph E. Milosh. *The scale of perfection and the English mystical tradition.* Madison, Wis., 1966; William A. Pantin. 'The monk-solitary of Farne, a fourteenth century English mystic', *EHR*, 59 (1944), 162—86.

1763   Hope, William H. St J. *The history of the London Charterhouse from its foundation until the suppression of the monastery.* 1925. See also David Knowles and William F. Grimes. *Charterhouse and its medieval foundations in the light of recent discoveries.* 1954.

1764   Howell, Margaret. *Regalian right in medieval England.* 1962. An extensive gloss on the two texts in which king John claimed the custody of vacant bishoprics and monasteries.

1765   James, Stanley B. *Back to Langland.* Sands, 1935. Discusses his spiritual teaching.

1766   Jamison, Catherine. *The history of the royal hospital of St Katherine by the tower of London.* 1952. Chiefly religious. Translates queen Philippa's ordinances of 1351.

1767   Kemp, Eric W. *An introduction to the canon law in the church of England: being the Lichfield cathedral divinity lectures for 1956.* 1957. Excellent elementary introduction; also *Counsel and consent.* 1961. A notable survey of the development of provincial councils of the church, especially in England. Mainly modern.

1768   King, Edwin J. *The grand priory of the order of the hospital of St John of Jerusalem in England: a short history.* 1924; also *The rule, statutes and customs of the Hospitallers, 1099—1310.* 1934.

1769   Knowles, David. *The episcopal colleagues of archbishop Thomas Becket.* Cambridge, 1949. A challenging analysis of the attitude of the bishops in the famous dispute; also *The medieval archbishops of York.* York, 1961. A lecture; *Great historical enterprises: problems in monastic history.* Edinburgh, 1963. A reprint of four presidential addresses to the Royal Historical Society; *The historian and character and other essays,* ed. Christopher N.L. Brooke *et al.* Cambridge, 1963. A *Festschrift* composed of Knowles' own writings. It contains 'The humanism of the twelfth century', 'Archbishop Thomas Becket: a character study', 'The censured opinions of Uthred of Bolden', 'The monastic buildings of England', 'Cardinal Gasquet as an historian', 'A bibliography of the writings of Dom David Knowles'; and David Knowles and John K.S. St Joseph. *Monastic sites from the air.* Cambridge Air Surveys, 1 (1952). Contains 138 photographs.

1770   Köhler, Hans. *Der Kirchenbegriff bei Wilhelm von Occam.* Leipzig, 1937. [Dissertation.]

1771   Leff, Gordon. *Bradwardine and the Pelagians: a study of his 'De causa Dei' and its opponents.* Cambridge Studies in Medieval Life and Thought, n.s., 5 (1957). An important study of post Aquinian thinking in England; also

Heiko A. Oberman. *Archbishop Thomas Bradwardine, a fourteenth-century Augustinian: a study of his theology and its historical context.* Utrecht, 1957. Contains much new material and some questionable conclusions.

1772 —— *Richard Fitzralph, a commentator on the Sentences: a study in theological orthodoxy.* Manchester, 1964. Regards Fitzralph as a critic an opponent of 'Ockhamism', but not yet a mature scholar; *Heresy in the later Middle Ages: the relation of heterodoxy to dissent c. 1250–c. 1450.* New York, 1967, 2 vols. A major contribution to religious and intellectual developments in the period.

1773 Little, Andrew G. *Studies in English Franciscan history.* Manchester, 1917. Of lasting importance; Andrew G. Little and Ruth C. Easterling. *The Franciscans and Dominicans of Exeter.* Exeter, 1927.

1774 Logan, F. Donald. *Excommunication and the secular arm in medieval England: a study in legal procedure from the thirteenth to the sixteenth century.* Toronto, 1968. A scholarly work on a neglected subject.

1775 Loserth, Johann. *Johann von Wicliff und Robert Grosseteste.* Vienna, 1918; also *Huss und Wiclif.* 2nd ed., Munich, 1925.

1776 Manning, Bernard L. *The people's faith in the time of Wyclif.* Cambridge, 1919. Still valuable.

1777 Matthew, Donald J.A. *The Norman monasteries and their English possessions.* Oxford, 1962. Carries the treatment to the end of the Middle Ages.

1778 Matthews, Walter R. and William H. Atkins (eds.). *A history of St Paul's cathedral and the men associated with it.* 1957. A good chapter by Christopher N.L. Brooke on the earliest times to 1485.

1779 Messenger, Ruth E. *Ethical teachings in the Latin hymns of medieval England.* Columbia University Studies in History, Economics, and Public Law. 321 (1930).

1780 Moorman, John R.H. *Church life in England in the thirteenth century.* Cambridge, 1945. An incomplete picture, but nevertheless scholarly and helpful, with a good bibliography.

1781 Mullin, Francis A. *A history of the work of the Cistercians in Yorkshire (1131–1300).* Washington, D.C., 1932.

1782 O'Sullivan, Jeremiah F. *Cistercian settlements in Wales and Monmouthshire, 1140–1540.* New York, 1947. Some serious weaknesses combined with much information.

1783 Owst, Gerald R. *Preaching in medieval England: an introduction to sermon manuscripts of the period c. 1350–1450.* Cambridge, 1926. A scholarly pioneer volume, including abundant extracts from unprinted materials; also Homer G. Pfander. *The popular sermon of the medieval friar in England.* New York, 1937; Mary Aquinas Devlin. 'Bishop Brunton and his sermons', *Speculum,* 14 (1939), 324–44; Durant W. Robertson, Jr. 'Frequency of preaching in thirteenth century England', *Speculum,* 22 (1949), 376–88; Phyllis B. Roberts. *Stephanus de Lingua-tonante. Studies in the sermons of Stephan Langton.* Toronto, 1968.

1784 Pantin, William A. *The English church in the fourteenth century.* Cambridge, 1955. The best survey of its kind that has yet appeared.

1785 Peckham, John L. *Archbishop Peckham as a religious educator.* Yale Studies in Religion, 7 (1934).

1786 Phillips, W. Alison (ed.). *History of the church of Ireland from the earliest times to the present day.* Vol. 2. *The movement towards Rome. The medieval church and the reformation.* Oxford, 1934. By various writers.

1787 Platt, Colin. *The monastic grange in medieval England: a reassessment.* 1969.

1788 Power, Eileen E. and William A. Pantin. *Report on the muniments of the dean and chapter of Durham.* 1939. [Printed for private circulation.]

1789 Roberts, A.K. Babette. *St George's chapel, Windsor castle, 1348–1416: a study in early collegiate administration.* Windsor, 1948.

1790 Roberts, H. Ernest. *Notes on the medieval monasteries and minsters of English and Wales.* 1949. S.P.C.K.

1791 Robinson, David. *Beneficed clergy in Cleveland and the East Riding, 1306–1340.* Borthwick Institute, St Anthony's Hall Publications, 37 (1969).

1792   Roth, Cecil. *Medieval Lincoln Jewry and its synagogue.* Jewish Historical Society, 1934.
1793   Roth, Francis X. *The English Austin friars 1249—1538.* New York, 1961, 2 vols. A definitive survey. Supersedes articles in *Augustiniana*, 8—17 (1958—67).
1794   Saunders, Herbert W. *An introduction to the obedientary and manor rolls of Canterbury.* 1930. Interesting, but at points debatable.
1795   Sayers, Jane E. (ed.). *Medieval records of the archbishopric of Canterbury.* 1962. Articles by Churchill, Kemp, Jacob, and Du Boulay; also Sayers. *Papal judges delegate in the province of Canterbury, 1198—1234: a study in ecclesiastical administration.* New York, 1971.
1796   Sheppard, Lancelot C. *The English Carmelites.* 1943.
1797   Smalley, Beryl. *English friars and antiquity in the early fourteenth century.* Oxford, 1960. A fascinating book dealing with some curiosities of medieval literature and some odd personalities.
1798   —— *The study of the Bible in the Middle Ages.* Notre Dame, Ind., 1964. A reprint of 2nd ed; first published, Oxford, 1952. Second ed. is greatly enlarged. The most important work in English in this field.
1799   —— *The Becket conflict and the schools: a study of intellectuals in politics.* Totowa, N.J., 1973.
1800   Smith, Herbert M. *Pre-Reformation England.* 1938. General survey.
1801   Smith, Jeremiah J. *The attitude of John Pecham toward monastic houses under his jurisdiction.* Washington, 1949. Scholarly but unoriginal.
1802   Smith, Reginald A.L. *Canterbury cathedral priory: a study in monastic administration.* Cambridge, 1943. Excellent study, showing detached and enquiring mind; also *Collected papers*, 1947. With a memoir of Dom David Knowles. Includes 'The central financial system of Christ Church Canterbury, 1186—1512' and 'The financial system of Rochester cathedral priory'.
1803   Smith, Waldo E.L. *Episcopal appointments and patronage in the reign of Edward II.* Chicago, 1938. Inadequate: marred by slips and palaeographical errors.
1804   Snape, Robert H. *English monastic finances in the later Middle Ages.* New York, 1968. First published Cambridge, 1926. A scholarly and indispensable work, but overshadowed by the problem of the dissolution.
1805   Sommer-Seckendorff, Eleonore M.F. *Studies in the life of Robert Kilwardby, O.P. Institutum Historicum F F. Praedicatorum Romae.* Fasc. 8. Rome, 1957.
1806   Talbot, Hugh. *The Cistercian abbeys of Scotland.* 1939.
1807   Thompson, A. Hamilton. *English monasteries.* 2nd ed., Cambridge, 1923. The plan and buildings of monasteries and sketch of monasticism. Also Thompson. *The Premonstratensian abbey of Welbeck.* 1938. Illustrations and plans; also *Diocesan organization in the Middle Ages: archdeacons and rural deans.* Oxford, 1944. Reprinted from *PBA*, 29 (1943), 153—94; and Thompson. *The English clergy and their organization in the later Middle Ages.* 2nd ed., Oxford, 1966. First published Oxford, 1947. An indispensable guide to the mechanism and the routine of church life.
1808   Thompson, E. Maunde. *The Carthusian order in England.* 1930. S.P.C.K. Full and thorough: a lasting contribution.
1809   Tierney, Brian. *Medieval poor law: a sketch of canonical theory and its application in England.* Berkeley, Cal., 1959.
1810   Tillmann, Helene. *Die päpstlichen Legaten in England bis zur Beendigung der Legation Gualas (1218).* Bonn, 1926.
1811   Watt, John A. *The church and the two nations in medieval Ireland.* Cambridge, 1970. An important study, breaking new ground.
1812   —— *et al.* (eds.). *Medieval studies presented to Aubrey Gwynn, S.J.* Dublin, 1961. Contents arranged under three headings, Ireland, England, Europe.
1813   Wenzel, Siegfried. *The sin of sloth: 'acedia' in medieval thought and literature.* Chapel Hill, N.C., 1960. A definitive treatment.
1814   Weske, Dorothy B. *Convocation of the clergy: a study of its antecedents and*

its rise, with special emphasis upon its growth and activities in thirteenth and fourteenth centuries. 1937. Still the most complete handling of the subject, but has serious weaknesses.

1815 Westlake, Herbert F. *Westminster abbey: the church, convent, cathedral and college of St Peter Westminster.* 1923, 2 vols. Illustrations. Folios.

1816 Williams, David H. *The Welsh Cistercians: aspects of their economic history.* Pontypool, 1969.

1817 Wood, Susan. *English monasteries and their patrons in the thirteenth century.* Oxford, 1955. Valuable, but lacking in warmth.

1818 Woodcock, Brian L. *Medieval ecclesiastical courts in the diocese of Canterbury.* 1952.

1819 Wood-Legh, Kathleen L. *Studies in church life in England under Edward III.* Cambridge, 1934. Scholarly survey.

1820 —— *Perpetual chantries in Britain.* Cambridge, 1965. Most comprehensive study to date: valuable and attractive.

4 Biographies

1821 Boulter, Benjamin C. *Robert Grossetête, the defender of our church and our liberties.* 1936. S.P.C.K.; also Lawrence E. Lynch. 'The doctrine of divine ideas and illumination in Robert Grosseteste', *MS*, 3 (1941), 161—73; Kathleen Major. 'The "familia" of Robert Grosseteste', in Daniel A.P. Callus (ed.). *Robert Grosseteste scholar and bishop.* Oxford, 1955, 216—41; Marjory M. Morgan. 'The excommunication of Grosseteste in 1243', *EHR*, 57 (1942), 244—47; William A. Pantin. 'Grosseteste's relations with the papacy and the Crown', in Daniel A.P. Callus (ed.). *Robert Grosseteste scholar and bishop.* Oxford, 1955, 178—215; Josiah C. Russell. 'Richard of Bardney's account of Robert Grosseteste's early and middle life', *Med et Hum*, 2 (1944), 45—54; also Russell's 'Some notes on the career of Robert Grosseteste', *Harvard Theological Review*, 48 (1955), 197—211; S. Harrison Thomson. 'The *Notuli* of Grosseteste on the Nichomachean Ethics', *PBA*, 19 (1935), 195—218; and Thomson's *The writings of Robert Grosseteste, bishop of Lincoln 1235—1253.* Cambridge, 1940; Brian Tierney. 'Grosseteste and the theory of papal sovereignty', *Journal of Ecclesiastical History*, 6 (1955), 1—17; James H. Strawley. 'Grosseteste's administration of the diocese of Lincoln', in Daniel A.P. Callus (ed.). *Robert Grosseteste scholar and bishop.* Oxford, 1955; Edwin J. Westermann. 'A comparison of some of the sermons and the *Dicta* of Robert Grosseteste', *Med et Hum*, 3 (1945), 49—68; Beryl Smalley. 'The biblical scholar', in Daniel A.P. Callus (ed.). *Robert Grosseteste scholar and bishop.* Oxford, 1955, 70—97. An authoritative interpretation.

1822 Brett-James, Norman G. 'John de Drokensford, bishop of Bath and Wells', *Transactions of the London and Middlesex Archaeological Society*, n.s., 10—11 (1947—54), *passim.* Includes the great robbery of 1303.

1823 Bulloch, James. *Adam of Dryburgh.* 1958. Late twelfth century Scottish Carthusian with a wide influence by his writings: a scholarly biography.

1824 Cazel, Fred A. 'The last years of Stephen Langton', *EHR*, 79 (1964), 673—97. Describes Langton's invalidism and increasing sanctity.

1825 Cheney, Christopher R. *Hubert Walter.* 1969. An expert treatment. See also Charles R. Young. *Hubert Walter, lord of Canterbury and lord of England.* Durham, N.C., 1968. Another scholarly study.

1826 Cummins, John I. 'St Robert of Knaresborough, hermit; 1218', *Pax*, 26 (1936), 101—06, 126—30, 176—80, 201—04.

1827 Douie, Decima L. *Archbishop Pecham.* Oxford, 1952. A scholarly volume. See also David Knowles. 'Some aspects of the career of archbishop Pecham', *EHR*, 57 (1942), 1—18, 178—201; Francis J. Taylor. 'A medieval primate and his suffragans', *Church Quarterly Review*, 134 (1942), 170—91, mainly about Pecham; Hilda Johnstone. 'Archbishop Pecham and the council of Lambeth', *EPTT*, 171—88; Decima L. Douie. 'Archbishop Pecham's sermons and collations', *SPFP*, 269—82.

1828 Fraser, Constance M. *A history of Anthony Bek, bishop of Durham, 1283– 1311.* Oxford, 1957. Objective, scholarly and definitive.

1829 Greenaway, George W. *The life and death of Thomas Becket.* London Folio Society, 1961. See also Nesta Pain. *The king and Becket.* New York, 1966. First published 1964; William H. Hutton. *Thomas Becket archbishop of Canterbury.* Cambridge, 1926; David Knowles. *Archbishop Thomas Becket: a character study.* 1949; and David Knowles. *Thomas Becket.* Stanford, Cal., 1971; Börje Schlyter. *La vie de Thomas Becket par Benoît [Beneit].* Copenhagen, 1941; Richard Winston, *Thomas Becket.* 1967. A clear and unpretentious biography; Johannes Haller. 'Die Tragödie Thomas Becket', *Welt als Geschichte,* 4 (1938), 97–124; Thomas F. Tout. 'The place of St Thomas of Canterbury in history. A centenary study', *BJRL,* 6 (1921), 235–65; Zachary N. Brooke. 'The register of Master David of London and the part he played in the Becket crisis', *EPRP,* 227–45. Revises Stubbs' estimate of the effect of Becket's murder on papal authority in England; Charles Duggan. 'The Becket dispute and criminous clerks', *BIHR,* 35 (1962), 1–28. Argues convincingly that with regard to criminous clerks Becket's position was sound; James W. Alexander. 'The Becket controversy in recent historiography', *JBS,* 9 (1970), 1–26; Anne J. Duggan and Christopher N.L. Brooke. 'Henry II's supplement to the constitutions of Clarendon', *EHR,* 87 (1972), 757– 71.

1830 Haines, Roy M. 'Wolstan de Bransford prior and bishop of Worcester *c.* 1280–1349', *UBHJ,* 8 (1962), 97–113.

1831 Lawrence, C. Hugh. *St Edmund of Abingdon. A study in hagiography and history.* Oxford, 1960. An admirable biography with much original matter.

1832 McFarlane, Kenneth B. *John Wycliffe and the beginnings of English nonconformity.* 1952, reprinted in 1966 as *The origins of religious dissent in England.* See also John Stacey. *John Wyclif and reform.* 1964; Margaret E. Aston. 'John Wyclif's Reformation reputation', *PP,* 30 (1965), 23–51; Joseph H. Dahmus. 'Did Wyclif recant?', *Catholic Historical Review,* 29 (1943), 155–68; also Dahmus. 'Wyclif was a negligent pluralist', *Speculum,* 28 (1953), 378–81; and 'John Wyclif and the English government', *Speculum,* 35 (1960), 51–68; O.L. Marti. 'John Wyclif's theory for the disendowment of the English church', *Anglican Theological Review,* 11 (1929), 30–44; Gunner Westin. 'John Wyclif och hans reformidéer?', *Kyrkohistorisk Årsskrift,* 36 (1936), 1–145; 37 (1937), 1–160; Lowrie J. Daly. *The political theory of John Wyclif.* Chicago, 1962; Herbert B. Workman. *John Wyclif, a study of the English medieval church.* 1926, 2 vols; M.E.H. Lloyd. 'John Wyclif and the prebend of Lincoln', *EHR,* 61 (1946), 388–94; Harry S. Cronin. 'Wycliffe's canonry at Lincoln', *EHR,* 35 (1920), 564–69; Johann Loserth. 'Johann von Wiclif und Guilelmus Peraldus, Studien zur Geschichte der Enstehung von Wiclifs Summa Theologiae', *Sitzungsberichte der Kaiserlichten Akademie der Wissenschaften,* 180 (1916), 1–101; also Loserth's 'Johann von Wicliff und Robert Grosseteste', *Sitzungsberichte der Kaiserlichten Akademie der Wissenschaften,* 186 (1918) [reprint] ; Edith C. Tatnall. 'John Wyclif and ecclesia Anglicana', *Journal of Ecclesiastical History,* 20 (1969), 19–43. Argues convincingly that this *ecclesia* was, to Wyclif, an inheritance by the English church of a body of law, custom and personal example, which created a distinct church-tradition peculiar to England. There are important articles by Beryl Smalley. 'John Wyclif's *Postilla super totam Bibliam*', *Bodleian Library Record,* 4 (1953), 186–205; 'The Bible and eternity: John Wyclif's dilemma', *Journal of the Warburg and Courtauld Institute,* 27 (1964), 73–89; 'Wyclif's *Postilla* on the Old Testament and his Principium', in *Oxford studies presented to Daniel Callus.* Oxford Historical Society, n.s., 16 (1964), 253–96. These articles contain a most illuminating discussion of one aspect of Wyclif's thought; Gordon Leff. *John Wyclif: the path to dissent.* Oxford, 1966; and Leff's 'Wyclif and the Augustinian tradition', *Med et Hum,* n.s., 1, 29–39; Paul de Vooght. *Les sources de la doctrine chrétienne d'après les théologiens* du XIVe siècle et du début du XVe. Bruges, 1954. Defends Wyclif against his critics.

1833   Morey, Adrian. *Bartholomew of Exeter bishop and canonist. A study of the twelfth century.* Cambridge, 1937. With charters, etc., and the text of Bartholomew's penetential from Cotton MS. Vitellius A XII.

1834   Pearce, Ernest H. *Walter de Wenlock, abbot of Westminster.* 1920. A good biography. With documents illustrating the rule of the abbot; also Pearce's *Thomas de Cobham, bishop of Worcester, 1312—1327.* S.P.C.K. A popular but scholarly biography.

1835   Powicke, Frederick M. 'Ailred of Rievaulx and his biographer Walter Daniel', *BJRL*, 6 (1921), 310—51. Reprinted with corrections. Manchester, 1922; see also Paul Grosjean. 'La prétendue canonisation d'Aelred de Rievaux par Célestin III', *Analecta Bollandiana*, 78 (1968), 124—29.

1836   ——— 'Stephen Langton: an oration delivered at Canterbury', *Theology*, 17 (1928), 83—96; see also Powicke's *Stephen Langton* [Ford lectures, 1927] Oxford, 1928. Reprinted New York, 1965.

1837   ——— 'Walter de Merton, bishop of Rochester, 1274—47', in *Annales Amicorum Cathedralis Roffensis*, (1938), 25—30.

1838   Saltman, Avrom. *Theobald archbishop of Canterbury.* 1956. The only recent biography. Prints extensively from sources.

1839   Scammell, Jean V. *Hugh du Puiset, bishop of Durham.* Cambridge, 1956. Based on a thorough knowledge of the records of the Durham treasury.

1840   Sharp, Dorothea E. 'The 1277 condemnation of Robert Kilwardby', *New Scholasticism*, 8 (1934), 306—18.

1841   Tout, Thomas F. 'John Halton, bishop of Carlisle', in James Tait and Frederick M. Powicke (eds.). *The collected papers of Thomas Frederick Tout.* Vol. 2, 101—42. Manchester, 1934. Halton died in 1324.

1842   Warren, Wilfred L. 'A reappraisal of Simon Sudbury, bishop of Lincoln (1361—75) and archbishop of Canterbury (1375—81)', *Journal of Ecclesiastical History*, 110 (1959), 139—52.

1843   Webb, Clement C.J. *John of Salisbury.* 1932; see also Richard H. and Mary A. Rouse. 'John of Salisbury and the doctrine of tyrannicide', *Speculum*, 42 (1967), 693—709; also Ernest F. Jacob. 'John of Salisbury and the *Policraticus*', in Fossey J.C. Hearnshaw (ed.). *The social and political ideas of some great medieval thinkers.* 1923, 53—84.

5 Articles

1844   Ackerman, Robert W. 'The traditional background of Henry of Lancaster's *Livre, l'esprit créateur*', II, 3 (1962), 114—18.

1845   Adams, Norma. 'The writ of prohibition to court christian', *Minnesota Law Review*, 20 (1936), 271—93; 'The judicial conflict over tithes', *EHR*, 52 (1937), 1—22. Common law appropriating what had once been considered the spiritual field of jurisdiction (thirteenth and fourteenth centuries).

1846   Aikins, Harold E. 'Bishops and monastic finance in fourteenth-century England', *University of Colorado Studies*, 22 (1935), 365—80.

1847   Appleby, John T. 'The ecclesiastical foundations of Henry II', *Catholic Historical Review*, 48 (1962), 205—15. Argues that Henry II's expenditure on religious foundations not generous.

1848   Arnould, Emile J.F. 'Richard Rolle and the Sorbonne', *BJRL*, 23 (1939), 68—101. Richard never a student at Sorbonne.

1849   Baildon, W. Percy (ed.). *Notes on the religious and houses of Yorkshire.* Vol. 2. *Yorks.Arch.Rec.*, 81 (1931).

1850   Barlow, Frank. 'The English, Norman and French councils called to deal with the papal schism of 1159', *EHR*, 51 (1936), 264—68.

1851   Bennett, John H.E. 'The White friars of Chester', *Journal of the Chester and North Wales Architectural Society*, n.s., 31 (1935), 5—54.

1852   Bethnell, Denis. 'English black monks and episcopal elections in the 1120's', *EHR*, 84 (1969), 673—98. Shows that there was, indeed, an attack on the black monks at this time, but that far from losing influence, these monks as a body actually gained it in the 1120's and 1130's.

1853   Bill, Peter A. *The Warwickshire parish clergy in the later Middle Ages.* Dugdale Society Occasional Papers, 26 (1969).

1854   Bishop, Edmund. 'The method and degree of fasting and abstinence of the Black monks in England before the Reformation', *Downshire Review*, 43 (1925), 184—237. Prints excerpts from sources.

1855   Bishop, Terence A.M. 'Monastic demesnes and the statute of mortmain', *EHR*, 49 (1934), 303—06.

1856   Boehmer, Heinrich. 'Das Eigenkirchtum in England', in *Texte und Forschungen zur englischen Kulturgeschichte. Festgabe für Felix Liebermann zum 20 Juli 1921.* Halle, 1921, 301—53.

1857   Bond, M. Francis. 'Chapter administration and the archives of Windsor', *Journal of Ecclesiastical History*, 8 (1957), 166—81. A valuable account of the history of chapter administration at St George's chapel, Windsor.

1858   Brandt, William J. 'Church and society in the late fourteenth century: a contemporary view', *Med et Hum*, 13 (1960), 56—67. Using sermons of Thomas Brinton, bishop of Rochester, 1373—89.

1859   Brooke, Christopher N.L. 'Gregorian reform in action: clerical marriage in England, 1050—1200', *CHJ*, 12 (1956), 1—21.

1860   ——— 'The deans of St Paul's *c.* 1090—1499', *BIHR*, 29 (1956), 231—44. Lists and brief notes.

1861   Browne, Austin L. 'The cathedral treasurer in the Middle Ages', *Church Quarterly Review*, 133 (1942), 197—207.

1862   Butler, L.H. 'Archbishop Melton, his neighbours and his kinsmen, 1317—1340', *Journal of Ecclesiastical History*, 2 (1951), 54—68.

1863   Burr, David. 'Ockham, Scotus, and the censure at Avignon', *Church History*, 37 (1968), 144—59.

1864   Burridge, A.W. 'L'immaculée conception dans la théologie de l'Angleterre médiévale', *Revue d'histoire ecclésiastique*, 32 (1936), 570—97.

1865   Cam, Helen M. 'The religious houses of London and the eyre of 1321', *SPAG*, 320—29.

1866   Cate, James L. 'The church and market reform in England during the reign of Henry III', in James L. Cate and E.N. Anderson. *Medieval and historiographical essays in honor of James Westfall Thompson.* Chicago, 1938, 27—65.

1867   Cheney, Christopher R. 'The papal legate and English monasteries in 1206', *EHR*, 46 (1931), 443—52. Prints injunctions. See also 'A visitation of St Peter's priory, Ipswich', *EHR*, 47 (1932), 268—72. Prints record from 1327—36; 'Legislation of the medieval English church', *EHR*, 50 (1935), 193—224, 385—417. A scholarly and thorough revision of Wilkin's *Concilia* for the twelfth to fourteenth century; 'Norwich cathedral priory in the fourteenth century', *BJRL*, 20 (1936), 93—120. Prints injunctions by William Bateman, bishop of Norwich, mostly in 1350, 1370 and 1379; 'The punishment of felonious clerks', *EHR*, 51 (1936), 215—36. Important: the clerk must prove his clergy; 'Some papal privileges for Gilbertine houses', *BIHR*, 21 (1946—48), 39—58. Prints fragments dating from 1178 and (probably) 1192; 'A neglected record of the Canterbury election of 1205—6', *BIHR*, 21 (1946—48), 233—38. Prints a letter of Innocent III; 'Master Philip the notary and the fortieth of 1199', *EHR*, 63 (1948), 342—50. Prints three letters regarding the tax imposed by pope in December 1199 for succour of the Holy Land; 'King John and the papal interdict', *BJRL*, 31 (1948), 295—317. A judicious estimate of the effect of the interdict; 'The earliest English diocesan statutes', *EHR*, 75 (1960), 1—29. Begun by Stephan Langton: an important stage in local lawmaking; 'A group of related synodal statutes of the thirteenth century', *SPAG*, 114—32; 'The so-called statutes of John Pecham and Robert Winchelsey for the province of Canterbury', *Journal of Ecclesiastical History*, 12 (1961), 14—34. A critical and expert examination; 'A papal privilege for Tonbridge priory', *BIHR*, 38 (1965), 192—200. Fragment, beautifully dated and reconstructed, and a letter of pope Celestine III (1191); 'A recent view of the general interdict on England, 1204—1214', in Geoffrey J. Cumming (ed.). *Studies in Church History*, 3 (1966), 159—

68. Strongly criticises Henry G. Richardson and George O. Sayles; 'England and the Roman curia under Innocent III', *Journal of Ecclesiastical History*, 18 (1967), 173—86.

1868　Cheney, Mary G. 'The compromise of Avranches of 1172 and the spread of canon law in England', *EHR*, 56 (1941), 177—97. Throws much new light; 'The recognition of pope Alexander III: some neglected evidence', *EHR*, 84 (1969), 474—97. An expert analysis.

1869　Chettle, Henry F. 'The friars of the Holy Cross in England', *History*, 34 (1949), 204—20.

1870　Cosgrove, A.J. 'The electors to the bishopric of Winchester 1280—2', *Studies in Church History*, 3 (1966), 169—78. Marks a stage in the diminution of the metropolitan jurisdiction over elections and the development of royal policy.

1871　Cowan, Ian B. 'The development of the parochial system in medieval Scotland', *SHR*, 40 (1961), 43—55.

1872　Davies, Cicily. 'The statute of provisors of 1351', *History*, 38 (1953), 116—33. Re-assesses Edward III's intentions.

1873　Deeley, Ann. 'Papal provision and royal rights of patronage in the early fourteenth century', *EHR*, 43 (1928), 497—527.

1874　Denholm-Young, Noël. 'A letter from the council to pope Honorius III, 1220—1', *EHR*, 60 (1945), 88—96.

1875　Dickinson, John C. 'Early suppressions of English Houses of Austin canons', in Veronica Ruffer and Alfred J. Taylor (eds.). *Medieval studies presented to Rose Graham*. Oxford, 1950, 54—77. A thoughtful analysis.

1876　Donkin, Robert A. 'Localisation, situation économique et rôle parlementaire des abbés cisterciens anglais (1295—1341)', *Revue d'histoire ecclésiastique*, 52 (1957), 832—41; also 'The urban property of the Cistercians in medieval England', *Analecta Sacri Ordininis Cisterciensis*, 15 (1959), 104—31; 'The Cistercian order and the settlement of Northern England', *Geographical Review*, 59 (1969), 403—16.

1877　Donnelly, James S. 'Changes in the grange economy of English and Welsh Cistercian abbeys', *Traditio*, 10 (1954), 399—458.

1878　Dunning, Patrick J. 'Irish representatives and Irish ecclesiastical affairs at the fourth Lateran Council', *SPAG*, 90—113.

1879　Edwards, Kathleen. 'The political importance of the English bishops during the reign of Edward II', *EHR*, 59 (1944), 311—48. An important survey; see also 'Bishops and learning in the reign of Edward II', *Church Quarterly Review*, 138 (1944), 57—86. A scholarly assessment; complementary to 'The social origins and provenance of the English bishops during the reign of Edward II', *TRHS*, ser. 5, 9 (1959), 51—79. A valuable analysis.

1880　Farmer, Hugh. 'The vision of Orm', *Analecta Bollandiana*, 75 (1957), 72—82. Prints text of the religious vision of a boy of thirteen.

1881　Flahiff, George B. 'Le bref royal de prohibition aux cours d'église en Angleterre (1187—1286)', *École nationale des chartes. Position des thèses*, 1935, 79—88.

1882　———— 'The use of prohibitions by clerics against ecclesiastical courts in England', *MS*, 3 (1941), 101—16. Shows that there was no clear-cut struggle between spiritual and temporal; 'The writ of prohibition to court christian in the thirteenth century', *MS*, 6 (1944), 261—313. Important study: examines the opposition to unjust royal prohibitions.

1883　Flanagan, Urban. 'Papal provisions in Ireland, 1305—78', *Historical Studies*, 3 (1961), 92—103.

1884　Fochtman, Vincent. 'The personality of Duns Scotus', *FS*, 23 (1942), 368—78. See also Johannes Binkowski. *Die Weltlehre des Duns Scotus*. Berlin, 1936; John K. Ryan and Bernadine M. Boansea (eds.). *John Duns Scotus, 1265—1965*. Washington, D.C., 1965; Etienne Gilson. 'L'existence de Dieu selon Duns Scot', *MS*, 11 (1940), 23—61.

1885　Fowler, Robert C. 'Faulk Basset's register and the Norwich taxation', *Transactions of the Essex Archaeological Society*, n.s., 18 (1928), 15—26, 119—34. Connected with English grievances at the Council of Lyons, 1245.

1886   Fryde, Natalie M. 'John Stratford, bishop of Winchester, and the crown, 1323—30', *BIHR*, 44 (1971), 153—61.
1887   Gabriel, J.R. 'Wales and the Avignon papacy', *ArchCamb*, 78 (ser. 3, 7) (1923), 70—86.
1888   Garlick, Vera F.M. 'Provision of vicars in the early XIVth century', *History*, 34 (1949), 15—27.
1889   Godfrey, Cuthbert J. 'Pluralists in the province of Canterbury in 1366', *Journal of Ecclesiastical History*, 11 (1960), 23—40. Returns of pluralists in the province of Canterbury.
1890   Goldthorp, L.M. 'The Franciscans and Dominicans in Yorkshire', *Yorks.Arch. J.*, 32 (1935—36), 264—320, 365—428.
1891   Graham, Rose. 'Cardinal Ottoboni and the monastery of Stratford Langthorne', *EHR*, 33 (1918), 213—25. Prints a record of the dispute over the right of visitation: 1265—68. Also 'An ecclesiastical tenth for national defence in 1298', *EHR*, 34 (1919), 200—05; 'A petition to Boniface VIII from the clergy of the province of Canterbury in 1297', *EHR*, 37 (1922), 35—46; 'The administration of Ely diocese *sede vacante*, 1298—9, 1302—3', *TRHS*, ser. 4, 12 (1292), 49—74; 'The conflict between Robert Winchelsey, archbishop of Canterbury, and the abbot and monks of St Augustine's Canterbury', *Journal of Ecclesiastical History*, 1 (1950), 37—50.
1892   Gransden, Antonia. 'The Peterborough customary and Gilbert de Stanford', *Revue bénédictine*, 70 (1960), 625—38. Describes a Peterborough customary of *c.* 1370: interesting details of monastic life; also 'The reply of a fourteenth-century abbot of Bury St Edmunds to a man's petition to be a recluse', *EHR*, 75 (1960), 464—67.
1893   Gray, J.W. 'Canon law in England: some reflections on the Stubbs—Maitland controversy', *Studies in Church History*, 3 (1966), 46—68. Questions the value of Maitland's constant reaffirmations of his anti—Stubbsian thesis; also 'The *ius praesentandi* in England from the constitutions of Clarendon to Bracton', *EHR*, 67 (1952), 481—509. Argues that the conflict of the jurisdictions over advowsons and presentations was not finally settled in the time of Bracton.
1894   Greenaway, William. 'The papacy and the diocese of St David's, 1305—1417', *Church Quarterly Review*, 161 (1960), 436—48; 162 (1961), 33—49; also 'Archbishop Pecham, Thomas Bek and St David's', *Journal of Ecclesiastical History*, 11 (1960), 152—63. The opposition of Thomas Bek to archbishop Pecham's attempt to visit the diocese of St David's.
1895   Gumbley, Walter. 'Provincial priors and vicars of the English Dominicans, 1221—1916', *EHR*, 33 (1918), 243—51. Supplemented by James Tait. *EHR*, 33 (1918), 496—500.
1896   Gwynn, Aubrey O. 'The sermon-diary of Richard Fitzralph, archbishop of Armagh', *Proceedings of the Royal Irish Academy*, 44 (1937—38), 1—57; also 'St Lawrence O'Toole as legate in Ireland (1179—1180)', *Analecta Bollandiana*, 68 (1950), 223—40.
1897   Hackett, M. Benedict. 'William Flete's "De remediis contra temptacionis" in its Latin and English recensions: the growth of the text', *MS*, 26 (1964), 210—30. The text was written before June 1359.
1898   Haines, Roy M.'The administration of the diocese of Worcester "sede vacante" 1266—1350', *Journal of Ecclesiastical History*, 13 (1962), 156—71; and 'Adam Oreleton and the diocese of Winchester', *Journal of Ecclesiastical History*, 23 (1972), 1—30.
1899   Hartridge, Reginald A.R. 'Edward I's use of his rights of presentation to benefices as shown by the patent rolls', *CHJ*, 2 (1928), 171—77. Suggests that work of conscientious prelates was frustrated by the complaisance of the Roman curia.
1900   Haskins, George L. and Ernst H. Kantorowicz. 'A diplomatic mission of Francis Accursius and his oration before pope Nicholas III', *EHR*, 58 (1943), 424—47. Accursius was an envoy of Edward I for the re-election of Robert Burnell to Canterbury.
1901   Hay, Denis. 'The church of England in the later Middle Ages', *History*, 53 (1968), 35—50. Historians should be less diffident in using the phrase.

1902   Hays, Rhys W. 'Rotoland, subprior of Aberconway and the controversy over the see of Bangor 1199–1204', *Journal of the Historical Society of the Church in Wales*, 13 (1963), 9–20.

1903   Highfield, John R.L. 'The English hierarchy in the reign of Edward III', *TRHS*, ser. 5, 6 (1956), 115–38. In the march towards a state-controlled Church there was a decisive step forward under Edward III. An important survey.

1904   Hill, Rosalind. 'The theory and practice of excommunication in medieval England', *History*, 42 (1957), 1–11. Over-much use caused it to degenerate from a tremendous spiritual sanction into a minor inconvenience.

1905   ——— 'Bishop of Sutton and the institution of heads of religious houses in the diocese of Lincoln', *EHR*, 58 (1943), 201–09. Between 1280 and 1299.

1906   ——— 'Public penance: some problems of a thirteenth century bishop', *History*, 36 (1951), 213–26.

1907   Hinnebusch, William A. 'The diplomatic activities of the English Dominicans in the thirteenth century', *Catholic Historical Review*, 28 (1942), 309–39; also 'The personnel of the early English Dominican province', *Catholic Historical Review*, 29 (1943), 326–46; 'The domestic economy of the English Dominicans', *Catholic Historical Review*, 30 (1944), 247–70.

1908   Holdsworth, Christopher J. 'John of Ford and English Cistercian writing 1167–1214', *TRHS*, ser. 5, 11 (1961), 177–36.

1909   Hussey, Arthur. 'Kent chantries', *Kent Archaeological Society Records Branch*, 12, pt. 2 (1934), 121–200.

1910   Jack, R. Ian. 'The ecclesiastical patronage exercised by a baronial family in the late Middle Ages', *Journal of Religious History*, 3 (1965), 275–95.

1911   Jacob, Ernest F. 'The medieval chapter of Salisbury cathedral', *Wiltshire Archaeological and Natural History Magazine*, 51 (1947), 479–95.

1912   ——— 'St Richard of Chichester', *Journal of Ecclesiastical History*, 7 (1956), 174–88.

1913   Jenkins, Claude. 'Sudbury's London register', *Church Quarterly Review*, 121 (1929), 222–54.

1914   Johnson, Charles. 'The reconciliation of Henry II with the papacy, a missing document', *EHR*, 52 (1937), 465–67. Prints a papal bull on the eve of submission.

1915   Keil, Ian. 'The abbots of Glastonbury in the early fourteenth century', *Downside Review*, 82 (1964), 327–48.

1916   King, Archdale A. 'Cistercian abbeys of Gloucestershire', *Pax* (1942), 5–12, 135–41; (1943), 30–40.

1917   Kingsford, Charles L. *et al.* 'Additional material for the history of the Grey friars, London', *Collectanea Franciscana*, 2 (1922), 61–169.

1918   Kissack, K.E. 'Religious life in Monmouth 1066–1536', *Journal of the Historical Society in the Church in Wales*, 14 (1964), 25–58.

1919   Knowles, David. 'The mappa mundi of Gervase of Canterbury', *Downside Review*, 48 (1930), 237–47; 'Essays in monastic history: IV. The growth of exemption', *Downside Review*, 50 (1932), 201–31, 396–436; V. 'The cathedral monasteries', *Downside Review*, 51 (1933), 73–96; VI. 'Parish organization', *Downside Review*, 51 (1933), 501–22; VII. 'The diet of the Black monks', *Downside Review*, 52 (1934), 275–99; also 'The excellence of the cloud', *Downside Review*, 52 (1934), 71–92; 'The revolt of the lay brothers of Sempringham', *EHR*, 50 (1935), 465–87. An important minor episode involving St Gilbert. Prints twelve original letters; 'The Canterbury election of 1205–6', *EHR*, 53 (1938), 211–20. Re-assesses Innocent's attitude; 'The cultural influence of English medieval monasticism', *CHJ*, 7 (1943), 146–59. Declining influence after the Norman conquest; 'Some developments in English monastic life, 1261–1336', *TRHS*, ser. 4, 26 (1944), 37–52. Discusses intellectual and economic development; 'English monastic life in the later Middle Ages', *History*, n.s., 39 (1954), 26–38. All Knowles' articles are the product of the finest scholarship; 'Religious life and organization', in Austin L. Poole (ed.). *Medieval England*. Oxford, 1958, 382—438; 'The twelfth and thirteenth centuries', in Charles R. Dodwell (ed.). *The English church and the continent*. 1959, 25—41. Solidarity of Western Christendom (including England) became explicit; 'The English bishops, 1070—1532', *SPAG*, 283—96.

1920 ———— and Richard N. Hadcock. 'Additions and corrections to medieval religious houses: England and Wales', *EHR*, 72 (1957), 60—87.

1921 Lambrick, Gabrielle. 'Abingdon and the riots of 1327', *Oxoniensia*, 29—30 (1964—65) 129—41; 'Abingdon abbey administration', *Journal of Ecclesiastical History*, 17 (1966), 159—83. From the tenth to the fifteenth century.

1922 Leeuwen, A. Van. 'L'église, régle de foi, dans les écrits de Guillaume d'Occam', *Universitas Catholica Loraniensis Sylloge*, 1934, 247—88.

1923 Leff, Gordon. 'Heresy and the decline of the medieval church', *PP*, 20 (1961), 36—51. A powerful analysis; recommended as prescribed reading.

1924 Leighton, Wilfred. 'The Black friars of Bristol', *Bristol and Gloucestershire Archaeological Society*, 55 (1934), 151—90.

1925 Little, Andrew G. 'A century of English Franciscan history (1224—1324)', *Contemporary Review*, 126 (1924), 449—58; 'A royal enquiry into property held by the mendicant friars in England in 1349 and 1350', *EHJT*, 179—189; 'The Franciscans and the statute of mortmain', *EHR*, 49 (1934), 673—76. Prints a letter of 1279—80; 'Grey friars of Salisbury', *Wiltshire Archaeological and Natural History Magazine*, 147 (1935), 36—54; 'Grey friars of Aylesbury', *Journal of the Architectural and Archaeological Society for Buckinghamshire*, 14 (1942), 77—98; 'Personal tithes', *EHR*, 60 (1945), 67—88; Andrew G. Little and Edward Stone. 'Corrodies at the Carmelite friary of Lynn', *Journal of Ecclesiastical History*, 9 (1959), 8—29.

1926 Lunt, William E. 'Collectors' accounts for the clerical tenth levied in England by order of Nicholas IV', [1291] *EHR*, 31 (1916), 102—19. Prints four accounts; also 'William Testa and the parliament of Carlisle', *EHR*, 41 (1926), 332—67. Prints reports; 'Clerical tenths levied by papal authority in England during the reign of Edward II', in Charles H. Taylor (ed.). *Haskins anniversary essays*. Boston, 1929.

1927 Lydon, James F. 'The Irish church and taxation in the XIVth century', *Irish Ecclesiastical Record*, ser. 5, 103, 158—65.

1928 Madden, James E. 'Business monks, banker monks, bankrupt monks; the English Cistercians in the thirteenth century', *Catholic Historical Review*, 49 (1963), 341—64. Suggests that the Cistercian business and banker monks became bankrupt in an effort to support their cherished exemption privilege.

1929 Major, Kathleen. 'The "familia" of archbishop Stephen Langton', *EHR*, 48 (1933), 529—53; also 'The Lincoln diocesan records', *TRHS*, ser. 4, 22 (1940), 39—66.

1930 Martin, Alan R. 'The Greyfriars of Walsingham', *Norfolk Archaeology*, 25 (1934), 227—71. The friary was founded in 1347; also the Greyfriars of Lincoln', *Archaeological Journal*, 92 (1936), 42—63.

1931 Martin, Edward J. 'The Templars in Yorkshire', *Yorks.Arch.J.*, 30 (1931), 135—56.

1932 Mayr-Harting, Henry. 'Hilary, bishop of Chichester (1147—1169) and Henry II', *EHR*, 78 (1963), 209—24. Hilary was a steadfast adherent of the king, in spite of papalist training; also 'Henry II and the papacy, 1170—1189', *Journal of Ecclesiastical History*, 16 (1965), 39—53.

1933 Meyer, Erwin T. 'Henri III d'Angleterre et l'église', *Revue de l'histoire des religions*, 97—8 (1928), 238—74.

1934 Mildner, Francis M. 'The immaculate conception in England up to the time of Duns Scotus', *Marianum*, 1939, 86—99, 200—21.

1935 Moorman, John R.H. 'The medieval parsonage and its occupants', *BJRL*, 28 (1944), 137—53; also 'The foreign element among the English Franciscans', *EHR*, 62 (1947), 289—303.

1936 Morgan, Marjorie M. 'The suppression of the alien priories', *History*, 26 (1941), 204—12.
1937 Niederstenbrugh, Alex. 'Die geistige Haltung Richard Rolles', *Archiv für das Studium neuern Sprachen*, 175 (1939), 50—64; also Émile J.F. Arnould. 'Richard Rolle and a bishop: a vindication', *BJRL*, 21 (1937), 55—77. Argues that Rolle did not conflict with ecclesiastical authority.
1938 O'Dwyer, B.W. 'The problem of Irish reforms in Cistercian monasteries and the attempted solution of Stephen of Lexington in 1228', *Journal of Ecclesiastical History*, 15 (1964), 189—91; also 'The impact of the native Irish on the Cistercians in the thirteenth century', *Journal of Religious History*, 4 (1967), 287—301.
1939 Orme, Margaret. 'A reconstruction of Robert of Cricklade's "Vita et Miracula S. Thomae Cantuariensis" ', *Analecta Bollandiana*, 84 (1966), 279—98.
1940 Otway-Ruthven, A. Jocelyn. 'The church lands of Co. Dublin', *SPAG*, 54—73.
1941 Pantin, William A. 'The general and provincial chapters of the English Black monks, 1215—1540', *TRHS*, 10 (1927), 195—263; also 'English monastic letter-books', *EHJT*, 201—223. Suggests that these form a valuable source of evidence for later Middle Ages; 'English monks and English friars', *Dublin Review*, 98 (1941), 98—112; 'Two treatises of Uthred of Bolden on the monastic life', *SPFP*, 363—85. Throws light on both fourteenth-century monasticism and intellectual life; 'The later Middle Ages', in Charles R. Dodwell (ed.). *The English church and the continent.* 1959, 42—59. Shows deep insight; 'Before Wolsey', in Hugh Trevor-Roper (ed.). *Essays in British history presented to Sir Keith Feiling.* 1964, 29—59. A scholarly discussion of the medieval site of Christ Church and neighbourhood; 'The letters of John Mason: a fourteenth-century formulary from St Augustine's Canterbury', *EPBW*, 192—219. An interesting and scholarly cross-section of the problems that faced a fourteenth-century abbot. Includes a number of original entries.
1942 Poole, Austin L. 'Outlawry as a punishment of criminous clerks', *EHJT*, 239—47. Shows that clerks were sometimes degraded and forced to abjure the realm, after 1170.
1943 Poole, Reginald L. 'John of Salisbury at the papal court', *EHR*, 38 (1923), 321—30.
1944 Powicke, Frederick M. 'The bull "Miramur plurimum" and a letter to archbishop Stephen Langton', *EHR*, 44 (1929), 87—93.
1945 Reid, W. Stanford. 'The papacy and the Scottish war of independence', *Catholic Historical Review*, 29 (1943), 1—24; 31 (1945), 282—301.
1946 Richardson, Henry G. 'Letters of the legate Guala', *EHR*, 48 (1933), 250—59. Three letters.
1947 ——— and George O. Sayles. 'The clergy in the Easter parliament, 1285', *EHR*, 52 (1937), 220—34. Important comment on the relations between church and state. Prints minutes of meeting between prelates and council.
1948 Robertson, Durant W., Jr. 'The cultural tradition of *Handlyng Synne*', *Speculum*, 22 (1947), 162—85. Regards it as a confessional manual. Important discussion.
1949 Ronan, Myles V. 'The diocese of Dublin and its beginnings. II. Bishops of Dublin', *Irish Ecclesiastical Record*, ser. 5, 43 (1934), 12—26, 137—54, 369—86, 485—509. Cf. *Irish Ecclesiastical Record*, ser. 5, 47 (1936), 28—44, 144—63, 459—68.
1950 Russell, Josiah C. 'The clerical population of medieval England', *Traditio*, 2 (1944), 177—212; also 'Medieval midland and northern migration to London, 1100—1365', *Speculum*, 34 (1959), 641—16.
1951 Sayers, Jane E. 'Canterbury proctors at the court of "Audientia Litterarum Contradictarum" ', *Traditio*, 22 (1966), 310—45. Transcripts and facsimiles.
1952 Sayles, George O. 'Ecclesiastical process and the parsonage of Stabannon in 1351. A study of the medieval Irish church in action', *Proceedings of the Royal Irish Academy*, 55 (1952—53), 1—23.
1953 Scammell, Jean V. 'Some aspects of medieval English monastic government:

the case of Geoffrey Burdon prior of Durham (1313–1321)', *Revue bénédictine*, 68 (1958), 226–50. New light on an unworthy prior.

1954   Seymour, St John D. 'The medieval church . . . ', in W. Alison Phillips (ed.). *History of the church of Ireland*. Vol. 2. Oxford, 1934, 3 vols.

1955   Sheehy, Stephen. 'The manner of appointing bishops in England. Its origin, growth and later developments', *Downside Review*, 55 (1937), 73–98.

1956   Smalley, Beryl. 'Stephen Langton and the four senses of scripture', *Speculum*, 6 (1931), 60–76. Important analysis of Langton's method.

1957   Smith, David. 'The rolls of Hugh of Wells, bishop of Lincoln 1209–35', *BIHR*, 45 (1972), 155–95.

1958   Spencer, Theodore. 'Chaucer's hell: a study in medieval convention', *Speculum*, 2 (1927), 177–200.

1959   Stegmüller, Friedrich. 'Robert Kilwardby, O.P. über die Möglichkeit der natürlichen Gottesliebe. (Quaestio de Dilectione Dei)', *Divus Thomus Piacenza*, 37 (1935), 306–19.

1960   Stenton, Frank M. 'Acta episcoporum', *CHJ*, 3 (1929–31), 1–14. Some details of twelfth-century ecclesiastical administration.

1961   Sutcliffe, Dorothy. 'The financial condition of the see of Canterbury, 1279–1292', *Speculum*, 10 (1935), 53–68. A scholarly analysis.

1962   Thompson, A. Hamilton. 'Notes on colleges of secular canons in England. Appendix: the statutes of the new collegiate church of St Mary Leicester, 1355–6 and 1490–1', *Archaeological Journal*, 74 (1917), 139–239; 'The registers of the archbishop of York', *Yorks.Arch.J.*, 32 (1935), 245–63; 'Ecclesiastical benefices and their incumbents', *Transactions of the Leicestershire Archaeological Society*, 22 (1942), 1–32; 'English colleges of chantry priests', *Ecclesiological Society Transactions*, n.s., 1 (1943), 92–108; 'William Beverley, archdeacon of Northumberland', in Veronica Ruffer and Alfred J. Taylor (eds.). *Medieval studies presented to Rose Graham*. Oxford, 1950, 216–32. Gives picture of life in the age of Chaucer.

1963   Ussery, Huling E. 'The status of Chaucer's monk: clerical, official, social, and moral', *Tulane Studies in English*, 17 (1969), 1–30.

1964   Walker, David. 'The medieval bishop of Llandaff', *Morgannwg*, 6 (1962), 5–33.

1965   Watkin, Aelred. 'The percentors, chancellors and treasurers in Wells cathedral', *Somerset Record Society*, 57 (1942), 51–103. A *fasti*, 1136–1940, with comments.

1966   Watson, Edward W. 'Collegiate churches', *Church Quarterly Review*, 91 (1921), 209–35.

1967   Waugh, William T. 'The great statute of praemunire', *EHR*, 37 (1922), 173–205. The significance of the statute of 1393. Now a little out of date.

1968   Williams, David H. 'The Cistercians in Wales: some aspects of their economy', *ArchCamb*, 114 (1965), 2–47.

1969   Williams, Glanmor. 'Religion in medieval Wales', in Arthur J. Roderick (ed.). *Wales through the ages*. Vol. 1. Aberystwyth, 1959, 160–67.

1970   Williamson, Dorothy. 'Some aspects of the legation of cardinal Otto in England, 1237–41', *EHR*, 64 (1949), 145–73; see also 'The legate Otto in Scotland and Ireland, 1237–1240', *SHR*, 28 (1949), 12–30.

1971   Wood-Legh, Kathleen L. 'The appropriation of parish churches during the reign of Edward III', *CHJ*, 3 (1929–31), 15–22. It was often beneficial; 'Some aspects of the history of the chantries during the reign of Edward III', *CHJ*, 4 (1932–34), 26–50. Suggests that chantries achieved greatest popularity well before the Black Death.

1972   Woodruff, C. Eveleigh. 'The election of Robert Winchelsey', *Church Quarterly Review*, 121 (1936), 210–32.

XII. HISTORY OF THE FINE ARTS

1 Printed Sources

1973   Colvin, Howard M. *Building accounts of Henry III*. Oxford, 1971; see also

'Building by king Henry III and Edward son of Odo', *Antiquaries Journal*, 28 (1948–49), 138–48; 29 (1950–51), 13–25.

1974   Friends of Canterbury Cathedral. *The Canterbury psalter.* 1935. Introduction by Montague R. James. Fifty-five pp. and 286 folios. Written *c.* 1150.

1975   Knoop, Douglas *et al.* (eds.). *The two earliest masonic MSS.: the "Regius MS. B.M. Bibl. Reg. 17.AI", and "Cook MS. B.M. Add. MS. 23198".* Manchester, 1938.

1976   Millar, Eric G. (ed.). *The Luttrell Psalter. (B.M. Add. MS. 42130).* [Published for the trustees of the British Museum] 1932. Plates and monochrome. A beautiful volume.

1977   Salzmann, Louis F. *Building in England down to 1540.* 2nd ed., Oxford, 1967. 148 pp. of original writings. Excellent survey of engineering and architectural operations.

2 Surveys

1978   Anderson, Mary D. *The medieval carver.* Cambridge, 1935. Really an anthology of medieval carving.

1979   Batsford, Harry and Charles Fry. *The cathedrals of England.* 6th ed., 1945. Ninety-seven plates. See also Thomas F. Bumpus. *The cathedrals of England and Wales.* 1937. First published 1905; Konrad Escher. *Englische Kathedralen.* Munich, 1929; John H. Harvey. *The English cathedrals.* 1950, scholarly and stimulating; A. Hamilton Thompson. *The cathedral churches of England.* 1926. S.P.C.K. Valuable; Peter Meyer *et al. English cathedrals.* 1950. Well illustrated.

1980   Boase, Thomas S.R. *The Oxford history of English art.* Vol. 3, *1100–1216.* Oxford, 1953. A standard work.

1981   Brieger, Peter. *The Oxford history of English art.* Vol. 4, *1216–1307.* Oxford, 1957. A standard work.

1982   Brown, R. Allen *et al. The history of the king's works. The Middle Ages.* 1963, 2 vols. HMSO. Important for students of military, ecclesiastical and civil architecture, as well as for economics and finance.

1983   Clapham, Alfred W. *Romanesque architecture in England.* 1950.

1984   Coltart, John S. *Scottish church architecture.* 1936.

1985   Coulton, George G. *Art and the Reformation.* 1928. A scholarly and important book, denigrating the importance of religion in medieval art.

1986   Cranage, David H.S. *Cathedrals and how they were built.* Cambridge, 1940.

1987   Crossley, Frederick H. *English church craftsmanship. An introduction to the work of the medieval period . . .* 1941; 2nd ed., 1947.

1988   Evans, Joan. *The Oxford history of English art.* Vol. 5, *1307–1461.* Oxford, 1949. A standard work, with ninety-six plates.

1989   Fellows, Arnold. *The wayfarer's companion: England's history in her buildings and countryside.* Oxford, 1937. Reprinted, with corrections, 1954. A courageous and searching book.

1990   Fichten, John. *The construction of Gothic cathedrals, a study of medieval vault erection.* Oxford, 1961.

1991   Frankl, Paul. *Gothic architecture.* Harmondsworth, 1962. An excellent survey.

1992   Hadow, William H. *English music.* 1931. A brilliant sketch. See also F. Llewellyn Harrison. *Music in medieval Britain.* 1958; Ernest Walker. *A history of music in England.* 3rd ed., revised, Oxford, 1952; H. Orsmond Anderton. *Early English music.* 1920.

1993   Hannah, Ian C. *Story of Scotland in stone.* Edinburgh, 1934.

1994   Harvey, John H. *Gothic England: a survey of national culture.* 1947. A study of the arts in England from the mid-fourteenth century to the Tudor period; also *The Gothic world 1100–1600: a survey of architecture and art.* New York, 1969. First published 1950. A remarkable and versatile reference book which should be in every library; also *The medieval architect.* New York, 1972.

1995   HMSO. *Royal commission on the ancient and historical monuments and construction in England.* 1911–70, 25 vols.; *Royal commission on ancient and historical monuments and construction in Scotland.* Edinburgh, 1909–67, 20 vols.

1996   Morey, Charles R. *Medieval art.* New York, 1942. A beautiful volume by a great expert.

1997   Prior, Edward S. *Eight chapters on English medieval art: a study in English economics.* Cambridge, 1922.

1998   Reese, Gustave. *Music in the Middle Ages, with an introduction on the music of ancient times.* New York, 1940. The first comprehensive study of medieval music to be written in the English language.

1999   Saunders, O. Elfrida. *A history of English art in the Middle Ages.* Oxford, 1932.

2000   Thompson, David V. *The materials of medieval painting.* New Haven, Conn., 1946. Not for specialists, but for all scholars and all interested in medieval art and life.

2001   Webb, Geoffrey. *Gothic architecture in England.* 1951; *Architecture in England in the Middle Ages.* 2nd ed., 1965. Authoritative.

2002   Young, Karl. *Drama of the medieval church.* Oxford, 1933. Product of a quarter of a century of research.

3 Monographs

2003   Addy, Sidney O. *The evolution of the English house.* 1933. First published 1898. Revised ed. enlarged from author's notes by John Summerson. See also Nathaniel Lloyd. *A history of the English house, from primitive times to the Victorian period.* 1931; Margaret E. Wood. *Thirteenth-century domestic architecture in England.* Supplement to *Archaeological Journal*, 105 (1950); *The English medieval house.* 1965. This volume will be a classic for many decades to come; H. Avray Tipping. *English homes.* 1920, 1937, 2 vols. [to 1558].

2004   Anderson, Mary D. *Design for a journey.* Cambridge, 1940. First-class study of medieval architecture. See also Mary Anderson's *Misericords. Medieval life in English woodcarving.* Cambridge, 1954. *Drama and imagery in English medieval churches.* Cambridge, 1963. By a sensitive expert.

2005   Arnold, Hugh. *Stained glass of the Middle Ages in England and France.* New York, 1955. First published in London, 1913. 2nd ed., 1939. A standard work. Fifty plates in colour.

2006   Borenius, Tancred. *St Thomas Becket in art.* 1932. Important contribution to the study of the cult of the Saint and to that of medieval iconography.

2007   Bradley, Elizabeth. *The story of the English abbey told in counties.* (The northern and eastern counties.) 1938–39, 2 vols.

2008   Brakspear, Harold. *The cathedral church of St Peter and St Paul at Bath, now generally known as Bath abbey.* 2nd ed., Gloucester, 1939.

2009   Caiger-Smith, A. *English medieval mural paintings.* Oxford, 1963. A useful and well-constructed study.

2010   Carpenter, Edward F. *et al. A house of kings, the history of Westminster abbey.* 1966. Popular survey of high quality. Plates. See also William R. Lethaby. *Westminster abbey re-examined.* 1925. See also Jocelyn H.T. Perkins. *Westminster abbey its worship and ornaments.* Oxford, 1938–52, 3 vols.; Winifride de L'hôpital. *Westminster cathedral and its architect.* 1919, 2 vols. Vol. 1 deals with the abbey; John G. Noppen. *Royal Westminster: a study of its origin and building . . . and of the coronation ceremony.* 1939. (A new ed. of *Royal Westminster and the coronation.* 1937.)

2011   Cave, Charles J.P. *Roof bosses in medieval churches.* Cambridge, 1948. Contains 368 photographs.

2012   Cook, George H. *Portrait of Durham cathedral.* 1948. Popular; *Portrait of Salisbury cathedral.* 1949. Popular, with beautiful illustrations; *Portrait of Lincoln cathedral.* 1950. Well illustrated; *The English medieval parish church.* 1954. Expertly told, with 180 photographs and fifty-four plans.

2013   Cook, Olive. *English abbeys and priories.* 1960; also Montague R. James.

Abbeys. With an additional chapter on monastic life and buildings by A. Hamilton Thompson. 1926.

2014 Couteur, John D. le. *English medieval painted glass.* Revised by Gordon McN. Rushforth. New York, 1926.

2015 Cranage, David H.S. *The home of a monk.* Cambridge, 1926. A succinct account of the buildings of a monastery.

2016 Crossley, Frederick H. *English church monuments, A.D. 1150—1550; an introduction to the study of tombs and effigies of the medieval period.* 1921; also *English church design, 1040—1540 A.D.; an introduction to the study of medieval building.* 1945; 2nd ed., revised 1948. A good survey; sixty-six plates; and Frederick H. Crossley with Maurice H. Ridgway. *Screens, lofts and stalls situated in Wales and Monmouthshire.* Reprinted from *Cambrian Archaeological Association,* 1947, 179—230; also Frederick H. Crossley and Maurice H. Ridgway. *Screens, lofts and stalls in Monmouthshire.* Newport, 1965.

2017 Cruden, Stewart. *Scottish abbeys.* Edinburgh, 1960. HMSO. An introduction to the subject.

2018 Davey, Henry. *History of English music.* 1895; 2nd ed., 1921.

2019 Dodwell, Charles R. *The Canterbury school of illumination 1066—1200.* Cambridge, 1954. An expert description with 291 photographs.

2020 Ede, William M. *Worcester cathedral . . .* 4th ed., Gloucester, 1937; 5th ed., 1939 by Ede and Harold Brakspear. A popular history and description.

2021 Egbert, Donald D. *The Tickhill psalter and related manuscripts.* New York, 1940. Possibly by Tickhill, prior of the Augustinian monastery of Worksop, 1303—1314. A permanent record finely illustrated (113 plates) with eight appendices: outstanding scholarship.

2022 Gardner, Arthur. *Alabaster tombs of the Pre-Reformation period in England.* Cambridge, 1940; *English medieval sculpture.* Cambridge, 1935; reprinted 1951. An abridged and up to date ed., abundantly illustrated, of Arthur Gardner and Edward S. Prior's *Account of medieval figure-sculpture.* 1912. A standard work. See also Fritz Saxl. *English sculptures of the twelfth century.* 1954; Lawrence Stone. *Sculpture in Britain: the Middle Ages.* Baltimore, Md., 1955.

2023 Gilson, Julius P. and Henry Poole. *Four maps of Great Britain designed by Matthew Paris about 1250.* 1928.

2024 Greene, Richard L. *The early English carols.* Oxford, 1935. A learned volume, showing the early connection with less worshipful lyrics. The carol had a learned as well as a popular source.

2025 Hamilton, A.H. *Song schools in the Middle Ages.* Church Music Society, Occasional Papers, 14 (1942).

2026 Harrison, Frederick. *English manuscripts of the fourteenth century (c. 1250 to 1400).* 1937. An expert account, with sumptuous illustrations.

2027 Harvey, John H. *Henry Yevele.* 1944. Also 'Henry Yvele, architect and his works in Kent', *Archaeologia Cantiana,* 56 (1944), 48—83; 'Henry Yevele reconsidered', *Archaeological Journal,* 108 (1951), 100—08; Douglas Knoop and Gwilym P. Jones. 'Henry Yevel and his associates', *Journal of the Royal Institute of British Architects,* ser. 3, 42 (1935), 801—09.

2028 Hastings, J. Maurice. *St Stephen's chapel and its place in the development of the perpendicular style in England.* Cambridge, 1955. Learned but over-enthusiastic.

2029 Hildburgh, Walter L. *English alabaster carvings as records of the medieval religious drama.* Oxford, 1949. Shows scholarship, originality and acumen. A good starting-point for further research.

2030 Horn, Walter and Ernest Born. *The barns of the abbey of Beaulieu at its granges of Great Coxwell and Beaulieu-St Leonards.* Berkeley, Cal., 1965. Magnificent illustrations. Mid-thirteenth century.

2031 Howard, Frank E. and Frederick H. Crossley. *English church woodwork during the medieval period A.D. 1250—1550.* 1917; 2nd ed., 1927. Text by Frank E. Howard. Good illustrations and diagrams.

2032 James, Montague R. *A Peterborough psalter and bestiary of the fourteenth century.* 1921. With photographic reproductions; *The Bohun manuscripts . . . executed in England about 1370.* Oxford, 1936. Sixty-eight plates.

2033   Kendrick, Albert F. *English needlework.* 1933; 2nd ed., 1967, revised by Patricia Wardle.

2034   Knowles, John A. *Essays in the history of the York school of glass-painting.* 1936.

2035   Leask, Harold G. *Irish churches and monastic buildings.* Dundalk, 1955. Valuable. Vol. 2 is on Gothic architecture to 1400. Numerous diagrams.

2036   Little, Andrew G. (ed.). *Franciscan history and legend in English medieval art.* British Society of Franciscan Studies, 19 (1937). Maintains a very high level.

2037   Lloyd, Terence H. *Some aspects of the building industry in medieval Stratford-upon-Avon.* Dugdale Society Occasional Papers, 14 (1961). Uses the archives of the Guild of Holy Cross at Stratford.

2038   Malden, Richard H. *The growth, building and work of a cathedral church.* Oxford, 1944.

2039   Martin, Alan R. *Franciscan architecture in England.* British Society of Franciscan Studies, 18 (1937). Stresses independent evolution. Original and scholarly.

2040   Millar, Eric G. *English illuminated manuscripts from the Xth to the XIIIth century.* Paris, 1928. Numerous plates; also *English illuminated manuscripts of the XIVth and XVth centuries.* Paris, 1928.

2041   Mooney, Canice. *Franciscan architecture in pre-Reformation Ireland.* Pt. 1. Reprint from *Journal of Royal Society of Antiquaries of Ireland,* 85 Pt. 2 (1955), 133–73.

2042   Mottram, Ralph H. *The glories of Norwich cathedral.* 1948. Well illustrated.

2043   Oman, Charles W.C. *English church plate, 597–1830.* 1957. An original and brilliant survey intended to describe the part which church plate has played in the national life.

2044   Palmer, R. Liddesdale. *English monasteries in the Middle Ages.* 1930. General survey of architecture.

2045   Pevsner, Nikolaus. *Middlesex.* Harmondsworth, 1951.

2046   Richardson, James S. *The medieval stone carver in Scotland.* Edinburgh, 1964.

2047   Saunders, O. Elfrida. *English illumination.* Florence, 1928, 2 vols. More than a hundred plates. An important book.

2048   Tristram, Ernest W. *English wall painting of the fourteenth century.* 1955; William R. Lethaby. 'Medieval paintings at Westminster', *PBA,* 13 (1927), 123–51; Edward T. Long. 'Some recently discovered English wall paintings', *Burlington Magazine,* 56 (1930), 225–32.

2049   Truby, Jeffrey. *The glories of Salisbury cathedral.* 1948. Popular account, well illustrated.

2050   Turner, Hilary L. *Town defences in England and Wales: an architectural and documentary study 900–1500.* Hamden, Conn., 1971.

2051   Warner, Stephen A. *Canterbury cathedral.* 1923.

2052   Webb, Geoffrey F. *Ely cathedral.* 1950.

2053   Woodforde, Christopher. *English stained glass and glass-painting in the fourteenth century.* 1939. From *PBA*; also *English stained and painted glass.* Oxford, 1954.

2054   Zarnecki, George. *Later English Romanesque sculpture 1140–1210.* 1953.

4 Articles

2055   Andrews, Herbert K. and Thurston Dart. 'Fourteenth century polyphony in a Fountains abbey MS. book', *Music and Letters,* 39 (1958), 1–12.

2056   Ashley, Judith. 'Medieval Christmas carols', *Music and Letters,* 5 (1924), 65–71.

2057   Atkinson, Thomas D. 'Medieval figure sculpture in Winchester cathedral', *Archaeologia,* 85 (1935), 159–67.

2058   Bilson, John. 'St Mary's church, Beverley', *Yorks.Arch.J.,* 25 (1920), 357–436. Plates and plan.

2059   Bonney, Helen. ' "Balle's Place", Salisbury, a 14th century merchant's house', *Wiltshire Archaeological and Natural History Magazine*, 59 (1964), 155–67.

2060   Bowles, E.Q. 'Haut and bas: the grouping of musical instruments in the Middle Ages', *Musica Disciplina*, 8 (1936), 268–76.

2061   Brieger, Peter H. 'A statue of Henry of Almain', *EPBW*, 268–76.

2062   Brooke, Christopher N.L. 'Religious sentiment and church design in the later Middle Ages', *BJRL*, 50 (1967–68), 13–33.

2063   Brooks, Frederick W. 'A medieval brick-yard at Hull', *JBAA*, ser. 3, 4 (1939), 141–74.

2064   Cheney, Christopher R. 'Church-building in the Middle Ages', *BJRL*, 34 (1951–2), 20–36.

2065   Crossley, Frederick H. 'On the constructional design of timber roofs in the churches of Cheshire', *Lancs.Antiq.*, 52 (1937), 81–150.

2066   Eames, Elizabeth. 'The royal apartments at Clarendon palace in the reign of Henry III', *JBAA*, ser. 3, 28 (1965), 57–85. Plates and plans.

2067   Girdlestone, C.M. 'Thirteenth century Gothic in England and Normandy: a comparison', *Archaeological Journal*, 102 (1945), 111–33.

2068   Harvey, John H. 'The medieval carpenter and his work as an architect', *Journal of the Royal Institute of British Architects*, 45 (1938), 733–43; also 'The medieval office of works', *British Archaeological Journal*, ser. 3, 6 (1941), 20–87; 'The Western entrance of the Tower' [of London], *Transactions of the London and Middlesex Archaeological Society*, n.s., 9 (1948), 20–34. Plans: building by Henry III or Edward I; 'The king's chief carpenters', *JBAA*, ser. 3, 11 (1948), 13–34; 'The masons of Westminster abbey', *Archaeological Journal*, 113 (1956), 82–101; 'The origin of the perpendicular style', in Edward M. Jope (ed.). *Studies in building history: essays in recognition of . . . B.H. St John O'Neil.* 1961, 134–65. The best account.

2069   Holmes, Martin. 'Henry III at Westminster: the building of the abbey', *History Today*, 14 (1964), 811–19.

2070   Hudson, Henry A. 'Carvings of medieval musical instruments in Manchester cathedral', *Lancs.Historic.*, 73 (1921), 100–26.

2071   James, Montague R. 'An English picture-book of the late thirteenth century', *Publications of the Walpole Society*, 25 (1937), 23–32.

2072   Knoop, Douglas and Gwilym P. Jones. 'Master Walter of Herefore, "cementarius" ', *Miscellanea Latomorum*, n.s., 24 (1939), 49–55. A thirteenth-century mason; 'A note on the mason in Wales', *ArchCamb*, 96 (1941), 11–22. See also Douglas Knoop and Gwilym P. Jones. *The medieval mason.* Manchester, 1933. Of permanent value; also *A short history of freemasonry.* Manchester, 1940.

2073   Leask, Harold G. 'The architecture of the Cistercian order in Ireland in the XIIth and XIIIth centuries', *North Munster Archaeological Journal*, ser. 3, 6 (1943), 61–68; 7 (1944), 53–61. Norman and later.

2074   Legg, J. Wickham. 'Windsor castle, New College, Oxford and Westminster College: a study in the development of planning by William Wykeham', *JBAA*, ser. 3, 3 (1939), 83–95.

2075   Loomis, Roger S. 'Were there theatres in the twelfth and thirteenth centuries?', *Speculum*, 20 (1945), 93–95. Commentary by Gustave Cohen. *Speculum*, 20 (1945), 96–98. Establishes good case.

2076   Marshall, Miriam H. 'Thirteenth-century culture as illustrated by Matthew Paris', *Speculum*, 14 (1939), 465–77. Shows Matthew as many-sided scholar.

2077   Noppen, John G. 'XIIIth century sculpture at Westminster abbey', *Apollo*, 20 (1934), 211–16.

2078   —— 'Building by king Henry III and Edward son of Odo', *Antiquaries Journal*, 28 (1948–49), 138–48; 29 (1950–51), 13–25.

2079   Olson, Clair C. 'Chaucer and the music of the fourteenth century', *Speculum*, 16 (1941), 64–91. Some important generalizations; also 'The minstrels at the court of Edward III', *Publications of Modern Language Association*, 56 (1941), 601–12.

2080   Pantin, William A. 'Medieval priests' houses in South-West England', *Medieval Archaeology*, 1 (1957), 118–46. Includes plans; also 'Chantry priests' houses and other medieval lodgings', *Medieval Archaeology*, 3–4 (1959–60), 216–58; 'Medieval inns', in Edward M. Jope (ed.). *Studies in building history: essays in recognition of . . . B.H. St John O'Neil.* 1961, 166–91.

2081   Reaney, Gilbert. 'Some little-known sources of medieval polyphony in England', *Musica Disciplina*, 15 (1961), 15–26.

2082   Reese, Gustave. 'Polyphony in the British Isles from XIIth century to the death of Dunstable', *Music in the Middle Ages*, 1941, 387–424.

2083   Sanders, Ernest H. 'Cantilena and discant in 14th century England', *Musica Disciplina*, 19 (1965), 7–52.

2084   Shelby, Lon R. 'The role of the master mason in medieval English building', *Speculum*, 39 (1964), 387–403. A useful survey.

2085   Smith, John T. and C.F. Stell. 'Baguley Hall: the survival of pre-conquest building traditions in the fourteenth century', *Antiquaries Journal*, 40 (1960), 131–51.

2086   Thompson, A. Hamilton. 'Medieval building documents and what we learn from them', *Proceedings of the Somerset Archaeological and Natural History Society*, 66 (1920), 1–25. Especial reference to William of Wykeham; also 'Cathedral builders of the Middle Ages', *History*, n.s., 10 (1925), 139–50. Interesting details about the craftsmen.

2087   Wormald, Francis. 'Paintings in Westminster abbey and contemporary paintings', *PBA*, 35 (1949), 161–76. Important change *c.* temp. Edward I.

XIII. INTELLECTUAL HISTORY

1 Printed Sources

2088   Allen, Percy S. and Heathcote W. Garrod (eds.). *Merton muniments.* Oxford, 1928. A beautiful volume, with twenty-six plates.

2089   Bacon, Roger. *Roger Bacon's 'opera inedita'.* ed. Ferdinand M. Delorme and Robert W. Steele. Oxford, 1909–40, 16 Vols.

2090   Burley, Walter. *Walter Burley's 'De sensibus'.* ed. Herman L. Shapiro and Frederick Scott. Munich, 1966; Walter's *De Deo, Natura et Arte.* ed. Herman L. Shapiro. *Med et Hum*, 15 (1963), 86–90.

2091   Campsall, Richard of. *The works of Richard of Campsall. I. Questiones super librum Priorum analecticorum. MS. Gonville and Caius 668.* ed. Edward A. Synan. Toronto, 1968. Richard was at Merton College: died *c.* 1350–60.

2092   Cornwall, Peter of. 'The disputation of Peter of Cornwall against Symon the Jew', *SPFP*, 143–56.

2093   Denholm-Young, Noël (ed.). *Letter book of Richard de Bury.* Roxburghe Club. 1948.

2094   Garland, John of. *Morale scolarium of John of Garland.* ed. Louis J. Paetow. Berkeley, Cal., 1927. Adds to our knowledge of thirteenth-century scholarship.

2095   Gibson, Strickland (ed.). *Statuta antiqua universitatis Oxoniensis.* Oxford, 1931.

2096   Grosseteste, Robert. 'The prooemium to Robert Grosseteste's Hexaemeron', ed. Richard C. Dales and Servus Gieben, *Speculum*, 43 (1968), 451–61. Print and discuss this neglected and important text.

2097   ———— 'The Hexameron of Robert Grosseteste: the first twelve chapters of part seven', ed. Joseph T. Muckle, *MS*, 6 (1944), 151–74.

2098   Highfield, John R.L. (ed.). *The early rolls of Merton college, Oxford; with an appendix of thirteenth-century Oxford charters.* Oxford, 1964. A valuable contribution to the history of medieval universities. The Introduction contains the life of Walter de Merton.

2099   Holkot, Robert. 'A quodlibet question of Robert Holkot, O.P. on the problem of the objects of knowledge and belief', ed. Ernest A. Moody, *Speculum*, 39 (1964), 58—74. Includes the text of Question six of Holkot's first Quodlibet dispute of 1332.

2100   Ockham, William of. *Summa logiae* . . . , ed. Philotheus H. Boehner. Louvain, 1951—.

2101   Pantin, William A. *Canterbury college Oxford.* Oxford Historical Society, n.s., 6—8 (1947—50), 3 vols.

2102   Parsons, Edward J.S. *The map of Great Britain, circa 1360, known as the Gough map.* Oxford, 1958. Facsimile and Introduction. Map produced temp. Edward III, after 1347. See also Gerald R. Crone. *The Hereford world map.* 1948. Drawn shortly before 1300 by Richard of Haldingham, canon of Lincoln and Hereford; Crone. *Early maps of the British Isles, A.D. 100—A.D. 1579.* 1961; Julius P. Gilson. *Four maps of Great Britain designed by Matthew Paris about 1250.* Cambridge, 1928; J. Conway Davies. 'The Kambriae mappa of Giraldus Cambrensis', *Journal of the Historical Society of the Church in Wales*, 2 (1950), 46—61; Noël Denholm-Young. 'The *mappa mundi* of Richard Haldingham at Hereford', *Speculum*, 32 (1957), 307—14.

2103   Richardson, Henry G. and William A. Pantin. *Formularies which bear on the history of Oxford c. 1204—1420.* Oxford Historical Society, n.s., 4 and 5 (1942). 2 vols.

2104   Salter, Herbert E. (ed.). *Medieval archives of the university of Oxford.* Oxford Historical Society, 52—53 (1920—21), 2 vols.; also *Snappe's formulary and other records.* Oxford, 1924. Important for Wyclif and the question of intellectual liberty; Salter and Charles L. Shadwell (eds.). *Oriel college records.* Oxford Historical Society, 85 (1926).

2 Surveys

2105   Baudry, Léon. *Lexique philosophique de Guillaume d'Ockham: Études des notions fondamentales.* Paris, 1958. Much more than a dictionary of technical terms.

2106   Giacon, Carlo. *Guglielmo di Occam, Saggio storico-critico sulla formazione e sulla decadenza della scolastica.* Milan, 1941, 2 vols.

2107   Kibre, Pearl. *The nations in medieval universities.* Cambridge, Mass., 1948. A thorough and scholarly work, including Oxford and Cambridge. See also Gray C. Boyce. *The English-German nation in the university of Paris during the Middle Ages.* Bruges, 1927; Astrik L. Gabriel. *English masters and students in Paris during the thirteenth century.* Antwerp, 1949.

2108   Leach, Arthur F. *The schools of medieval England.* New York, 1969; first published, 1915.

2109   Leff, Gordon. *Paris and Oxford universities in the thirteenth and fourteenth centuries: an institutional intellectual history.* New York, 1968. Penetrating study, especially of Grosseteste and the Oxford school.

2110   Oberman, Heiko A. *Forerunners of the reformation: the shape of late medieval thought.* New York, 1966. Includes Robert Holkot and Thomas Bradwardine.

2111   Poole, Reginald L. *Illustrations of the history of medieval thought and learning.* 2nd ed., 1920. A classic, especially on Wyclif.

2112   Rashdall, Hastings. *The universities of Europe in the Middle Ages*, ed. Frederick M. Powicke and Alfred B. Emden. New ed., Oxford, 1936, 3 vols. Standard: valuable for bibliographies as well as corrections of earlier works.

2113   Sorley, William R. *A history of English philosophy.* 1930; 2nd ed., Cambridge, 1937.

3 Monographs

2114   Attwater, Aubrey L. *Pembroke college, Cambridge: a short history*, ed. Sydney C. Roberts. Cambridge, 1936. Introduction and postscript by Roberts.

INTELLECTUAL HISTORY

2115   Blair, David O.H. *In Victorian days and other papers.* 1939. Includes 'The
       Black monks at Oxford university'.
2116   Callus, Daniel A.P. (ed.). *The condemnation of St Thomas at Oxford.* 2nd
       ed., 1955. Examines actions of Kilwardby and Pecham.
2117   —— *Introduction of Aristotelian learning to Oxford.* 1944. Reprinted
       from *PBA*, 29 (1943), 229—81. By the end of the thirteenth century,
       movements famous in the fourteenth century had already gained impetus.
2118   —— *Oxford studies presented to Daniel Callus.* Oxford Historical Society,
       n.s., 16 (1964). Foreword by Richard W. Southern. Important essays on
       university life in Oxford by Alfred B. Emden, William A. Pantin, William
       A. Hinnebusch, Richard W. Hunt, Charles T. Martin, James A. Weisheipl,
       and Beryl Smalley, with list of Callus' writings.
2119   Cassidy, Vincent H. *The sea around them: the Atlantic Ocean A.D. 1250.*
       Baton Rouge, La., 1968. Informative and entertaining. Sets out to tell
       what intelligent men of the thirteenth century knew about the Atlantic,
       but does not entirely succeed.
2120   Chibnall, Albert C. *Richard de Badew and the university of Cambridge 1315—
       1340.* Cambridge, 1963. Throws much new light on scholars active in the
       university at this time.
2121   Cobban, Alan B. *The king's hall within the university of Cambridge in the
       later Middle Ages.* Cambridge, 1969.
2122   Crowley, Theodore. *Roger Bacon: the problem of the soul in his philosophical
       commentaries.* Louvain, 1950. A real contribution to the history of earlier
       thirteenth-century philosophy and to the problem of Bacon's place in his-
       tory. See also Edward Lutz. *Roger Bacon's contribution to knowledge,*
       FS, 17 (1936); Andrew G. Little. 'Roger Bacon', *PBA*, 14 (1928), 265—
       96. An important re-appraisal; Eugenio Massa. *Ruggero Bacone: etica e
       poetica nella storia dell' 'Opus maius'.* Rome, 1955. Brings out the
       thoughts of Bacon in convincing relief.
2123   Emden, Alfred B. *Donors of books to St Augustine's abbey, Canterbury.*
       Oxford, 1968.
2124   —— *An Oxford hall in medieval times: being the early history of St
       Edmund Hall.* 1927; re-issued Oxford, 1968, with new Preface.
2125   Forbes, Mansfield D. (ed.). *Clare college 1326—1926.* Cambridge, 1928,
       1930, 2 vols. (University Hall 1326—46; Clare Hall 1346—1856.)
2126   Gwynn, Aubrey O. 'Richard Fitzralph, archbishop of Armagh'. Pts. 3—6.
       Studies, 23 (1934), 359—411; 25 (1936), 81—96. See also Louis L.
       Hammerich. *The beginning of the strife between Richard FitzRalph and
       the mendicants, with an edition of his autobiographical prayer and his
       proposition 'Unusquisque'.* Det Kgl. Danske Videnskabernes Selskab.
       Historisk-filogiske Meddelselser, 36 (1938).
2127   Helbling-Gloor, Barbara. *Natur und Aberglauben im Policraticus des
       Johannes von Salisbury.* Zurich, 1956. Deals with methods of divination
       and magical practices as classified and criticized in Bks. 1 and 2 of the
       Policraticus.
2128   Hodgkin, Robert H. *Six centuries of an Oxford college: a history of Queens
       college, 1340—1940.* 1949.
2129   Kingsford, Charles L. *et al.* (eds.). *Collecteana Franciscana.* Manchester, 1922.
       Contains essays on libraries.
2130   Lacombe, George and Beryl Smalley. *Studies on the commentaries of Car-
       dinal Stephen Langton.* 1930. Indispensable for serious students of
       Langton. It also contains indices of rubrics and incipits. See also
       Langton's *Questiones* by Alys L. Gregory.
2131   Little, Andrew G. *Franciscan papers, lists, and documents.* Manchester, 1943.
       Collected articles, including one on the Franciscan school at Oxford, and
       another on the role of the Franciscans in the founding of the faculty of
       theology at Cambridge. Also a résumé on Roger Bacon and Bacon scholar-
       ship. The lists contain data illustrating the organization of the order. A
       most distinguished group of essays.
2132   —— and Franz Pelster. *Oxford theology and theologians, c. 1282—1302.*
       Oxford, 1934.

2133 Magrath, John R. *The Queen's college*. Oxford, 1921, 2 vols.
2134 Mallet, Charles E. *A history of the university of Oxford*. Vol. 1. The medieval university and the colleges founded in the Middle Ages. 1924.
2135 Mansbridge, Albert. *The older universities of England: Oxford and Cambridge*. 1923.
2136 Mietke, Jürgen. *Ockham's Weg zur Sozialphilisophie*. Berlin, 1969; Helmer Junghans. *Ockham im Lichte der neuren Forschung*. Berlin, 1968. Ernest A. Moody. *The logic of William of Ockham*. 1935; *Wilhelm Ockham (1349–1949) Aufsätze zu seiner Philosophie und Theologie*. Munster, 1950. Includes bibliography of works concerning Ockham published in preceding thirty years; Léon Baudry. *Guillaume de Occam. Sa vie, ses oeuvres, ses idées sociales et politiques*. Paris, 1949; Ernest F. Jacob. 'Some notes on Occam as a political thinker', *BJRL*, 20 (1936), 332–53; Georges de Lagarde. 'Marsile de Padoue et Guillaume d'Occam', *Revue des sciences réligieuses*, 17 (1937), 167–86, 428–55; A. Van Leeuwen. 'William of Occam †1349, en ziyn plaats in de geschiedenis van de theologie', *Studia Catholica*, 13 (1937), 181–208; Gordon Leff. 'Knowledge and its relation to the status of theology according to Ockham', *Journal of Ecclesiastical History*, 20 (1969), 7–17; Philotheus H. Boehner. *Philosophical writings of William of Ockham*. 1957. A selection with an Introduction and bibliography; Eloie M. Buytaert (ed.). *Collected articles on Ockham*. St Bonaventure, N.Y., 1958; Max A. Shepard. 'William of Occam and higher law', *American Political Science Review*, (1932), 1005–23; Robert Guelluy. *Philosophie et théologie chez Guillaume d'Ockham*. Louvain, 1947. Deals with the central problem of the relation between reason and faith: a profound and valuable study.
2137 Moorman, John R.H. *The Grey friars in Cambridge, 1225–1538*. Cambridge, 1952. Suggests that they exercised considerable influence.
2138 Plimpton, George A. *The education of Chaucer. Illustrated from the school-books of his time*. Oxford, 1935. See also Hugh Graham. 'Chaucer's educational background', *Thought*, 9 (1934), 222–35.
2139 Powicke, Frederick M. *The medieval books of Merton college*. Oxford, 1931. Concerns books distributed among the fellows at periodic intervals. Helps to form a picture of Oxford life in thirteenth and fourteenth centuries.
2140 Robson, John A. *Wyclif and the Oxford schools: the relation of the 'Summa de ente' to scholastic debates at Oxford in the later fourteenth century*. Cambridge, 1961. Breaks new ground in relating Wyclif's later views to his earlier teaching at Oxford; also Gordon Leff. 'Wyclif and the Augustinian tradition, with special reference to his *De trinitate*', *Med et Hum*, n.s., 1 (1970), 29–39.
2141 Roensch, Frederick J. *Early Thomistic school*. Dubuque, Ia., 1964. Gives careers of five English and nine French Dominican Thomists between 1277 and 1323: bibliographical.
2142 Sharp, Dorothea E. *Franciscan philosophy at Oxford in the thirteenth century*. British Society of Franciscan Studies, 16. 1930. Solid and enduring.
2143 Thompson, A. Hamilton. *Cambridge and its colleges*. 6th ed., 1926.
2144 Walter, Ludwig. *Das Glaubensverständnis bei Johannes Duns Scotus*. Munich, 1968.
2145 Walz, Rudolf. *Das Verhältnis von Glaube und Wissen bei Roger Bacon*. Freiburg, Switzerland, 1928. Careful and judicious.
2146 Wormald, Francis and Cyril E. Wright (eds.). *The English library before 1700*. 1958. Important chapters by various writers: generally useful and stimulating.

4 Biographies

2147 Denholm-Young, Noël. 'Richard de Bury (1287–1345)', *TRHS*, ser. 4, 20 (1937), 135–68. 'The greatest bibliophile of medieval Europe'. See also Richard de Bury. *The Philobiblion*. Berkeley, Cal., 1948. Reprint of trans. (1889) by Andrew F. West, new Introduction by Archer Taylor.
2148 Holmes, James S. and Hans C. Van Marle (trans.). *Johan Huizinga's Men and Ideas*. New York, 1959. Includes 'John of Salisbury: a pre-Gothic mind'.

2149 Morey, Adrian. *Bartholomew of Exeter, bishop and canonist; a study in the twelfth century.* Cambridge, 1937.
2150 Oberman, Heiko A. *Archbishop Thomas Bradwardine.* Utrecht, 1957.
2151 Pelster, Franz. *Thomas von Sutton. O. Pr.* Innsbruck, 1922. Pamphlet on a contemporary of Duns Scotus.
2152 Woodruff, F. Winthrop. *Roger Bacon, a biography.* 1938.

5 Articles

2153 Betts, Reginald R. 'Richard Fitz Ralph, archbishop of Armagh, and the doctrine of dominion', in David B. Quinn *et al.* (eds.). *Essays in British and Irish history in honour of James Eadie Todd.* 1949, 46−60. Distinguishes between 'original' and 'civil' lordship.
2154 Boehner, Philotheus H. '*In propria causa.* A reply to professor Pegis concerning of Ockham', *FS*, n.s., 5 (1945), 37−54; Anton C. Pegis. 'Concerning William of Ockham', *Traditio*, 2 (1944), 465−80; Philotheus H. Boehner. 'Ockham's theory of truth', *FS*, n.s., 5 (1945), 138−61.
2155 Brampton, Charles K. 'Duns Scotus at Oxford, 1288−1301', *FS*, 24 (1964), 1−20; Beraud de Saint-Maurice. *Johns Duns Scotus, a teacher for our times.* trans. Columbus Duffy, 1955.
2156 Cobban, Alan B. 'Edward II, pope John XXII and the university of Cambridge', *BJRL*, 47 (1964−65), 49−78. Argues that the establishment of an arm of the Chapel Royal in Cambridge was a crucial expedient intended to buttress the power of the monarchy.
2157 Daly, Lowrie J. 'The conclusions of Walter Burley's commentary on the *Politics. Bks. 1−4*', *Manuscripta*, 12 (1968), 79−88; also 'Some notes on Walter Burley's commentary on the *Politics*', *EPBW*, 250−69. Gives some insight into what the medieval professor thought it was important for the student of the *Politics* to know.
2158 Dunn, Charles W. 'Ireland and the twelfth century renaissance', *University of Toronto Quarterly*, 24 (1954), 70−86.
2159 Emden, Alfred B. 'Northerners and Southerners in the organization of the university to 1509', in *Oxford studies presented to Daniel Callus.* Oxford Historical Society, n.s., 16 (1964), 1−30. List of proctors from 1267−68 to 1510.
2160 Flahiff, George B. 'The censorship of books in the twelfth century', *MS*, 4 (1942), 1−22. Much concerned with Ralph Niger in the last quarter of the twelfth century.
2161 Francerchini, Enzio. 'Robert Grosseteste, vescovo di Lincoln, et le sue traduzione latine', *Reale Instituto Veneto Atti*, 93, Pt. 2 (1933−34), 1−138.
2162 Gieben, Servus. 'Traces of God in nature according to Robert Grosseteste. With the text of the dictum: *Omnia creatura speculum est*', *FS*, 24 (1964), 144−58.
2163 Grabmann, Martin. *Die Aristoteleskommentare des Simon von Faversham.* Munich, 1943.
2164 Haskins, George L. 'The university of Oxford and the "ius ubique docendi" ', *EHR*, 56 (1941), 281−92. Prints some relevant letters.
2165 Hays, Rhys W. 'Welsh students at Oxford and Cambridge in the later Middle Ages', *WHR*, 4 (1964), 325−44.
2166 Hinnebusch, William A. 'Foreign Dominican students at Oxford Blackfriars', in *Oxford studies presented to Daniel Callus.* Oxford Historical Society, n.s., 16 (1964), 101−34.
2167 Holdsworth, Christopher J. 'John Ford and English Cistercian writing 1167−1214', *TRHS*, ser. 5, 11 (1961), 117−36. Discusses the writing in a period of change.
2168 Hunt, Richard W. 'The library of Robert Grosseteste', in Daniel A.P. Callus (ed.). *Robert Grosseteste, scholar and bishop.* Oxford, 1955, 121−45.
2169 ———— 'Oxford grammar masters in the Middle Ages', in *Oxford studies presented to Daniel Callus.* Oxford Historical Society, n.s., 16 (1964), 163−93. Gives excerpts from MSS.
2170 ———— 'English learning in the late twelfth century', in Richard W. Southern

(ed.). *Essays in medieval history selected from the 'transactions' of the Royal Historical Society on the occasion of its centenary*. 1968. From *TRHS*, 19 (1936), 106—28.

2171 Kantorowicz, Ernst H. and Beryl Smalley. 'An English theologian's view of Roman law', *Medieval and Renaissance Studies*, 1 (1943), 237—52.

2172 Knowles, David. 'The censured opinions of Uthred of Boldon', *PBA*, 37 (1951), 305—42. Throws light on teaching at Oxford in the fourteenth century. Prints original documents.

2173 Kuttner, Stephan and Eleanor Rathbone. 'Anglo-Norman canonists of the twelfth century', *Traditio*, 7 (1949—51), 279—358.

2174 Leff, Gordon. 'Thomas Bradwardine's *De causa Dei*', *Journal of Ecclesiastical History*, 7 (1956), 21—29. The *De causa* the response of faith to scepticism; 'The fourteenth century and the decline of scholasticism', *PP*, 9 (1956), 30—41. Analysis of the divorce between theology and philosophy. Includes Ockham and Bradwardine; 'The changing pattern of the earlier fourteenth century', *BJRL*, 43 (1961), 354—72. Argues in favour of a radical break both in tone and topics.

2175 Little, Andrew G. 'Thomas Docking and his relation to Roger Bacon', *EPRP*, 301—31. Expert comments on a not well-known Oxford teacher.

2176 ——— 'The friars and the university of Cambridge', *EHR*, 50 (1935), 686—96. Prints the Instrument of Concord, June 1306.

2177 ——— 'Theological schools in medieval England', *EHR*, 55 (1940), 624—30. Discusses disputations outside of Oxford and Cambridge.

2178 Loewe, Raphael. 'Alexander Neckham's knowledge of Hebrew', *Medieval and Renaissance Studies*, 4 (1958), 17—34. Alexander lived from 1157—1217.

2179 Longpré, Ephrem. 'Robert Grosseteste et Duns Scotus', *France Franciscaine*, 21 (1938), 1—16.

2180 Mackinnon, Hugh. 'William de Montibus, a medieval teacher', *EPBW*, 32—45. Presents a convincing case for regarding William as an important figure in a new movement in teaching sacramental theology to the parish priests.

2181 Macloughlin, James. 'Higher education in medieval Ireland', *Irish Ecclesiastical Record*, ser. 5, 44 (1934), 55—66, 167—87, 267—81.

2182 Martin, C. 'Walter Burley', in *Oxford studies presented to Daniel Callus*. Oxford Historical Society, n.s., 16 (1964), 194—230.

2183 Morrall, John B. 'Some notes on a recent interpretation of Ockham's political philosophy', *FS*, 9 (1949), 417—42.

2184 Pantin, William A. 'The *Defensorium* of Adam Easton', *EHR*, 51 (1936), 675—80; 'The halls and schools of medieval Oxford: an attempt at reconstruction', in *Oxford studies presented to Daniel Callus*. Oxford Historical Society, n.s., 16 (1964), 31—100; 'John of Wales and medieval humanism', *SPAG*, 297—319.

2185 Pelster, Franz. 'Adam von Bocfeld (Bockingfold), ein Oxforder Erklärer des Aristoteles um die Mitte des 13 Jahrhunderts. Sein Leben und seine Schriften', *Scholastik*, 11 (1936), 196—224.

2186 Pelzer, Auguste. 'Les 51 articles du Guillaume Occam censuré en Avignon, en 1326', *Études d'histoire sur la scholastique médiévale*. Louvain, 1964, 508—19.

2187 Poole, Reginald L. 'The early correspondence of John of Salisbury', *PBA*, 11 (1924), 27—53.

2188 Powicke, Frederick M. 'Master Simon of Faversham', in *Mélanges d'histoire du moyen âge offerts à M. Ferdinand Lot*. Paris, 1925, 649—58.

2189 ——— 'Robert Grosseteste and the Nichomachean ethics', *PBA*, 16 (1930), 85—104.

2190 ——— 'Some problems in the history of the medieval university', *TRHS*, ser. 4, 17 (1934), 1—18.

2191 ——— 'England and Europe in the thirteenth century', in *Independence, convergence and borrowing in institutions, thought and art*. Cambridge, Mass., 1937, 137—50. Paper contributed to a collection.

2192 ——— 'The alleged migration of the university of Oxford to Northampton in 1264', *Oxoniensia*, 8—9 (1945), 107—11.

2193 Pratt, Robert A. 'The importance of manuscripts for the study of medieval education as revealed by the learning of Chaucer', *Progress of Medieval and Renaissance Society*, 20 (1949), 43–51.

2194   Richards, R.C. 'Ockham and skepticism', *New Scholasticism*, 42 (1968), 345–63.

2195   Richardson, Henry G. 'The schools of Northampton in the twelfth century', *EHR*, 56 (1941), 595–605; 'Business training in medieval Oxford', *AHR*, 46 (1941), 595–605; 'Oxford law school under John', *LQR*, 57 (1941), 319–38.

2196   Russell, Josiah C. 'The early schools of Oxford and Cambridge', *Historian*, 5 (1943), 61–76.

2197   —— 'Richard of Bardney's account of Robert Grosseteste's early and middle life', *Med et Hum*, 2 (1944), 45–54; 'Phases of Grosseteste's intellectual life', *Harvard Theological Review*, 43 (1950), 93–116.

2198   Salter, Herbert E. 'The Stamford schism', *EHR*, 37 (1922), 249–53.

2199   —— and John Carter. 'Town and gown', *Oxford*, 4 (1937), 56–61, 70–79.

2200   Sharp, Dorothea E. 'Further philosophical doctrines of Kilwardby', *New Scholasticism*, 8 (1934), 306–18.

2201   Tornay, Stephen C. 'William of Ockham's nominalism', *Philosophical Review*, 45 (1936), 245–67.

2202   Trakhtenberg, O.V. 'William of Ockham and the prehistory of English materialism', *Philosophy and Phenomenological Research*, 6 (1945), 212–24.

2203   Tweedale, Martin. 'Scotus and Ockham on the infinity of the most eminent being', *FS*, 23 (1963), 257–67.

2204   Usher, Gwilym. 'Welsh students at Oxford in the Middle Ages', *BBCS*, 16 (1955), 193–99.

2205   Watt, Donald E.R. 'University clerks and rolls of petitions for benefices', *Speculum*, 34 (1959), 213–29.

2206   Weisheipl, James A. 'Curriculum of the faculty of arts at Oxford in the early fourteenth century', *MS*, 26 (1964), 143–85.

2207   —— 'Developments in the arts curriculum at Oxford in the early fourteenth century', *MS*, 28 (1966), 151–75.

XIV. HISTORIOGRAPHY

1 Printed Sources

2208   Bishop, Terence A.M. (ed.). *Scriptores regis. Facsimiles to identify and illustrate the hands of royal scribes in original charters of Henry I, Stephen, and Henry II*. Oxford, 1961. Identifies the handwriting of forty-eight scribes. A tour de force of palaeography. See also Noël Denholm-Young. *Handwriting in England and Wales*. Cardiff, 1954; 2nd ed., 1964. A helpful guide; Vivian H. Galbraith. 'Handwriting', in Austin L. Poole (ed.). *Medieval England*. Oxford, 1958, II, 541–58; Leonard C. Hector. *The handwriting of English documents*. 1958; 2nd ed., 1966. An expert commentary, with thirty-two facsimiles; Charles Johnson and C. Hilary Jenkinson. *English court hand, A.D. 1066 to 1500*. 1915; reprinted New York, 1967, 2 vols. Still invaluable: includes numerous plates.

2 Monographs

2209   Bell, Henry E. *Maitland, a critical examination and assessment*. 1965; also Roy Stone de Montpensier. 'Maitland and the interpretation', *American Journal of Legal History*, 10 (1966), 259–81; Theodore F.T. Plucknett. 'Maitland's view of law and history', *LQR*, 67 (1951), 179–94.

2210   Elton, Geoffrey R. *The future of the past: an inaugural lecture*. Cambridge, 1968. Begins his stimulating but somewhat provocative career as an expert on the writing of history.

2211   Galbraith, Vivian H. *The literacy of medieval English kings*. Milford, 1935.

Includes diplomatic. Slight sketch by a great expert. All Galbraith's works are authoritative and stimulating.

2212 ——— *Roger Wendover and Matthew Paris.* Glasgow, 1944. Comments by an outstanding authority. See also 2214, 2219 below.

2213 ——— *Studies in the public records.* Edinburgh, 1948. Reprinted 1949. See also Galbraith's *An introduction to the use of the public records.* Oxford, 1952. First published 1934. Masterly discussions.

2214 ——— *Historical research in medieval England.* 1951. Some valuable observations on a number of chronicles.

2215 Haselden, Reginald S. *Scientific aids for the study of manuscripts.* Bibliographical Society Supp, 10 (1935). Includes bibliographies.

2216 Hector, Leonard C. *Palaeography and forgery.* York, 1959. A pamphlet by a distinguished expert. From *c.* 1200 to Judge Jeffreys.

2217 Hollaender, Albert E.J. (ed.). *Essays in memory of Sir Hilary Jenkinson.* 1962. The essays include articles on archival and palaeographical sciences.

2218 Jenkins, Claude. *The monastic chronicler and the early school of St Albans.* 1923. S.P.C.K. Popular but scholarly.

2219 Kingsford, Hugh S. *Seals.* Helps for Students of History, 30 (1920). Helpful introduction to the subject. Includes bibliography.

2220 Knowles, David. *Great historical enterprises: problems in monastic history.* Edinburgh, 1963. Collaborative and individual contributions to the realization of historical truth: includes an essay on the Rolls Series.

2221 Lloyd, John E. *The Welsh chronicles.* 1929. Reprint from *PBA*, 14 (1928), 369—91.

2222 Powicke, Frederick M. *Modern historians and the study of history.* 1955. Historiographical essays, and biographies of modern writers.

2223 Taylor John. *Medieval historical writing in Yorkshire.* St Anthony's Hall Publications, 19 (1961). Brief but helpful survey. Four plates.

2224 ——— *The 'Universal Chronicle' of Ranulf Higden.* Oxford, 1966. Higden is presented as the most significant English historian between Matthew Paris and Thomas of Walsingham.

2225 Wright, Cyril E. *English vernacular hands from the twelfth to the fifteenth centuries.* Oxford Palaeographical Handbooks. Oxford, 1969. Authoritative. Includes plates. Series ed. by Richard W. Hunt *et al.*

3 Biographies

2226 Edwards, J. Goronwy. *William Stubbs.* Historical Association Pamphlet, no. G 22. (1952); see also Robert Brentano. 'The sound of Stubbs', *JBS*, 6 (1965), 1—14.

2227 Holland, Henry A. *Frederic W. Maitland, 1850—1906.* Selden Society lecture. 1953; William W. Buckland. 'F.W. Maitland', *Cambridge Law Journal*, 1 (1923), 279—301.

2228 Shears, Frederick S. *Froissart chronicler and poet.* 1930. Fresh and interesting introduction to Froissart.

2229 Vaughan, Richard. *Matthew Paris.* Cambridge, 1958. Thorough and scholarly: significant for an understanding of both Matthew and medieval historiography. See also Frederick M. Powicke. 'Notes on the compilation of *Chronica majora* of Matthew Paris', *Modern Philology*, 38 (1941), 305—17; also 'The compilation of the *Chronica majora* of Matthew Paris', *PBA*, 30 (1944), 147—60. Reprinted Oxford, 1944. Illuminating comments.

4 Articles

2230 Anglo-American Historical Committee. 'Report on editing historical documents', *BIHR*, 1 (1924), 6—25.

2231 Barlow, Frank. 'Roger of Howden', *EHR*, 65 (1950), 352—60. Valuable correction to Stubbs.

2232 Cheney, Christopher R. 'Notes on the making of the Dunstable annals, A.D. 33 to 1242', *EPBW*, 79—98. An important reassessment of the value of the *Annals*; 'Magna carti beati Thome: another Canterbury forgery', *BIHR*, 36 (1963), 1—26.

2233 Christopher, Henry G.T. *Palaeography and the archives*. 1938.

2234 Clarke, Maude V. and Noël Denholm-Young. 'The Kirkstall chronicle 1355—1400', *BJRL*, 15 (1931), 100—37.

2235 Coulton, George. 'Two ways of history', *History*, 9 (1924), 1—13. See also rejoinder by Frederick Powicke. *History*, 9 (1924), 13—17. A very spirited exchange; also *Fourscore years: an autobiography*. Cambridge, 1943.

2236 Crump, Charles G. 'A note on the criticism of records', *BJRL*, 8 (1924), 140—49; 'On sealing letters close', *EHR*, 37 (1922), 267—72.

2237 Denholm-Young, Noël. 'Thomas de Wykes and his chronicle', *EHR*, 61 (1946), 157—79.

2238 Galbraith, Vivian H. 'The *Historia aurea* of John, vicar of Tynemouth, and the sources of the St Albans chronicle (1327—77)', *EPRP*, 379—98. Expertly demolishes views about the continuity of historical writing at St Albans under Edward III.

2239 ——— 'Seven charters of Henry II at Lincoln cathedral', *Antiquaries Journal*, 12 (1932), 269—78. Prints facsimiles and comments on the Angevin chancery.

2240 ——— 'Thomas Walsingham and the St Albans chronicle, 1272—1422', *EHR*, 47 (1932), 12—30.

2241 ——— 'A new charter of Henry II to Battle abbey', *EHR*, 52 (1937), 67—73. Discusses new formulae for royal charters, *c.* 1175. Prints charter possibly dated in April, 1176.

2242 ——— 'The St Edmundsbury chronicle, 1296—1301', *EHR*, 58 (1943), 51—78. Valuable comments.

2243 ——— 'An autograph MS. of Ranulph Higden's *Polychronicon*', *Huntington Library Quarterly*, 23 (1959—60), 1—18. Outlines the growth of Higden's *Polychronicon*.

2244 Holt, James C. 'The St Albans chroniclers and Magna carta', *TRHS*, ser. 5, 14 (1964), 67—88. Illuminating comments on Matthew Paris and Roger of Wendover.

2245 Jenkins, Claude. *The monastic chronicler and the early school of St Albans*. 1922. S.P.C.K. A short but valuable essay on historical writing at St Albans.

2246 Jenkinson, C. Hilary. 'The study of English seals: illustrated chiefly from examples in the P.R.O.', *JBAA*, ser. 3, 1 (1937), 93—127.

2247 Kay, Richard. 'Wendover's last annal', *EHR*, 84 (1969), 779—85. Discusses the text of Wendover's *Flores historiarum*.

2248 Kinghorn, Alexander M. 'Scottish historiography in the 14th century: a new introduction to Barbour's Bruce', *Studies in Scottish Literature*, 6 (1969), 131—45.

2249 Lawrence, C. Hugh. 'Robert of Abingdon and Matthew Paris', *EHR*, 69 (1954), 408—17. Suggests where Matthew got his literary sources for his life of St Edmund.

2250 Little, Andrew G. 'The authorship of the Lancaster chronicle', *EHR*, 31 (1916), 269—79.

2251 Otway-Ruthven, Jocelyn. 'Medieval Ireland, 1169—1485', in Theodore W. Moody (ed.). *Irish historiography 1936—70*. Dublin, 1971, 16—22.

2252 Powicke, Frederick M. 'Alexander of St Albans: a literary muddle', *EPRP*, 246—60. Expert work of detection.

2253 Reynolds, Susan. 'The forged charters of Barnstaple', *EHR*, 84 (1969), 699—720. Questions authenticity of charters twelfth—fourteenth century, and suggests tests for authenticity of such charters.

2254 Richardson, Henry G. 'The exchequer year', *TRHS*, ser. 4, 8 (1925), 171—90; *THRS*, ser. 4, 9 (1926), 175—76.

2255 Salter, Herbert E. 'Two forged charters of Henry II', *EHR*, 34 (1919), 65—68. Valuable.

2256 Searle, Eleanor. 'Battle abbey and exemption: the forged charters', *EHR*, 83 (1968), 449—80. Illustrates the attitude of the monks of Battle towards their traditions of exemption and the defence of these by forgery over some sixty years.

2257   Stenton, Doris M. 'Roger of Howden and Benedict', *EHR*, 68 (1953), 574—82. Examines Roger's experiences and methods: modifies views of Stubbs.

2258   Stones, Edward L.G. 'Two points of diplomatic', *SHR*, 32 (1953), 43—51. On witness and dating.

2259   Wilkinson, Bertie. 'The later middle ages in England: continuity, transition or decline?', *Transactions of the Royal Society of Canada*, ser. 4, 11 (1973), 243—54. Deals with the writing of history, with special reference to the high Middle Ages in England.

INDEX OF AUTHORS, EDITORS, AND TRANSLATORS

Numbers are entry numbers